A Forensic Approach to Political and State Violence

A Forensic Approach to Political and State Violence applies a forensic lens to the study of risk in relation to political and state violence.

Divided into three parts, the book outlines the nature and function of political and state violence and the historic development of contributions from forensic practice. It then considers the distinction between political and state violence and the foundations for this. This is followed by a review of developments of current research and practice looking at future development and the ways in which forensic practice might more effectively contribute to risk reduction and management. The text will argue that the basis of much current forensic practice, in relation to political and state violence, is unduly limited and has failed to integrate relevant scientific research into practice. The role of market-led approaches to work in these areas will also be considered, in relation to the way this has influenced and distorted practice and delayed progress. Drawing on theories derived from psychology and other areas of research, the book considers how evidence might inform improvements, using the risks and uncertainties that surround politically motivated violence to illustrate this. Real cases of political and state violence are considered, with topics including military conflict, terrorism, use of torture and hostage taking to highlight current failings and weaknesses. Barriers to implementing better forensic practice in terms of both professional, economic and policy interests are also explored.

It will be an essential read for all students or practitioners in the areas of forensic psychology, criminal justice, or violence risk management.

David Crighton is Professor of Forensic Psychology at Durham University, UK. He was previously Acting Chief/Deputy Chief Psychologist at the Ministry of Justice, UK.

New Frontiers in Forensic Psychology

Series Editors

Graham Towl is Professor of Forensic Psychology at Durham University and was formerly Chief Psychologist at the Ministry of Justice, UK. He is the recipient of the British Psychological Society Awards for Distinguished Contributions to Professional Practice and forensic academic knowledge.

Roxanne Khan is a multi-award-winning academic researcher. For over 18 years, she was based at the University of Central Lancashire where she was a Senior Lecturer in Forensic Psychology and led a Forensic Psychology course ranked top in the UK in a national student survey. Dr. Khan is Founder and Director of HARM—Honour Abuse Research Matrix. As Director of onEvidence, Dr. Khan is an independent chair and author for Domestic Homicide Reviews and Child Safeguarding Practice Reviews.

New Frontiers in Forensic Psychology brings together contemporary, cutting-edge research in core and emerging topics, to present new and original areas of investigation at the forefront of 21st century forensic psychology theory, policy, and practice.

We welcome proposals in all areas of forensic psychology – especially those bringing a fresh perspective on traditional lines of enquiry, or innovative and novel perspectives that are excluded from the main discourse.

Equity, diversity, and inclusion are embedded within each book in this series, which is underpinned by a values-based approach to forensic psychology and its applications.

The Psychology of Honor Abuse, Violence, and Killings
Roxanne Khan

A Forensic Approach to Political and State Violence
Uncertainty, Ambiguity and Risk
David Crighton

A Forensic Approach to Political and State Violence

Uncertainty, Ambiguity and Risk

David Crighton

R Routledge
Taylor & Francis Group

LONDON AND NEW YORK

Designed cover image: Getty © guvendemir

First published 2026
by Routledge
4 Park Square, Milton Park, Abingdon, Oxon OX14 4RN

and by Routledge
605 Third Avenue, New York, NY 10158

Routledge is an imprint of the Taylor & Francis Group, an informa business

British Library Cataloguing-in-Publication Data
A catalogue record for this book is available from the British Library

ISBN: 9781032552187 (hbk)
ISBN: 9781032552170 (pbk)
ISBN: 9781003429579 (ebk)

DOI: 10.4324/9781003429579

Typeset in Times New Roman
by Newgen Publishing UK

Contents

Series foreword

It is with great pleasure that we introduce this timely and significant contribution to the field of forensic psychology. As Editors of the "New Frontiers in Forensic Psychology" series, our aim is to curate cutting-edge research that addresses both foundational and emerging topics, offering fresh perspectives on traditional enquiries and introducing innovative approaches often excluded from mainstream discourse. This book unequivocally meets these criteria, offering an essential analysis of political and state violence, an area of increasing relevance in our complex and fragile world.

What sets this book apart is its critical engagement with forensic practice in the context of political and state violence. It reminds us of the necessity to uphold professional ethics and scientific standards, particularly in the face of the growing marketisation and privatisation of forensic practice. Prof Crighton expertly navigates the narrow scope of much current forensic practice, revealing its limitations when applied to the complexities of political and state violence.

Key themes explored in this book include the following:

- The limitations of relying on a narrow empirical base and manualised 'toolkit' approaches, which are ill-suited to the multifaceted nature of political and state violence.
- The critical need to maintain professional ethics and scientific standards in forensic practice, particularly concerning state-involved actions.
- The risks of naively transferring ideas and methods from routine clinical practice to the context of politically motivated violence without sufficient evidence or understanding.
- The importance of acknowledging and addressing the uncertainty inherent in understanding and responding to political and state violence.

This book is of paramount importance to forensic psychology and forensic psychologists because it challenges conventional thinking and encourages a more nuanced, ethical and evidence-informed approach to understanding and addressing political and state violence. In a world, where such violence is increasingly prevalent, this book offers vital insights for practitioners, policymakers and researchers alike. The book considers the impact of war and conflict on civilian populations, as seen in the Gaza Strip and Northern Ireland, with its long period of civil disorder, insurgency and later terrorism, which raises serious ethical considerations. These are matters that should concern all psychologists as the world witnesses the horror of war repeat itself in the 21st century.

We commend Prof Crighton for writing this transformative book. It is not only a significant contribution to our forensic series, but to the field much more widely too. We are confident that it will stimulate critical discussion and inform more effective and ethical responses to political and state violence. The contents of this book may serve to encourage forensic psychologists to consider the broader implications of forensic practice in an ever more complex world. Its comprehensive approach and critical analysis make it an indispensable resource for students building their foundational knowledge, researchers seeking to advance the field, and practitioners striving for ethical and effective interventions.

Professor Graham Towl and Dr Roxanne Khan
Series Editors

Preface

This book provides an introductory review of the political and state violence and the contributions that forensic practitioners have made and could make in future. There has been a significant growth of interest in this area and indeed other forms of politically motivated violence, which has been marked in the 'West' following the attacks on the United States the 9th September 2001 and related attacks in Europe. Yet, these events were a continuation of high levels of politically motivated violence in other parts of the world, which had been resulting in death and trauma for many years.

Forensic practice has a limited history in this area of violence, with a marked preference for focusing on individual 'psychopathology' and violence. Periods of interest have been limited but have often carried over this focus on individual psychology and treatment. Systemic drivers of the aggression and violence, stemming from social and economic forces, have been relatively neglected. In relation to politically motivated forms of violence though, this has been a very serious limitation. More recently, there have been some moves towards addressing this, as part of the resurgence of interest in why people undertake the most extreme acts in pursuit of such goals.

Answers to politically motivated violence are necessarily multi-disciplinary in nature. No single discipline can hope to address such questions fully and fields, such as sociology, criminology, political economy, international relations and the evidence base on risk and risk management are central. Contributions from these fields often dominate this area, so understanding some of the key concepts and models involved is important in understanding the current evidence base. This includes an understanding of how concepts such as violence, the state and government have been defined. For forensic practitioners, thinking around questions of risk and uncertainty are crucial. Understanding the underpinnings and limits of notions of 'risk' is essential to competent policy and practice in this area.

At the outset, the aim of this text was to give a useful introduction to the area of political and state violence by critically addressing recent contributions from forensic practice. Here, the sometimes diminished, maintenance of professional ethics and scientific standards has been a major concern. This continues to be highly relevant to forensic policy and practice, and this area is looked at across areas of practice. An analysis of this area seems timely and important, in view of the growing marketisation and privatization of forensic practice. This has been based on an increasingly mechanistic approach, based on a manualised 'toolkit' industry, drawing on a narrow empirical base. This seems to be particularly ill-suited to the area of political and state violence and as a result the discussion here is somewhat critical. One theme of the text is concerned with the narrowness of much current forensic practice, in relation to political and state violence. This appears very limited, failing to integrate much of the relevant scientific research into practice. Market-led approaches to work in these areas have it seems influenced and distorted practice and delayed progress. This includes a persistent and undue emphasis on individual psychopathology and intervention at this level.

Another theme addresses the disturbing fact that, for such a young discipline, forensic practice already has a concerning ethical track record. In recent years, psychologists have faced the most serious allegations of using specialist knowledge and skills to facilitate violent abuses by state actors. Professional codes of conduct have been criticised for deteriorating into a form of 'guild' ethics, which seek to balance fundamental rights against professional self-interest. However uncomfortable it may be, such serious failings need to be dealt with if ethical standards are to be maintained and practice is to be improved.

The text has been broadly divided into three parts. The first of these addresses some of the main definitional issues and challenges that surround politically motivated violence and state violence. Here, the focus is largely on those forms of violence that have political aims and objectives, whether these are intentionally carried out by non-state actors or state actors. This necessarily involves limiting the scope of what is covered. A great deal of the violence inflicted by states is not captured here. This would include violence that is not intended or is disapproved of by the state. This excludes acts in some states such as the abuse of prisoners, where there is no explicit or implicit sanction for this. It would though include such violence where states are sanctioning this violence for political motives. Similarly, addressing areas such as the use of mass imprisonment has not been attempted here.

The second part of the text looks across the question of whether political and state violence are distinct entities or not. The practice of separating these seems to be built on weak foundations. It often appears to involve treating identical acts as different and the reasons for this are briefly reviewed. The example of the United Kingdom is used to illustrate this. This is also used as a vehicle to look at some of the policy and practice difficulties that have emerged in this area. The United Kingdom provides a useful example of a state here. As a result of its imperial history, its people have been involved in a particularly wide range of political and state violence. Indeed, much of the political violence seen in the world today cannot be adequately understood without reference to the histories of the states that now make up the United Kingdom.

The third part of the text moves on to critically review the main current contributions of forensic practice. This includes efforts to psychologically profile those engaged in politically motivated violence and efforts to profile the acts themselves. The other major area of work looked at covers efforts to deal with the risk, ambiguity, uncertainty and intractability involved in such violence. Here, there has been a worrying trend of naïvely transferring ideas and methods from areas of routine clinical practice. There appears to have been a largely unthinking adoption of market-based approaches from other areas and has already been associated with catastrophic failures. Events at Fishmongers Hall in London provide a graphic example of this, where two young volunteers were murdered and others seriously injured or traumatised. This was at the hands of someone who had successfully completed a 'rehabilitation programme' of this kind. Failure though is not inevitable here. There are promising areas of work with great potential to contribute in future to more effective responses to the risk and uncertainty involved in this area.

In writing this book, I am deeply indebted to the series editors, Prof Graham Towl and Dr Roxanne Khan for their support, comments on earlier drafts and thoughts on this area. I am very grateful to Prof John Monahan, Prof Dennis Fischbacher-Smith and Prof Gerd Gigerenzer for their previous comments and thinking around risk, uncertainty and intractability. I am also grateful to my editor at Routledge, Annabelle Harris for her support and guidance throughout.

David Crighton,
Durham, UK

1 Aggression and violence

An adequate consideration of terrorism, state and non-state violence necessarily starts with some consideration of issues of definition. This is a complex area and has therefore also been a fraught and contested one. At the outset, it is perhaps worth being clear that this has been an area where widespread agreement has often been hard to reach. Universal agreement has not been achieved and given the complexities of the field remains a largely unrealistic quest. A more realistic aim has been to achieve growing consensus, around the 'core' characteristics that may be seen to describe these constructs. Indeed, this has increasingly emerged from work in the area, going on to form a stronger basis for academic research, policy development and applied practice. As a starting point, it therefore seems helpful to start with efforts to develop consistency in the use of the concept of violence, an adequate understanding of which can be seen as an essential foundation, before looking at efforts to define complex and more ideologically positioned concepts such as 'state violence' and terrorism.'

Violence

Violence is defined by the Collins English Dictionary as "behaviour which is intended to hurt, injure, or kill people" (Collins, 2024). This broad definition of violence is one that generally accords with common use of the term. It does though raise significant issues and so provides a poor basis for research and developing practice in this area. Broad dictionary definitions of violence focus on behaviour, performed by parties with a broad intent to harm others, but there are clear problems with this. For example, by its focus on interpersonal behaviour, it excludes many areas of what has often been called 'structural violence.' Here essentially, it is organisational structures that are seen to act to create harms, rather than specific individual behaviours (Galtung, 1969). Equally, it is unclear why the focus of violence in the example given is limited to acts to harm a person or persons. Even in common usage, many if not most people would consider the brutal treatment of non-human species as a violent act. Indeed, it is difficult to see a firm basis for limiting violence to human-to-human acts, although historically it has been common to do so. The focus on intent is also important and has

DOI: 10.4324/9781003429579-1

similarly been questioned, with some arguing that definitions of violence should be extended to include unintentional and intentional acts. For example, in criminal justice, distinctions are made between intentional killing or murder and unintentional killing which is described using terms including manslaughter and culpable homicide, although both forms may attract the most severe criminal penalties. It is perhaps also worth noting that such a definition is remarkably narrow in these respects but also remarkably broad in other respects. A vast range of behaviours could be seen to intentionally cause some hurt or injury to others. Any form of criticism or negative feedback, however mild, warranted, or constructive, could potentially fall within such a definition of violence. For the purposes of understanding the kinds of acts involved in terrorism or state violence, few would therefore argue that these kinds of definitions provide an adequate basis for research, policy and practice development.

Various dictionary definitions do though begin to capture an essence of violence as involving conflict, disputed ends and behaviours seen in response to these. Adequately defining violence though needs to go beyond this: it needs to address, or try to address, its normative, theoretical and descriptive aspects. Taking these in turn, the normative aspect of violence suggests that such acts are wrong or morally bad by definition and so require special justification over non-violent acts (Wyckoff, 2013). Theoretical concepts of violence need to address the negative effects of violence, where such acts can be destabilising and dehumanising. Additionally, violence can frequently be linked to an increased probability of unstable resolutions (some would argue inevitably so) along with a lowering of the threshold for further violence and linked evils, of repression and increasing authoritarianism. The descriptive aspect refers to the need for good concordance between the theoretical concept of violence and more commonly held understanding of it (Pontara, 1978).

It is worth noting that some schools of thought in the social sciences start from a position of very largely rejecting notions of legitimate authority. Anarchist and libertarian approaches, for different reasons, reject to varying degrees the idea of legitimate impersonal authority, in favour of individual agency (Chomsky, 1970). In line with such views, many forms of social control are therefore seen as being the exercise of illegitimate force or violence. Such views potentially expand the definition of violence, to include many routine forms of state compulsion, with these argued to be unwarranted and illegitimate uses of power. Such views though appear to stray a long way from commonly held concepts of violence, where the concept of legitimate state power is generally accepted within contested limits (Morris, 2008).

Such ideas become more salient and it can be suggested more important when looking at the question of the limits on state violence and the idea of state terrorism. Wide acceptance of laws that allow for compulsion does not suggest that accepting the concept of legitimate impersonal authority implies that this is unlimited. Clearly, such acquiescence can be and frequently has been abused by states, with the use of unauthorised violence by legitimate authorities being an evident and recurring fact. Similarly, even the use of legitimated authority, in widely accepted ways, does not negate the fact that the use of violence by authorities can have brutalising effects.

The most obvious example of this is perhaps the widespread use of imprisonment by states, which has a range of adverse effects.

Focusing on physical force and physical injury

Within the literature on violence, there has often been an undue stress on the use of physical force and physical injury following on from this. This bias has gone largely unquestioned in forensic practice, where the professional norm has increasingly been to focus on individual rather than systemic or structural aspects of violence. This is discussed in greater detail when looking at the question of how to operationally define terms. For present purposes though, it is worth noting that this is problematic since it excludes a wide range of violence and harm that can be seen to derive from it. One topical example here would be the suspension of aid to civilian populations during periods of conflict, as reported in Gaza strip from 2023 to 2025 (Kim and Rabin, 2024). This does not involve the use of physical force, but such acts may have similar or more severe effects than doing so. On this basis, it is difficult to argue that similar ethical considerations do not arise. The distinction between killing someone by shooting them, or intentionally leaving them to starve to death, appears reflective of a difference in the means used to achieve a similar end. The suggestion that the use of one means reflects violence and the other non-violence, conflicts with common sense notions of what violence is. The use of boycotts and industrial action may raise similar issues, although here they are generally in less acute form. For example, where healthcare staff withdraw their labour, putting patients at risk of death or serious injury. Concerns around the perception of such acts as violence perhaps explains, at least in part, why those involved generally go to great lengths to avoid the most serious forms of harm.

The focus on physical injury is also problematic from both ethical and philosophical standpoints. One implication of this is that psychological distress is less relevant, or has no relevance at all, to violence. This appears at best to be a highly questionable assumption and one that generates practical issues when trying to develop an adequate definition of violence. The basis for distinguishing between physical and psychological injury seems to be fundamentally weak on multiple grounds. To take an example, the use of a chemical gas attack known to generate severe feelings of anxiety and distress seems to accord with common notions of a violent act. So too would the destruction of homes and treasured possessions as a means of generating fear and distress. The effects following on from such actions may be more damaging in the medium to long term than severe physical injury which heals more quickly. Therefore, to exclude psychological injuries from the study of violence appears both arbitrary and unhelpful (Osofsky, 1995). At a more fundamental level, it is also far from clear where to draw the line between psychological and physical harm (Vasterling, Proctor, Amoroso et al., 2006).

That said, it has been argued that the extension of the concept of violence to areas such as social injustice takes the recognition of psychological harms too far and the question of thresholds is important. Some have suggested that over-extending the definition of violence to include all psychological harms is both unhelpful and unnecessary, whilst others have argued that capturing the actions or inactions of social and political systems that cause harm is important (Pontara, 1978; Dewi and Cahyani, 2020). Other exclusions have, less convincingly, been argued for. Of these, the idea of restricting violence to those acts directed at human beings has been argued to be philosophically and pragmatically poorly grounded (Singer, 1993; Korsgaard, 1996). It is difficult to see the persuasive basis for excluding other species and certainly any sentient species, from the ability to experience violence. Such a division appears to be largely arbitrary and at a practical level would unhelpfully define acts of animal abuse and cruelty as non-violent.

Violence and aggression

Adopting a scientific approach to the study of any phenomena rests on a high degree of clarity about what is being dealt with. This has been notably absent in much of the historic literature on the area of violence and the much narrower subject areas of political and state violence. Evidence in these areas has clearly quite often begun from very different starting points and involved differing assumptions. To progress there has been a pressing need for better operational definitions, with some progress being made in this respect. In looking at the broad area of violence, it has been suggested that four widely used and influential approaches have come to dominate the area (Hamby, 2017a):

(1)   Exemplar-based
(2)   Public health
(3)   Social–psychological
(4)   Biological–psychological

Exemplar-based approaches

The use of exemplar-based definitions of violence is perhaps the longest standing way of going beyond general dictionary definitions. This approach to definition is seen commonly across legal systems and legal thinking in this area, with violence being defined in terms of specific acts and a range of contexts (Ashworth and Horder, 2013). This way of defining violence is largely based on using specific examples of behaviours to define what is and is not violent. To take the UK as an example, crimes such as murder, kidnap, rape and physical assaults are all used to provide such exemplars of violence. Other offences though are not defined as violence in this manner, for example, burglary, theft and fraud, even though these offences will undoubtedly often cause serious harms and distress. Such division differs to some degree across different legal systems but is based largely on salient features of the behaviour observed and the nature of its impact. A stress has typically been placed here on serious physical injury, although there has been a growing recognition of more severe forms of psychological injury. Issues of intent are also an important part of these kinds of exemplar-based definitions, with the exclusions of many forms of behaviour that may cause serious injury, where intent to cause harm is judged to be absent, or is not judged to be malicious, or indeed where the behaviour is viewed as being justified.

Exemplar-based approaches to the definition of violence have often dominated the discussion of the area, and it has often been adopted, apparently uncritically, in areas of forensic practice. It is though also the least compelling approach in terms of analysis, suffering as it does from several key weaknesses. Most strikingly perhaps, adopting a definition based on specific examples fails to define clear and consistent boundaries between different acts determined to be violent or non-violent (Hamby, 2017a). Different legal systems, although showing clear areas of overlap, will also develop quite different and inconsistent decisions about what to include and what to exclude, when defining violence by exemplars. In turn, a range of political and policy considerations will be involved in making such distinctions, which will in turn be driven by various competing interests and concerns. The value of exemplar-based approaches to developing a better understanding of violence at a fundamental level is therefore necessarily quite circumscribed.

Public health approaches

Public health efforts to define violence have adopted a quite different approach, which has not generally been based on specific exemplars of violence. Rather public health approaches have sought to provide a broad-based definition that may encompass the full range of violence, independent of specific acts or requirements that such acts are defined as criminal. Public health approaches in contrast to exemplar-based ones can be seen as treating violence as closely analogous to disease, suggesting very different responses at policy and practice levels. The analogy with disease leads to a stress on notions such as 'treatment' and 'cure,' based in turn on empirical evidence, rather than categorisation with a view to determining culpability and punishment. Identification of the causes of violence, and effective early and preventative interventions, typically drawing on health and social care services, are generally stressed here (Brown, 2019). Within this kind of definition, violence is typically seen more broadly, including behaviours that are likely to have significant harms on defined notions of health. One widely used example of this type of approach is perhaps illustrative of this, with the World Health Organization (WHO) defining violence as:

> The intentional use of physical force or power, threatened or actual, against oneself, another person, or against a group or community, that either results in or has a high likelihood of resulting in injury, death, psychological harm, maldevelopment, or deprivation.
>
> (World Health Organization, 2024)

Public health approaches do not generally rest on any specific examples of violent behaviour and as such have several clear advantages, when compared to exemplar-based approaches. Most obviously, in avoiding definition based on specific examples, they may provide a more conceptual definition of violence. As a result of this, many of the boundary issues seen in exemplar-based definitions may be avoided. The WHO definition above also defines violence in terms of threat or behaviour likely to cause harm, suggesting that the generation of fear itself may constitute violence and that the occurrence of harm is in turn probabilistic in nature. Whether harm does or does not follow on from an act though, it may still fall within such a definition of violence. The WHO example above also broadens out the nature of harm, well beyond that typically seen in exemplar-based approaches. Here, this would include not just physical injury or psychological harm but also 'maldevelopment' and 'deprivation.' This serves to bring a wide range of acts within the scope of violence, such as the use of political and bureaucratic power to increase levels of deprivation. In this way, public health approaches to defining violence can also encompass ideas of 'structural violence.' In essence, ideas of structural violence stress the role of organisations and institutions in undertaking acts that can result in significant physical and psychological harms to individuals and groups (Galtung, 1969; Herrick and Bell, 2022).

Several criticisms of public health approaches to defining violence can be made. The analogy between violence and disease, or sometimes infectious disease, can be criticised as being weakly grounded or for being misleading. Public health definitions of violence have also, often with justification, been criticised for being over-inclusive. The WHO definition outlined above provides a clear illustration of this, with acts that are clearly carried out with the best of intentions seeming to fall clearly within scope as violence, similarly to malign and intentional acts, on the basis that both have negative effects on health outcomes (Hamby, 2017a). So here, a healthcare practitioner carrying out a policy of mass immunisation that has some likelihood of causing harm to individuals would potentially fall within the definition of violence, alongside malicious actors who, for example, commit serious physical assaults on patients. This appears to be an over-inclusive approach, but it also seems to be missing important distinctions in behaviour.

Critics have also noted that in public health definitions, some behaviours have often been excluded, without apparent justification. Most strikingly, 'child neglect' has often been excluded as a form of violence, apparently on the basis that this is defined as involving acts of omission rather than commission. Here, later additional commentary from the WHO can be seen to have sought to address this in their definition of violence, bringing such behaviours within scope, albeit at the expense of a rather more complex definition. Public health definitions have also been criticised for an at times curious use of language and here again the WHO definition is illustrative, having been heavily criticised for the use of the term 'abuse' rather than 'violence' when referring to some public health areas. This is evident in references to 'sexual abuse' and 'child sexual abuse' which have both been criticised and challenged as inappropriate. The basis for adopting terms such as 'abuse' in this context rather than sexual violence is at best questionable and behaviours that appear to otherwise clearly meet the definition of violence are perhaps better described as such (Hamby, 2017a). Worse still perhaps is the adoption of terms such as 'grooming' across a range of health settings to describe a range of physical and systemic violence. Again, it is unclear what legitimate function is served by the adoption of these forms of opaque and misleading language (Ristroph, 2010; San Kuay and Towl, 2021).

Social psychological approaches

These approaches typically start by distinguishing between two forms of behaviour: aggression and violence. Here, aggression is seen as behaviours that are unwanted by the recipient and have the intent to cause some level of harm. Violence is then defined as an aggressive act that causes extreme physical harm, serious injury or death (DeWall, Anderson and Bushman, 2011). This represents a marked improvement over some earlier attempts at psychological definition, such as violence being "a response that delivers a noxious stimuli to another organism" (Buss, 1961). This earlier attempt at an operational definition can be seen to be over-inclusive and to raise additional questions, such as the suggestion of violence as a response. Later, efforts have sought to address issues of intent and the unwanted nature of the behaviours. This has served to reduce the over-inclusiveness of earlier definitions by excluding such things as accidental injury and what would generally be seen as positive behaviours, such as pharmacological, medical and surgical interventions.

These kinds of social–psychological definitions do though have some limitations and have been criticised on this basis. The definition of aggression has been challenged, particularly on the basis that it is inconsistent with other, better developed definitions, used in other areas of psychology and other fields such as biology. For example, such definitions are often not consistent with those used in cross-species research, biological psychology and areas such as ethology (Lorenz, 1981; Natarajan and Caramaschi, 2010). The focus on immediate physical harms, to the exclusion of psychological and longer-term negative effects, has also been criticised (Hamby, 2017a). This is perhaps a particularly striking omission for an explicitly psychological approach to defining violence. There have also been significant criticisms around the way that intent is dealt with in such models. Here, aggression is defined as an act based on intent, but this is not directly addressed in relation to violence, arguably resulting in an over-inclusive definition. To take an example here, acting in self-defence may involve intentional aggression that causes serious harm. As such, it would not be distinguished, within such a definition of violence, from an unprovoked assault on others.

Bio-psychological approaches

More 'biological' approaches to behaviour have also sought to define violence, although here the aim has typically involved definitions that can be applied equally to non-human species. This work has been largely, though not exclusively, focused on behavioural models in other species. Here, aggression has been seen as an adaptive cross-species behaviour (Natarajan and Caramaschi, 2010; De Boer, 2018). It is typically defined as a form of social communication with clear functionality or 'functional endpoints.' These would include such things as getting and retaining food, shelter, mates and less clearly attaining social status. The advantage of behaviours that achieve these aims, in terms of survival and reproduction, generally seem clear. Extensive work in this area has suggested that different species have developed a range of behaviours, suited to their needs. In addition, there appears to be a range of linked inhibitory mechanisms that serve to reduce and mitigate the levels of aggression normally seen. An example here would be dogs growling and escalating this to the baring of their teeth to warn off others, rather than immediately attacking by biting. Indeed, most species can be seen to have a range of escalatory and de-escalatory behaviours that can be used to avoid the potentially high costs associated with aggression.

Within these models, violence can be defined as a pathological form of aggression which, largely, is not subject to these kinds of inhibitory mechanism. As such, violence can be seen as a form of social communication that has lost its function and may have become dysfunctional (Koolhaas, de Boer and Buwalda, 2010; Natarajan and Caramaschi, 2010). Such violence in other species has been observed to have several characteristics:

(i) There is minimal or no pre-escalatory or ritualistic behaviours.
(ii) Attacks are longer, with lower levels of withdrawal, even when appropriate defeat and submission postures are adopted by the other animal.
(iii) Attacks are independent of the context and indiscriminate.
(iv) Attacks and bites tend to be directed to vulnerable areas resulting in severe injuries.

Such biologically based definitions of violence have some significant strengths. First of these being that they provide a focus on clear operational definition, with this being based on observable behaviours. This provides a sound foundation for systematically approaching research into the understanding of violence, since this is not fixed to any specific examples of violent acts. As a result, many of the difficulties that are associated with exemplar-based approaches to definition can be largely avoided, since the definition here is independent of specific examples of behaviour and is species-independent as well. The approach also shows some overlap with social psychological approaches, sharing some common elements. Most importantly perhaps being the clear distinction drawn between aggression and violence.

Elements of violence

In a systematic review of this area, it has been suggested that conceptual, as opposed to an exemplar-based, definitions of violence require four 'core elements' (Hamby, 2017a). To be described as violent, it is suggested that the behaviour needs to meet the criteria of being: non-essential, unwanted, harmful and intentional. Each of these requirements in turn raises some subsidiary issues, with the effect that the boundaries around each of these aspects may, in some cases, become difficult to define precisely. Even so, such a framework provides a sound starting point to better understand violence.

Non-essential

The idea that violence involves non-essential aggression, or aggression that is more than what is necessary, has often been missing from work concerning humans. This contrasts with work on other species, where such behaviour is routinely described as maladaptive. Behaviour of this kind can be seen as only rarely being helpful, or functional, either to the individual or to the wider group. Something which appears to be the case even for high-ranking individuals within groups. This suggests that much of what has often been discussed as aggression in research into humans might more appropriately be seen as violence. This would include for example areas such as many forms of bullying, child neglect and aggressive and controlling behaviours towards intimate partners (Hamby, 2017b). This is because in such cases what has often been described as aggression serves no legitimate function that could not be achieved, or better achieved, in other non-violent ways.

To take bullying as an example here, most children can achieve social status amongst peers and others, with most seeking to do so (Coie, Dodge and Kupersmidt, 1990). Importantly, many children will do this without resort to violence, suggesting that such behaviour is not essential to achieving such goals. Equally, not all children who enjoy high social status amongst their peers engage in violence, showing it to be non-essential to the attaining of high status. Indeed, violent children often have low social status amongst their peers and others, with the effects of their behaviour appearing to be negative in the medium to long term (Lereya, Copeland, Costello et al., 2015). However, this association appears to be moderated as a function of age, sex, type of aggression and social status resulting from having peer-valued characteristics. Some aggression in boys, with peer-valued characteristics, was linked to higher levels of popularity and power than those who did not show such characteristics (Vaillancourt and Hymel, 2006).

This aspect of defining violence may also mean that some behaviours, previously not classed as violent, need to be recategorised. Most obviously, here, perhaps, is the physical punishment of children. The use of severe aggression by adults towards children is something that has been reported throughout history. Although as already noted, it has not typically been described as violence. Rather, terms such as 'child abuse,' 'punishment,' 'corporal punishment' and so on have been used. Historically, this normally took place within families, although more recently, with the growth of formal education outside kin groups, it became common for unrelated adults in positions of authority to engage in similar behaviours towards children. This use of violence was often justified based on being 'natural' by reference to analogous behaviours seen in families or essential as a means of control over large groups of children. It is though clear that such behaviour does not meet the threshold of being essential, and in fact, such behaviours can often appear gratuitous. For children, there are alternative means of controlling and modifying unwanted behaviours that are more effective, with the use of violence being associated with long-term negative effects (Gershoff and Bitensky, 2007).

The need for behaviour to be essential also works in the opposite direction, to exclude other behaviours from being classified as violence. Use of even very high levels of aggression, when in defence of others or in self-defence, would not here be defined as violence. It would rather be seen as functional aggression. Equally, where individuals lack a sufficient behavioural repertoire, their even severe aggressive behaviour would not be classified as violence. This would include young children who lack the language and social skills to achieve goals in other ways. It would, on similar grounds, include many of those with intellectual disabilities or neuropsychological conditions such as dementia. Applying the test of whether the behaviour is essential would also avoid classifying most healthcare interventions as violence, even where these might involve the inflicting of severe injuries, for example, the use of invasive cardiopulmonary resuscitation (CPR). This result is counterintuitive in that it leads to describing some apparently 'violent' encounters as 'aggressive.' This can though be seen to overlap with efforts across legal systems to deal with some of the difficult questions that emerge around violence. Legal notions such as 'proportionality,' 'reasonable treatment,' 'reasonable force' and 'best interests' of others have developed there to address such distinctions (Kopelman, 1997; Newton and May, 2014).

Unwanted

Distinguishing between wanted and unwanted acts is crucial to defining violence, since it serves to separate acts that are often innocuous or 'pro-social' from those which are violent (Hamby, 2017a). This would include a wide range of behaviours that can be captured under the broad term of 'play.' Such things as free play in children, organised games and competitions may all involve acts that would otherwise be defined as violent. All may involve high levels of aggression, although this is moderated and controlled. The requirement for violent behaviour to be unwanted also excludes areas such as appropriate medical treatment from classification as violence. Within this group of behaviours, there are a range of inhibiting mechanisms that exist to reduce the risk of serious harm. These would include the consensual nature of the activities and the ability to withdraw consent. Other mechanisms would include such things as the rules of the game, the presence of officials to enforce these and prevent abuse or the legal regulation of healthcare staff. Notably, where such mechanisms are ignored or subverted, then the definition of the act may fundamentally change. What is normally seen as competitive aggression may become violence (Hardman, 2019) and what is seen as medical treatment may become violent assault (Thomas-Peter and Lawday, 2021).

The degree to which an experience is unwanted can be seen as a falling along a continuum, and as a result, it is common that coerced consent is guarded against (Hamby and Koss, 2003). Limits to consent are also linked to this, with the determination that there are some behaviours that individuals cannot consent to. This is demonstrated in past case law, where it has been argued that individuals had consented to severely injurious acts. A clear example of this is provided by the case R v Brown [1993] UKHL 19 (11 March 1993) where five appellants were convicted on various criminal offences of violence, under the Offences against the Person Act 1861, for injuries that had been inflicted during consensual homosexual sadomasochist activities. Here, the trial judge ruled that the consent of the victim conferred no defence and this was subsequently confirmed, with one dissenting opinion, on appeal. Legal systems have generally been careful to guard against issues of coerced or invalid consent and to balance this with protections against viewing individuals as, for various reasons, incompetent to consent. As such, the wanted aspect of the definition is not absolute and wanted behaviours may still meet the criteria of violence. The opposite may also be true and when deemed necessary, some unwanted behaviours may not meet the criteria for violence. Examples here would be showing high levels of aggression in self-defence or some healthcare interventions involving those deemed unable to provide valid consent. Increasingly, notions of such consent are seen to require active engagement rather than passive compliance (DiSantis and Towl, 2025).

Harmful

A key aspect of definitions of violence has been the presence of harm. Usually, this has included a marked stress on physical harm and the severity of effects. This focus on physical harm has been extensively criticised and has even been described as a 'bordering on the irrational' (Hamby, 2017a). There are persuasive arguments against limiting or even largely focusing on harm only as physical effects. Such limitations would typically include acts that result in only minor physical harms as violence, whilst excluding or diminishing many acts that result in severe psychological harms. Perhaps the most vivid example of this would be the area of combat stress. Here, individuals may be subject to severe psychological harm linked to prolonged periods of extreme psychological stress (Kormos, 2014). It seems unreasonable to exclude this kind of severe injury but include much less serious incidents of physical harm. Other examples here would include the downplaying of effects of incidents of severe neglect of young children: primarily on the basis that the harm done is often psychological rather than physical. This appears an unhelpful distinction to draw. The view taken here is that the distinction is unjusti-fied and that taking harms, both psychological and physical, as an important part of defining violence is essential to an adequate understanding. Given this assumption, three further questions can be seen to arise. These include the question of where to set the thresholds for violence, how to address the probabilistic nature of harm and how to deal with the interactive nature of harm.

The threshold question concerns issues of severity of harms but also moral judgements and the point at which it is deemed appropriate to consider harm as ser-ious enough to constitute violence. Clearly, it can be suggested that any aggression at all may have weak and transient negative effects on individuals or groups. Most acts of this kind have though generally been excluded from consideration as vio-lence. They have been widely though not universally seen as an inadequate and potentially misleading basis for defining violence. The focus has typically been on behaviour associated with longer-term and more severe effects (Walby, Towers, Balderston et al., 2017). Notions of 'extreme' harm have at times been used, but these can be seen as generally unhelpful, with such terminology often being poorly defined and typically raising more questions than it answers. A better approach perhaps and one that has been increasingly adopted has been the use of operational definitions of harm (Hamby, 2017a). These have served to separate transitory distress and momentary physical pain from psychological and physical harms, so distinguishing unpleasant events and experiences from violent ones.

The probabilistic nature of harm refers to the fact that effect does not follow cause in a simple and mechanistic way after an act. An event needs to have a relatively high likelihood of causing harm to be counted as violence. For some individuals, minor acts may cause harm, but it seems unreasonable to treat these as violence, since this would lead to over-inclusiveness. The interactive nature of harm is linked to this probabilistic nature and in part provides an explanation. Here, individual characteristics intervene between acts and responses, with some experiencing ordinary behaviours very negatively, whilst others will show a high tolerance to adverse experiences. This does not though justify redefining such behaviours. As an example, the rejection of a request for an intimate relationship, or social meeting, cannot reasonably be seen to constitute a violent act, even where an individual may perceive this as aggressive and experience psychological harm. As noted already, harm alone should not be seen as sufficient to determine an act to be violent and harm may follow from normal social behaviours, accidents or simply unpleasant experiences of not getting what we desire. Harm is though a necessary part of an adequate consideration of violence. Many unpleasant experiences in life are non-essential, unwanted and intentional but do not meet the definition of being harmful. Without a requirement for harm and one that sets this clearly above the threshold of transitory unhappiness or frustration, then much of normal experience ranging from receiving junk mail to the ups and downs of interpersonal relationships would be inappropriately classified as violence (Follingstad, 2017).

Intentional

Intent to harm is seen in most definitions of violence and serves to exclude many neutral and positive events, as well as some harmful ones. Notions of intent are not though without significant difficulties. Intent may often be unclear or hard to discern. It is generally not observable in the way that many harms are but needs to be inferred. Intentions can also be mixed or confused and the area is one replete with case law that has grappled with these complexities. Even where intent seems to be clearly absent, issues of recklessness and negligence may arise. For example, murder is clearly defined in UK law as intentionally killing another, an archetypal example of violence. In cases where such intent is lacking though, convictions for manslaughter or culpable homicide are an option, usually where someone has been reckless as to the outcome of their behaviour, or severely negligent in their actions (Ashworth and Horder, 2013).

Capacity for intent is also important and similar behaviours may be viewed quite differently where individuals lack the capacity to form an intent to act in given ways. An example here would be from common law and the concept of *dolus incapax*, where young children are seen to lack the capacity to form necessary intent. As a result, they are not held to be accountable for what would be defined as violent criminal acts in most adults. Intent also needs to be clearly separated from motive. Motives may be illegitimate, delusional or real, but all may be distinguished from forming the intention to undertake specific acts. It is possible to have motive without any intent to act or to form an intention based on spurious or irrational motives.

It has been suggested that intent is best viewed as a continuum of disposition to act with three general ranges of intent discernible (Hamby, 2017a):

(1) Clearly malicious intent. This would include a range of intent seen in criminal violence, for example, the offence of murder (Finkelhor, 2008).
(2) Unintentional harmful outcomes, such as those seen in sporting events or during medical procedures. Here, the outcomes are harmful but were not intended to be and as such would not meet the requirements to be defined as violent crime.
(3) Perhaps the largest group comprised of those events falling between (1) and (2) where the acts are intentional but lack malicious intent, which would for example include harms caused by systemic failings and omissions, such as decisions to under-resource crucial services to maximise profits.

Issues of recklessness and negligence have been largely unaddressed in psychological approaches to the definition of violence, and they have proved difficult to model in cross-species and biological research. They have though been extensively considered in socio-legal approaches. Violence cannot in practice be defined solely based on a specific malicious intent to enact given outcomes, and the reality is more nuanced than this. Notions of behaving in a reckless way or ways that are indifferent to negative outcomes need to be adequately captured in this area. Cases of child neglect perhaps show this most clearly. Here, it is often acts of omission rather than commission that are involved, with these often better construed as recklessness or 'callous disregard' for the welfare of children. Some public health models have perhaps captured this better as violence than psychological models. Similarly, the case of sexual abuse often sees the question of intent being complicated and, as suggested by some, overcomplicated (Hamby, 2017b). Here, the behaviours seen are often using illegitimate means to pursue widely desired goals of sexual activity. There may in some instances be no direct intent to cause harm but rather a reckless indifference or disregard as to whether it is caused.

What violence is not

There have been many other efforts to define what violence is and it is not possible, or indeed helpful, to try to discuss all these here. It may though be useful to briefly consider some of the most popular approaches that are widely viewed in the literature as unproductive or unhelpful in defining violence. First amongst these is perhaps historic definitions that have seen violence as primarily a violation of social norms. This has a superficial appeal but is in fact not a reliable way to define violence. It shares many of the problems seen in exemplar-based approaches to definition but adds to these. Social norms are themselves unstable constructions, and they have changed over time and can indeed also be actively changed at a policy level (Neville, 2015; Van Kleef, Gelfand and Jetten, 2019). Taking some obvious examples from history, it is only comparatively recently that rape within marriage has been accepted in many states as a violent criminal offence or that family violence has been seen as a matter for the criminal justice system. A reliance on a social norms-based definition of violence then would suggest that in some places, these are violent acts, and in others, they are not. Similarly, it might lead to the view that prior to being socially proscribed by being made illegal, these acts were not violence. Furthermore, it is notable that states have at times reverted to earlier views, driven largely by a desire to return to what are seen by those in power as historic social norms, with the laws changed accordingly. Clearly, such a shifting and inconsistent approach to definition of what constitutes violence is not a helpful basis for study (Hamby, 2017a).

Another approach to defining violence has been to focus on it simply as an aspect of anger and hostility. Confounding these emotional states with aggression and violence is though a serious error that leads to undesired effects on definition. Anger is a universal, or near universal, emotion. Feelings of hostility may clearly stem from this and as an emotional state this can in fact be highly functional and adaptive (Towl and Dexter, 1994). It may have clear survival value for humans and indeed other species (Wilson, 2000). Anger does though need to be regulated and self-regulated for it to remain functional, and it can also very clearly become dysfunctional (Cavell and Malcolm, 2007). Critically though, anger and hostility are not an essential characteristic of violence. It is entirely possible to see violence in the absence of any anger or feelings of hostility, with violence being carried out in what is often termed 'cold blood' or associated with some other emotional state. Examples here might include the use of state-sanctioned torture or the use of extra-judicial killings.

Finally, efforts have often been made to define violence in terms of the nature of the act, or the personal or situational characteristics of those involved. This appears in many respects like exemplar-based definitions of violence. It is problematic for some of the same reasons, placing an excessive focus on some types of violence and excluding others. This has often led to an undue focus on some forms of criminal physical violence. As a result, the approach often neglects other acts such as 'child neglect' or 'sexual abuse.' A focus on personal or situational characteristics exacerbates this by frequently limiting the focus to specific sub-groups involved in violence.

The importance of good definition

Good operational definitions are important to the scientific study of any subject area. In forensic practice, they provide the bedrock of systematic assessment, theory development and hopefully effective interventions. The area of violence has, historically, suffered from a wide range of vague and unhelpful terminology, which has in turn been associated with over and under-inclusive definitions of violence. Forensic psychology has traditionally been prone to limiting the focus to the area of direct person-to-person violent acts, whilst neglecting systemic and structural aspects of violence, thus creating a misleading picture of the subject area.

In addition, there has also been the issue of shifting definitions over time and often muddled debates following from these. Discussion of the area of violence has often been conducted at cross purposes about quite different concepts, and this can reasonably be seen to have held back progress in understanding. It is not a way in which scientific understanding can progress. In line with this, it is stressed here that the use of clearer terminology is helpful and indeed fundamental. The use of terms such as 'sexual violence' in place of 'sexual abuse' or 'caregiver violence' in place of 'child abuse' seems an important part of this clarification, with more descriptively accurate terminology contributing to better measurement, theory, policy and practice development. At the same time, it may be best to finally abandon the popular euphemism of 'grooming' leaving this as a term perhaps best reserved for areas such as equine care (DiSantis and Towl, 2025).

Definition also greatly affects measurement. Poorly defined concepts, it seems clear, are not ones that can be accurately measured. Theory development also rests on clarity of definition, and much of the existing work in this area has been guilty of relying on vague or weak definitions. This, it can be suggested, has been associated with the development of inadequate single motive models seeking to account for violence. Examples here would include feminist models of violence. Similarly, social–psychological models of violence have often proved inadequate, tending to draw on a range of risk factors for aggressive acts but failing to address the essential elements for violence, or how these risk factors link to intent and then to violence. Models such as the general aggression model pay little attention to the role of underlying behavioural goals (DeWall, Anderson and Bushman, 2011). As a result, they tend to suggest interventions that block behaviours, rather than develop replacement with a broader repertoire of functional behaviour.

Public health models have adopted an apparently similar focus on risk factors and have been similarly lacking when it comes to integrating these into an analysis of underlying causes (Hamby, 2017a). An illustrative example of this is the Haddon matrix which was derived from the study of natural disasters, accidents and unintentional acts (Haddon, 1970). This matrix was subsequently applied to the analysis of violence, in terms of the agents of violence, such as the types of weapons used and a range of environmental factors (Hemenway, 2009). Such modelling has been descriptively and practically useful but has been relatively weak in terms of theory development, as well as largely neglecting the role of human factors, such as recklessness, in violence.

Summary and conclusions

The development of good operational definitions to define key terms is a fundamental aspect of systematic inquiry into any given topic. Progress in scientific research, policy and practice depends largely on having a common frame of reference. The area of violence has long suffered from the use of weak definitions and the use of inconsistent or incompatible terminology. Concepts such as anger or aggression have often been conflated with violence. Such weaknesses have been further complicated by the use a wide variety of explanatory models, drawing from very different foundations, in areas such as law, public health, sociology and psychology. Forensic practice has tended to place undue focus on direct person-to-person acts of violence at the expense of considering systemic violence and group-based effects. This has acted to distort work in this area, to the detriment of important aspects of violence and aggression, and there is a case for strong corrective action here.

The approach adopted here and throughout this text builds primarily on psychological models of violence, drawing mainly from social and biological and comparative psychology. The position taken here is that violence and areas such as social injustice and inequality are better treated separately. An extension of the concept of violence to include broader aspects of political, social and economic policies appears to be an unhelpful over extension of the concept of violence. Although often unintended, this detracts from rather than enhances effective study. It is undoubtedly the case that social injustice exists but this is, it has been argued, better studied as an economic and social phenomenon distinct from violence, which is not to suggest that this is not an area that forensic practice needs to be mindful of, as part of the wider context surrounding aggression and violence (Armstead, Wilkins and Nation, 2021).

A distinction is drawn between aggression and violence. Aggression is seen here as an adaptive and functional behaviour, seen across many species. As such, aggression is not seen as a negative or dysfunctional behaviour. Appropriate use and control of aggression is seen as part of normal human development and something fundamental to normal human development. In contrast, violence is seen as maladaptive and lacking functional goals, such as self-defence. In summary, it can be argued that violence needs to be understood in terms of four definitional components, which in combination may clearly separate it from other behaviours. Firstly, violent acts concern the expression of non-essential behaviours. Secondly, they involve behaviours that are seen as unwanted. Thirdly, violence is seen as causing significant harm exceeding some threshold. Finally, violence is seen as behaviour that is intentional or if not intentional then reckless over causing harm.

Effectively defining aggression and violence are foundational to efforts to study violence in a scientific manner. This is similarly the case for efforts to understand and respond positively to political and state violence, where clarity of definition is central to the development of effective policy and practice. A lack of a clear definition of these areas in forensic practice has contributed to serious weaknesses and failings.

References

Armstead, T. L., Wilkins, N., and Nation, M. (2021). Structural and social determinants of inequities in violence risk: a review of indicators. *Journal of Community Psychology*, *49*(4), 878–906.

Ashworth, A., and Horder, J. (2013). *Principles of Criminal Law*. Oxford: Oxford University Press.

Brown, J. (2019). *How is the Government Implementing a 'Public Health Approach' to Serious Violence?* London: House of Commons Library.

Buss, A.H. (1961). *The psychology of aggression.* New York: Wiley.

Cavell, T. A. and Malcolm, K. T. (Eds.) (2007). *Anger, Aggression, and Interventions for Interpersonal Violence* (1st ed.). London: Routledge.

Chomsky, N. (1970, May 21). Notes on Anarchism. *New York Review of Books*. New York: Hederman. https://archive.org/details/NotesOnAnarchism/mode/2up

Coie, J. D., Dodge, K. A., and Kupersmidt, J. B. (1990). Peer group behavior and social status. In S. R. Asher and Coie, J. D. (Eds.), *Peer Rejection in Childhood*. New York: Cambridge University Press.

Collins. (2024). *Collins English Dictionary*. Glasgow: Collins.

De Boer, S. F. (2018). Animal models of excessive aggression: implications for human aggression and violence. *Current Opinion in Psychology*, *19*, 81–87.

DeWall, C. N., Anderson, C. A., and Bushman, B. J. (2011). The general aggression model: theoretical extensions to violence. *Psychology of Violence*, *1*(3), 245–258.

Dewi, K. U. and Cahyani, D. P. (2020). The United States zero tolerance immigration policy: an analysis of structural violence. *Global Strategic*, *14*(1), 31–44.

DiSantis, C. and Towl, G. J. (2025). *Addressing Student Sexual Violence in Higher Education: A Good Practice Guide* (2nd ed.). Leeds: Emerald Publishing.

Finkelhor, D. (2008). *Childhood Victimization: Violence, Crime, and Abuse.* Oxford: Oxford University Press.

Follingstad, D. (2017). The challenges of measuring violence against women. In C. Renzetti, Edleson, J., and Bergen, R. (Eds.), *Sourcebook on Violence against Women* (3rd ed.). Thousand Oaks: Sage.

Galtung, J. (1969). Violence, peace, and peace research. *Journal of Peace Research*, *6*(3), 167–191.

Gershoff, E. T. and Bitensky, S. H. (2007). The case against corporal punishment of children: converging evidence from social science research and international human rights law and implications for U.S. public policy. *Psychology, Public Policy and Law*, *13*, 231–272.

Haddon, W., Jr. (1970). On the escape of tigers: an ecologic note. *American Journal of Public Health and the Nation's Health*, *60*(12), 2229–2234.

Hamby, S. (2017a). On defining violence, and why it matters. *Psychology of Violence*, *7*(2), 167–180.

Hamby, S. (2017b). A scientific answer to a scientific question: the gender debate on intimate partner violence. *Trauma, Violence, and Abuse*, *18*(2), 145–154.

Hamby, S. and Koss, M. P. (2003). Shades of gray: a qualitative study of terms used in the measurement of sexual victimization. *Psychology of Women Quarterly*, *27*, 243–255.

Hardman, R. (2019). 'Deviant' or Criminal? On-field 'Sports Violence' and the Involvement of Criminal Law in English Rugby Union. Unpublished Doctoral dissertation, Durham University. http://etheses.dur.ac.uk/13351/1/Thesis_(Final_Version)_.pdf

Hemenway, D. (2009). *While We Were Sleeping: Success Stories in Injury and Violence Prevention*. Berkeley: University of California Press.

Herrick, C. and Bell, K. (2022). Concepts, disciplines and politics: on 'structural violence' and the 'social determinants of health.' *Critical Public Health*, *32*(3), 295–308.

Kim, V. and Rabin, R. (2024, 25 Jan). Protests resume at the Israel-Gaza border after aid trucks were rerouted. *New York Times* [Digital Edition].

Koolhaas, J. M., de Boer, S. F., and Buwalda, B. (2010). Neurobiology of offensive aggression. In G. Koob, Moal, M. L., and Thompson, R. (Eds.), *Encyclopedia of Behavioral Neuroscience*. San Diego: Elsevier Press.

Kopelman, L. M. (1997). The best-interests standard as threshold, ideal, and standard of reasonableness. *Journal of Medicine and Philosophy*, *22*(3), 271–289.

Kormos, H. R. (2014). The nature of combat stress. In C. R. Figley (Ed.), *Stress Disorders Among Vietnam Veterans: Theory, Research and Treatment*. London: Routledge.

Korsgaard, C. M. (1996). *The Sources of Normativity*. Cambridge: Cambridge University Press.

Lereya, S. T., Copeland, W. E., Costello, E. J., and Wolke, D. (2015). Adult mental health consequences of peer bullying and maltreatment in childhood: two cohorts in two countries. *The Lancet Psychiatry*, *2*, 524–531.

Lorenz, K. (1981). *The Foundations of Ethology*. Vienna: Springer.

Morris, C. (2008). State legitimacy and social order. In J. Kühnelt (Ed.), *Political Legitimization without Morality?* Dordrecht: Springer Netherlands.

Natarajan, D. and Caramaschi, D. (2010). Animal violence demystified. *Frontiers in Behavioral Neuroscience*, *4*, 9–16.

Neville, F. G. (2015). Preventing violence through changing social norms. In P. Donnelly and Ward, C. (Eds.), *Oxford Textbook of Violence Prevention*. Oxford: Oxford University Press.

Newton, M. and May, L. (2014). *Proportionality in International Law*. Oxford: Oxford University Press.

Osofsky, J. D. (1995). The effects of exposure to violence on young children. *American Psychologist*, *50*(9), 782.

Pontara, G. (1978). The concept of violence. *Journal of Peace Research*, *1*, 19–32.

Ristroph, A. (2010). Criminal law in the shadow of violence. *Alabama Law Review*, *62*, 571–621.

San Kuay, H. and Towl, G. (2021). *Child to Parent Aggression and Violence: A Guidebook for Parents and Practitioners*. London: Routledge.

Singer, P. (1993). *Practical Ethics* (2nd ed.). Cambridge: Cambridge University Press.

Thomas-Peter, B. A. and Lawday, R. (2021). Role of safeguarding in overcoming persistent harmful practice in forensic mental health. In D. A. Crighton and Towl, G. J. (Eds.), *Forensic Psychology* (3rd ed.). Chichester: BPS Wiley.

Towl, G. and Dexter, P. (1994). Anger management in prisons: an empirical investigation. *Groupwork London*, *7*, 256–259.

Vaillancourt, T. and Hymel, S. (2006). Aggression and social status: the moderating roles of sex and peer-valued characteristics. *Aggressive Behavior: Official Journal of the International Society for Research on Aggression*, *32*(4), 396–408.

Van Kleef, G. A., Gelfand, M. J., and Jetten, J. (2019). The dynamic nature of social norms: new perspectives on norm development, impact, violation, and enforcement. *Journal of Experimental Social Psychology*, *84*, 103814.

Vasterling, J. J., Proctor, S. P., Amoroso, P., Kane, R., Heeren, T., and White, R. F. (2006). Neuropsychological outcomes of army personnel following deployment to the Iraq war. *JAMA*, *296*(5), 519–529.

Walby, S., Towers, J., Balderston, S., Corradi, C., Francis, B., Heiskanen, M., ... and Strid, S. (2017). *The Concept and Measurement of Violence against Women and Men.* Bristol: Policy Press.

Wilson, E. O. (2000). *Sociobiology: The New Synthesis.* Cambridge: Harvard University Press.

World Health Organization. (2024). *Definition and Typology of Violence.* Geneva: World Health Organization.

Wyckoff, J. (2013). Is the concept of violence normative? *Revue Internationale de Philosophie, 265*(3), 337–352.

2   Defining political violence

The current use of the term 'terrorism' can be traced to the French Revolution of 1789, where reference was made to 'the Terror' or the Jacobin Terror. This is not to suggest, of course, that some of the acts seen in that period did not pre-date it, rather that this is widely seen to be the derivation of the terminology. This period of history also serves to highlight some of the complexities and contradictions that were present and have remained inherent in the language used. The Jacobin Terror took place between June 1793 and July 1794, at which point the violent overthrow of the revolutionary leader Maximilien Robespierre led to a decline in violence, at least in its legalised form stemming from the French state.

Three principle causes of the Jacobin Terror have subsequently been suggested:

(1) The strength of the counter-revolutionary response to the 1789 Revolution and the rapid escalation of this between 1791 and 1793.
(2) The absence of any Parliamentary tradition in France, with the revolution-aries having no experience of forming political parties, coalitions, majority voting or tolerating opposing views. This followed from the French state moving directly from an absolute Monarchy with those in charge falling back on abstract Universalist principles and vague 'enlightenment rhetoric,' with politics becoming increasingly divisive and having little scope for legitimised opposition.
(3) Most significantly, an explicitly counter-revolutionary war with an alliance of foreign powers had started in 1792. In turn this led to growing demands for a wartime economy, increasing polarisation of political views and active encouragement of denunciations of suspected 'counter-revolutionaries' (Linton, 2012).

By 1793, this war against Austrian, Prussian, British and Spanish allied powers was clearly seen to be going badly, with concerns that there was a high risk of invasion. Civil war had also broken out in parts of France (the Vendee Civil War) in 1793, motivated partly by the threat of military conscription. By that summer, leaders of the revolution were seen to be blaming others for increasingly difficult conditions. Views were also becoming increasingly radical, with further support

DOI: 10.4324/9781003429579-2

being sought from radicals drawn largely from the 'lower orders' (the so-called 'Sans Culottes'). The revolts that took place in France were not always counter-revolutionary in nature, but such distinctions were quickly lost as revolutionary leaders focussed on two key aims: winning the war and imposing their ideology throughout the state. Here, creating terror within the French population was used to achieve both aims, as well as being used as a means of enforcing the weakening legitimacy of the regime, through the notorious Committee of Public Safety (Linton, 2012).

Popular mythology has suggested that most of deaths that resulted from the Jacobin Terror occurred in Paris and involved aristocrats, who could reasonably be seen as reactionary and hostile to the aims of the revolution. This is though not the case, with the great majority of victims being drawn from the peasantry. Most of the deaths were those who had, for a variety of reasons, taken up arms against the Jacobin revolution. Aristocratic émigrés who had returned to France were certainly amongst the victims, since many were assumed to be spies. Priests who resisted the new ideology were also more liable to be executed. Both groups though only formed a minority of those who were killed. Similarly, the notion that most executions occurred in Paris has been shown to be misleading. In fact, analysis of official records suggests that Paris saw 16,549 'legal' death sentences. Far more deaths than this occurred across the various war zones in France. Here, credible estimates have suggested that around 250,000 of those deemed 'insurgents' and around 200,000 republicans were killed during a war that was marked, on both sides, by terrible atrocities (Linton, 2012).

Terrorism, insurgency, guerrilla war and hybrid war

Terrorism, insurgency, guerrilla and hybrid war can each be seen as differing forms of politically motivated violence. There is though no agreement on how to define these terms by prospective grouping into a firm typology, or by retrospective grouping into a logically coherent taxonomy, based on clear and distinct criteria. This lack of solid agreement in defining terms is the result, in large part, of a lack of common understanding across the area. There are widely differing perspectives around the ethics of such violence, its history and the political basis underpinning the concepts (Ramraj, 2006).

Insurgency has been defined in terms of resistance, revolt or violent armed rebellion against a state. As such, it involves unequal or asymmetric conflict between parties. Here, the existing state will typically have far greater strength, in terms of military and security resources. The resulting asymmetry, in capacity and availability in the use of force, in turn suggests differences in strategy and tactics. In an insurgency, this conflict does not reach the level of an organised revolution, although it may transition into this. Insurgency is not defined in international law in the same way as warfare, so those engaged in insurgent acts lack the protections normally now afforded to combatants in war, such as the Geneva Conventions. Many examples of insurgent actions can be seen in recent history, including the many insurgencies that emerged as part of the decolonisation movements. For example, these were seen following the end of World War II across much of Asia and Africa.

Guerrilla warfare, in contrast to insurgency, is typically defined as a form of war (Taber, 1970). It is distinguished from warfare in that it involves 'irregular' troops, often engaged in small-scale actions against a more powerful opponent and focussed on military or armed police targets. On occasion though, it may also involve actions against rival anti-state actors. Guerilla warfare may be undertaken independently, or as part of a broader military–political strategy, and the term can be traced back to the Peninsula War (1808–1814) in Europe. Here, Spanish and Portuguese irregulars (called guerrilleros) fought to drive the French occupying forces out of the Iberian Peninsula. Those who engage in guerrilla warfare have attracted a wide variety of names including rebels, irregulars, insurgents, partisans and mercenaries. They have also frequently been described as 'terrorists' typically by those targeted by guerrilla attacks.

Hybrid warfare is a more recently coined term and has evolved and been refined over its short history (Hoffman, 2007; Johnson, 2018). This idea builds on other theories concerning 'Fourth Generation Warfare,' 'Compound War' and 'Unrestricted Warfare.' These theories have in common a stress on convergence in warfare of the methods of violence used. The hybridisation here primarily concerns a blending of the lethality of state actors, directly or through proxy actors, with the strong belief systems and the organisational structures and methods seen in other forms of politically motivated violence (Hoffman, 2007). This typically involves the power of state actors being used in the context of insurgencies and civil wars. In recent years, this has been seen increasingly to involve multi-dimensional approaches to violence, exploiting modern information technology and integrating this into violent operations. An early example of this process was the conflict between Hezbollah and Israel in 2006, which provided a clear example of a modern hybrid challenge with the use of rapidly developing information technology with politically motivated violence (Hoffman, 2007). Hybrid threats can be seen to involve a full range of methods including conventional capabilities, use of irregular formations, terrorist acts, indiscriminate violence and varied forms of non-political criminal behaviour. Use of such methods may be undertaken by distinct units or by units engaged in more conventional tactics. These units can be operationally and tactically directed to use hybrid methods with the aim of achieving synergistic effects, both physical and psychological. As a result, hybrid war has come to be seen as distinct from previous forms of warfare in this blurring of methods seen at lower organisational levels. Many wars in the past have involved these kinds of actions and have involved use of both regular and irregular forces, along with the development and use of what have been termed 'psychological operations.' These are argued to be distinct from hybrid warfare, on the basis that they were strategically coordinated and took place in different 'theatres' of conflict or were undertaken by distinct formations (Roberts, 2018). In contrast, it has been argued that hybrid warfare has seen a blending and blurring of these kinds of distinction extending down to operational and tactical levels (Hoffman, 2007). The notion of hybrid warfare is also subject to some significant criticisms at a conceptual level. Most significantly perhaps, has been the suggestion that hybrid warfare is simply a relabelling of something that has existed for a long time, with the term not describing anything new or distinctive (Green, 2020). Certainly, many of the characteristics involved can be seen in conflicts that took place during the Cold War of the 1950s and 1960s, when both superpowers engaged in such actions. Critics of the term have also suggested that it simply describes some evolution in tactics (Galeotti, 2016). The use of new and emerging forms of technology has been common here and the use of current information technology can be seen as a continuation, albeit with very powerful technology, of this trend. There appears to be validity to these kinds of criticisms. Despite this though, the terminology of hybrid warfare has gone on to form part of orthodox military thinking and language in US and other defence circles.

The term 'terrorism' is highly contentious and has probably enjoyed the lowest levels of agreement around its definition. It is characterised by its perceived illegitimacy and has strongly negative connotations. The term also engages intense emotions that are attached to its use. This lack of agreement around definition has led to the study of terrorism being approached from a range of very different perspectives. There is a large body of research which has looked at terrorism in terms of conceptual definitions (Ganor, 2002; Saul, 2005; Goodwin, 2006; Crenshaw, 2010). Other approaches have focussed on terrorism in specific contexts, such as the study of the role of terrorism in civil wars (Kalyvas, 2004; Sambanis, 2008; Findley and Young, 2012; Jones and Pedahzur, 2013). Others have stressed the importance of looking at the relationship between terrorism and other forms of political violence and its function as a tactic or method (Harmon, 2001; Kydd and Walter, 2006).

Most of the approaches taken to terrorism can be seen as being action-based, meaning that they have defined it in terms of the status of the targets and the violence used (Harmon, 2001; Ganor, 2002; Kalyvas, 2004; Kydd and Walter, 2006; Sambanis, 2008). This has included lone-actor and multiple actor-based studies concerned with the perpetrators of terrorism (Wilson, 2000; Sánchez-Cuenca and De la Calle, 2009). Linked to this have been various studies which have tried to develop useful typologies or profiles of terrorists (Kydd and Walter, 2006; Stepanova, 2008). A markedly different approach to research has focussed on the development of conceptual legal definitions of terrorism, rather than focussing on actors or actions involved (Golder and Williams, 2004). At least since the mid-20th century, there have been concerted efforts to develop agreed legal frameworks for terrorism. These have often drawn on ontological approaches, which have sought to identify the characteristics of political violence, violent uprisings and the perceived legitimacy of the cause (Gibbs, 1989; Barber, 2007).

The bulk of existing studies into terrorism have used criteria that are argued to exist simultaneously. Typically, these have stressed organisation at a sub-state level, the use of threats or violence against civilian populations and the presence of political motives and goals that underpin these actions (Schmid, 2004; Saul, 2005; Goodwin, 2006; Crenshaw, 2010). Amongst action-oriented approaches to terrorism, a primary concern has been the nature, form and purpose of violence.

Violence here is commonly seen as a tool to achieve some ends rather than being the end product of terrorism. So terrorist violence is seen as being used with the aim of taking forward some political goal which motivates the individual and group undertaking the act (Kalyvas, 2004). An important distinction suggested here, between insurgents and terrorists, is that the former enjoy wider public support and sympathy and may often see this as important to their cause. For terrorist groups though, the generation of public fear and anxiety is seen as the primary aim and public support may or may not be important (Zartman, 2006). The extent to which such a distinction can be supported in reality is open to challenge and such division may be unclear. In practice, both insurgent and terrorist groups may be largely concerned with keeping parts of the populace on side and may aim to increase feelings of anxiety and fear in other parts of the populace. Given such blurred boundaries, some have suggested the adoption of terms such as 'militant terrorist group' or 'revolutionary terrorism' to distinguish those groups where the primary function is to generate feelings of fear and terror in the wider popula-tion, from those which use terrorist methods as part of broader political insurgency (Crenshaw-Hutchinson, 1972; Stepanova, 2008; Crenshaw, 2010; Belge, 2011; Ünal, 2014, 2016a, 2016b).

Critics of this separation of different forms of politically motivated violence have countered that these need to be studied and understood together, rather than in isolation, as part of a broad continuum of politically motivated violence. The pri-mary reason often put forward for avoiding such separation is that these differing forms commonly coexist, complementing each other and indeed being used inter-changeably (Findley and Young, 2012). Additionally, there may often be links between these differing forms of violence and studying each in isolation will, at best, give a limited understanding of the area. Others have argued that whilst this may be true of the progression from insurgency through to civil war, this does not apply to terrorism which is in fact distinct, having separate and different causes which need to be studied as such (Sambanis, 2008). In line with this, it has been suggested that terrorism cannot normally evolve into civil war, except as a method used in the very early stages of an insurgency. Insurgents at this early stage, it is suggested, will exploit whatever works in the circumstances that pertain and will exploit terrorist methods wherever possible, as the easiest method of political struggle (Merari, 1993). As political struggles evolve and change, different forms of political violence may be favoured. In large part this may be due to the high costs of terrorism, as a form of political signalling, relying amongst other things on intimidation, provocation and attrition (Kydd and Walter, 2006; Ünal, 2016a).

Method versus movement

This debate, around whether terrorism is best seen as a distinct phenomenon or as part of a broader continuum of political violence, which may overlap with insur-gency, guerrilla war and civil war, is an important one. The distinction is important because terrorism is generally used as a highly pejorative term. This can lead to neglect of genuine grievances and concerns that may be the drivers for violence. In contrast, insurgency and guerrilla war may be used to suggest at least some degree of legitimacy. Views on this have diverged with some stressing the differences that are involved in resorting to terrorism, as contrasted with the other forms of political violence. Following on from this, it has been argued that terrorism is most usefully viewed as a distinct form that can be further broken down into multiple terrorist strategies, each with distinct purpose and reason (Sambanis, 2008). Others have countered this view stressing that such distinctions can be misleading, preferring to see terrorism as one method that may be used by some along with other forms of political violence. As such, terrorist violence would be seen as a complementary or supplementary method of political violence and a by-product of a political claim that cannot be easily distinguished from other forms (Findley and Young, 2012).

Use of terrorist methods has been seen as part of a strategy in insurgencies and civil wars and as an aspect of some armed conflicts. Resort to terrorist methods is not universal though. It is evident that, for example, some insurgent movements have not used and indeed have actively renounced terrorist methods, whilst others have embraced them (Stepanova, 2008). Such decisions may be linked to concerns such as perceived legitimacy, levels of public support, likelihood of progression to civil war, capacity to undertaken guerilla warfare and the perceived likelihood of replacing the current state. Typological analysis has been suggested as a useful means of explaining why such differences have been observed. To take one example of this kind of analysis, it has been argued that terrorism can be subdivided. This would include distinguishing international from domestic terrorism. A further division based on motivation (nationalistic, religious, etc.) is suggested. Finally, a distinction based on functional factors is suggested with terrorism being divided in 'Classic' and 'Conflict related' forms, the latter being where terrorism is used as part of a broader conflict such as an insurgency (Stepanova, 2008).

There is some indirect support for such typologies. Within state insurgencies mostly appear to employ guerrilla warfare as a method of conflict, and indeed, in some cases, the two terms may appear to be used synonymously (Goodwin, 2006; Frisch, 2012). As a result, some have suggested combining the terms, with reference to guerrilla insurgency (Joes, 2006). One example of this blending is the Marxist Theory of Peoples War. This was adopted as an approach to political violence, for example, by Mao Tse Tung in the post-World War II period. This relied on guerrilla warfare techniques which are to be achieved by mobilising urban workers and peasants to engage initially in insurgence, escalating to guerrilla warfare and civil war. On successful completion, this guerrilla army would then be converted into the regular state armed forces (Rich, 1984).

Insurgencies have been distinguished as being politico-military in nature. This suggests that they actively draw on social, political and economic means, in addition to violent conflict typically targeting military forces. All this forms part of a broad-based campaign against a state or similar power (Nagl, Amos, Sewall et al., 2008). Such actions though have been reported to increasingly draw on the use of terrorist methods in recent years, as well as diversifying into the use of more high-tech digitally based methods. This is complicated by examples of the use of similar methods by state actors, as a means of simulating home-grown insurgencies as part of security and military operations. One example of this would be the use by the actions of the Russian Federation in some neighbouring states (Galeotti, 2015).

Directness of challenge or fight

An alternative way of distinguishing types of political violence has been suggested, which draws on how direct or indirect the challenge presented is. Here, insurgencies, guerrilla warfare and civil war are seen as increasingly direct forms of challenge, involving increasingly direct violence directed against the dominant power or state (Joes, 2006). Terrorism by contrast is characterised as an indirect challenge, where the primary aim is to create fear, anxiety and intimidation. The intention here is to provoke a political reaction or over-reaction (Ganor, 2002; Schmid, 2004). This is not though a universally accepted viewpoint, and some have argued that terrorism may involve very direct challenge (Crenshaw-Hutchinson, 1972). Terrorism though rarely brings about political change in isolation.

Structure and goals

These do not necessarily differ between various types of political violence in consistent ways, although as noted, terrorist violence can be seen as the most indirect. It also tends to have the weakest direct links between the actions undertaken and overall goals, relying as it does on the intermediate response of the state or individuals (Crenshaw, 2011). Terrorism also tends to be more clandestine than other forms of political violence (Crenshaw-Hutchinson, 1972; McCormick and Giordano, 2007), where some level of public support is needed to sustain protracted direct conflict (Joes, 2006; Sambanis, 2008). As such, underground cell structures and formations are more often used (McCormick and Giordano, 2007; Sánchez-Cuenca and De la Calle, 2009). This compares to more centralised decision making and representative management bodies that can engage in talks more often seen in insurgent and guerrilla groups.

Legal definitions of terrorism

Although the types of violent behaviour involved in terrorism go back throughout human history and the term itself can be traced back to the 18th century, legal efforts to define the term appear to be more recent. Efforts at legal definition nationally and internationally can be seen from the 20th century onwards. Here, initial attempts at universal definition appeared largely unsuccessful. The 21st century and particularly the events of 9/11 in New York saw renewed and concerted efforts to achieve agreement in this area, although progress has again been limited. Following the attack on the United States, enhanced state powers were put in place across several states. This created a need for a clearer legal meaning of terrorism to limit the scope of this kind of legislation. Limitation here was crucial to protect civil liberties, such as rights to privacy and to protect the rule of law more widely. Several key difficulties though contribute to this intractability in achieving an agreed definition of terrorism, which can reliably distinguish it from other forms of political or other violence. Some of these have already been touched on above but warrant more detailed consideration. In doing this, some normative points are assumed:

(1) That terrorism presents a serious threat to national security.
(2) That the law needs to respond to this threat.
(3) That the capacity of law to respond is limited.
(4) That legal response needs to be proportionate.
(5) That legal response needs to be compliant with human rights and the rule of law.

Definitions in international law

Different states have taken up distinct and often very different political positions on terrorism. One of the most intractable differences seen here involves the question of whether the actions of states can be viewed as terrorism. Another major area of dispute has been whether national liberation movements can legitimately be viewed as terrorist. Such questions have remained largely unresolved and instead what can be seen as an inductive method has dominated the area. This focuses on the description and proscription of specific acts, analogous to the exemplar-based approach to aggression and violence discussed in Chapter 1. This contrasts with the more usual deductive legal approach of trying to achieve and apply overarching or conceptual definitions (Golder and Williams, 2004).

The use of this kind of specific inductive approach to definition has had various effects. Most strikingly perhaps, it has often supported a shift of focus on to specific presentations of terrorism over time, rather than the concept itself. In doing this, international law has largely sidestepped the political aspects of terrorism (Sorel, 2003). This approach can also be seen to have led to the growth of multiple international conventions, for example, the International Convention Against the Taking of Hostages 1316 UNTS 205 which is focussed on one form of terrorist act. The utility of this kind of act-by-act approach to particular acts is open to multiple criticisms (Sorel, 2003; Walker, 2004). Most significant of these is perhaps the suggestion that the lack of internationally agreed legal definitions has had very negative impacts on areas such as policy development, policing and enforcement.

Universal conventions in this area do exist though and examples of the bodies responsible would include the International Civil Aviation Organisation (ICAO), the International Maritime Organization (IMO), the International Atomic Energy Agency (IAEA) and the General Assembly of the United Nations (UN). Conventions in various areas have been relatively well developed, but the extent of definition within them has been generally limited to enumerating and describing relevant acts. As a result, they can be criticised for often being confused and overlapping, lacking clarity around meaning. In addition, they have tended to be depoliticised, in a way that is inconsistent with the nature of terrorism as a form of politically motivated violence (Sorel, 2003).

This has led to some suggestions that legal definition of terrorism is unnecessary, with the UN Security Council, suggesting in 2001 that the term was redundant and unnecessary, reflecting a pejorative term for some forms of political violence. As a result, it has been argued that a range of international law will be applicable to terrorism, rather than there being a need for an international law of terrorism (Higgins and Flory, 1997). The suggestion here seems to be that that terrorism is largely or exclusively a term of convenience, lacking clear legal meaning, so that a reliance on descriptive approaches is justified. Reliance on description to capture terrorism risks would see the term itself as a social judgement rather than a social phenomenon (Sorel, 2003).

Such debates around the effective definition of terrorism in law, nationally or internationally, need to be separated from questions of legitimacy. This stresses that terrorism cannot be persuasively defined by dominant powers, simply to serve their own interests. The problems that can emerge from this are illustrated by the case of Osama Bin Laden. Here, it may be recalled, Bin Laden went from being described as a 'freedom fighter' to a 'terrorist' by the US. Similarly, Nelson Mandella went the other way, from being defined as a 'terrorist' to later being defined as a 'freedom fighter' and subsequently statesman and head of state. In fact, credible definition needs to rest on a proper 'normative order,' rather than models of police state control. Put more simply, it has been suggested that definition needs to rest on specified values that cannot be infringed, rather than being based on the suppression of criticism and protest (Sorel, 2003). The importance of this has been highlighted, even within the most mature democratic societies, by efforts to move towards exactly this kind of suppression of dissent (Ferstman, 2024).

Efforts to define terrorism based on specified values will not be perfect. It has though been suggested that such definition would need to incorporate several key elements. This would include a need to refer to illicit acts, which disturb public order. In addition, these need to be serious and indiscriminate. Critically, they also need to generate an atmosphere of terror, with this generation of emotion intended to influence political actions (Sorel, 2003). This in turn raises additional questions, about how to deal with linked activities, that have to date proved largely intractable. Here, the role of financing and the 'laundering' of money to support politically motivated violence present clear challenges. Conventions exist in this area within international law. To date though, they have proved to be largely ineffectual. Estimates by the International Monetary Fund (IMF) have suggested that between 2% and 5% of global gross domestic product annually has been subject to 'non-distrainable' laundering. Non-distrainable here essentially referring to forms of laundering that mean authorities cannot seize these funds. There are varied reasons for this, which would include the variety of methods used for this financial activity, allowing funds to be moved and redefined across international borders. This includes such actions as the use of innocuous third parties (sometimes called 'Smurfs') to move funds around. Similarly, the use of multiple shell companies and 'tax havens' can be used to make it increasingly difficult to know where funds come from or what use they are being put to (Aninat, Hardy and Johnston, 2002). Notably, there has also been a lack of adequate investigation and enforcement in this area. Large numbers of specialists may use client confidentiality as a convenient means of restricting or avoiding scrutiny. This extends across law, banking and finance but also goes beyond this to include insurance and property services. Such specialists are generally more generously resourced than the agencies charged with regulation and enforcement and indeed may recruit from these agencies. Even in the wake of 9/11, the US and UK Governments were noted to have strongly resisted giving the International Criminal Court (ICC) a role in this area (Sorel, 2003).

Examples of national approaches

Taking the US as the first example, following the terrorist attacks of 9/11, it quickly issued an executive order on terrorism. This defined terrorism as acts that involved violence, intimidation or coercion of a civilian population, involved influence by coercion or intimidation of Government policy and involved mass destruction, assassination, kidnapping or hostage taking. This was followed up by the United States Congress, on 25 October 2001, which developed its own, more extensive, definition of terrorism. It was noted that this was passed with only one dissenting vote in the US Senate and sixty-six dissenting votes in the US House of Representatives (Golder and Williams, 2004). This went on to be called the *Uniting and Strengthening America by Providing Appropriate Tools Required to Intercept and Obstruct Terrorism Act of 2001* which came to be widely known as the 'Patriot Act.' This amended the definition of 'domestic terrorism' within the US (Golder and Williams, 2004). It also set out a definition of 'international terrorism' as involving violent acts or acts dangerous to human life in violation of criminal laws that appeared to be intended to intimidate or coerce a civilian population, influence government policy or affect the conduct of a government by mass destruction, assassination or kidnapping. The definition of 'domestic' terrorism was generally similar but limited to actions within the territorial jurisdiction of the US.

This approach has been subject to considerable criticism. These include the breadth and vagueness of the definitions, which would potentially capture a very wide range of legitimate activities in a democracy. Indeed, the distinguished political philosopher Ronald Dworkin described it as a '...new, breathtakingly vague and broad definition of terrorism' (Dworkin, 2002). The risks that may arise from such breadth, in relation to individual rights and to the US constitution more widely, seem largely self-evident.

Canada

The Canadian approach to defining terrorism was somewhat unusual in that it emerged not from the legislature but from case law, in *Suresh v Canada (Minister of Citizenship and Immigration)* 44 (*'Suresh'*). Here, the Supreme Court of Canada was called on to define terrorism and terrorist organisations. These terms had been used previously but had not been adequately defined in existing legislations. In this case, the Court noted that no universally accepted definition existed but held that the term provided sufficient basis for them to adjudicate. Whilst acknowledging the difficulty of conceptual definition, they chose to rely on the *International Convention for the Suppression of the Financing of Terrorism.* Drawing on this, the view was taken that terrorism refers to acts intended to cause death or serious bodily injury to someone not involved in military conflict. The purpose of such acts was also seen as critical, involving an intention to intimidate or compel individuals or a government.

Shortly, before terrorism was judicially defined in *Suresh,* the Canadian Parliament had enacted its own legislative definition in the *Anti-terrorism Act,* RSC 2001. This defined 'terrorist activity' as involving acts or omissions in or outside Canada that, if committed in Canada, would be one of several offences. In addition, the act was wholly or partly motivated by a political, religious or ideological purpose. In addition, the intention of intimidating the public and compelling individual or government action was recognised.

United Kingdom

The United Kingdom (UK) has a lengthy history of anti-terrorism law which continues to date. In terms of modern examples, the Prevention of Terrorism (Temporary Provisions) Act 1974 was brought in. This was a response to a growing crisis in Northern Ireland. This was followed by the *Terrorism Act 2000* (UK) which contained a definition of terrorism. This definition takes terrorism to involve the use or threat of action designed to influence the government, an international governmental organisation or to intimidate the public. In addition, this needs to be made to advance a political, religious, racial or ideological cause. Such acts are limited to serious violence against a person, serious damage to property and endangering others. More contentiously, this is extended to acts that create serious risk to the health or safety of the public or part of the public, or that is designed seriously to interfere with or seriously to disrupt an electronic system. Threats of action involving firearms or explosives is also included, along with actions outside the UK.

The same definition was carried over unamended in the *Anti-terrorism, Crime and Security Act 2001* (UK), which was the UK's response to the 11 September terrorist attacks (Walker, 2004). It was also added to by the Terrorism Act 2006, although this was primarily concerned with ancillary acts, such as promotion of terrorism. This did not seek to revised the definition and as with the US response, what were called the 'vague contours' of this definition have been commented on. The main concern here was that the definition used was again very broad and so placed significant trust in 'good sense' of the police, security services, prosecutors, judges and jurors (Williams, 2003; Walker, 2004, 2011).

Problems with legal definitions of terrorism

The first problem that arises from legal efforts to define terrorism is the issue of whether to use specific or general definitions. This was made explicit in the Canadian Supreme Court judgement, which stressed the extent to which the term was open to abuse, through political manipulation and polemic interpretation *Suresh* (2002) 1 SCR 3 (94). This can be seen as an argument for a more specific definition to reduce the risk of the various forms of misuse. However, even efforts to produce specific definitions often struggle to define the essence of terrorism and may capture a wide range of non-terrorist acts, such as criminal behaviours with no political motivations, for example, capturing criminal hostage taking, undertaken for financial gain, along with terrorist hostage taking which is motivated by some political aim. Highly specified definitions that list relevant acts though create the risk of missing new and developing forms of terrorism, such as the development and growth in use of cyber-attacks. Attempts to address this may then simply lead to ever growing lists of specific acts. Indeed, the creation of highly specific laws very much invites responses, in the form of innovation and new tactics that may circumvent existing legislation. This can be seen to be one motivation behind the vagueness of definitions such as that seen in the UK approach, or the over-inclusive nature of the US approach: although both come with high costs in terms of creating potential for abuse. Such difficulties have also raised the question of why there is a need to have specific laws for terrorism at all. If the concept itself is so hard to pin down and the development of an overarching concept of terrorism presents so many serious difficulties for legislatures and Courts, then some have suggested that persistent efforts in this area are misplaced. It can be argued that it would be easier and better, in terms of protecting existing rights, to simply prosecute the acts involved under existing criminal law. A primary concern here though has been that, however difficult to legally define, terrorism is qualitatively different from other forms of violent crime. The often international nature of such acts also means domestic criminal law is often unsuited to address it; failing to recognise this may increase the vulnerability of states to attack (Buchhandler-Raphael, 2011).

Although there are differences in the exact way terrorism is defined there is currently a high level of agreement around a few core features:

(1) That there is a political, religious or ideological motivation to violence.
(2) That there is some harm to people or property.
(3) That there are coercive aims, either directed at the civilian population or government.
(4) That instilling fear is a goal.

But this level of agreement results in a definition that is much too broad to be of much practical use, since it would potentially capture instances of civil disobedience, public protest and also industrial actions such as the withdrawal of labour. This is not just a theoretical possibility either. To take recent examples from the UK, a long-running industrial dispute by nursing staff was open to a threat of action falling within the law covering terrorism. Specifically here, the use or threat of acts designed to influence the government made for the purpose of advancing a political cause. Here, acts could also be described as endangering life, other than that of the person committing the action and creating a serious risk to the health or safety of the public or a section of the public. Similarly, recent student protests over the

2024 invasion of Gaza could conceptually be caught under different sub-sections of the same UK anti-terror legislation. As noted above, the avoidance of such over-inclusion rests largely on trust.

Taking the examples above, it could be suggested that both are not intended to be acts of terrorism. Equally though, it might be argued that the absence of specific exemptions for industrial action or political protest suggests this is exactly what Parliament intended, so tying the Courts hands (Golder and Williams, 2004). The deductive approach to definition adopted in the US can be seen as presenting similar problems. Here though, the US Bill of Rights provides an overarching constitutional protection of 'free speech' to offset this, at least in terms of public protests. In the UK, Human Rights legislation provides much more limited protection in this respect. Some other common law jurisdictions though provide no such protections, as for example in Australia, where this has resulted in the use of such legislation as a means to silence environmental protests (Golder and Williams, 2004).

Who should define terrorism?

Definitions of terrorism have typically come from the legislative or executive branches of governments, although one major exception to this is given in the example outlined above from Canada. Here, at least initially definition was left in the hands of the Judiciary. This stress on legislative definition has at times led to a polarisation of views, between the political and legal. This has generally been most evident where governments have responded quickly, typically in reaction to high-profile events, with the judiciary and courts subsequently viewing the results of this as often being unduly hasty and ill considered. Such differences are not though inevitable and legislation, in states that operate under rule of law, can serve as a positive starting point for legal interpretation. On this basis, it has been argued that the real question becomes how best to divide the tasks involved in definition of terrorism within legal systems (Moses, 2003). In common law systems, it is suggested that statute only ever provides general guidance and key elements, with the interpretation of detail being done through the consideration of case law. Within codified systems of law, there is in theory less scope for case-by-case interpretation but even here, independent courts will have considerable scope to interpret the intentions of legislators. Others have argued that it would be inconceivable that democracies would leave such a contested area entirely to the judiciary and juries, without providing some defined terms (Golder and Williams, 2004). The use of statute law here serves to reduce and circumscribe the scope for interpretation of meaning. It has also been highlighted as a check against what has been described as judicial development and manipulation of precedent (Boyle, 1985; Gerhardt, 2011). Others have expressed greater concern around the risk of erosion of the separation of powers between governments and the courts, with the attendant damage to the ability of courts to check executive and legislative abuses (Haggard and Tiede, 2024).

In summary, it is notable that there are not universally agreed criteria by which to evaluate legal definitions of terrorism. Three main conclusions though can be drawn from the literature concerning what makes a good definition in this case. First of these is the adoption of a general approach, by which is meant the incorporation of a general description of the phenomena of concern, although this does not exclude the incorporation of some specific elements. Use of a general approach, it has been argued, allows for stronger political statements and legal responses to such acts of violence. In contrast, specific approaches are seen as likely to result in the generation of multiple ad hoc regulations. Secondly, it has been argued that a good legal definition needs to carve out specific exceptions, which need as a minimum to include acts relating to advocacy, dissent and industrial action. The importance of this is in the protection of democracy, even in the face of this being inconvenient, disruptive, costly and widely unpopular (Ferstman, 2024). One historic example of the dangers here would be the imprisonment in the US, on entirely spurious grounds, of Eugene Debs, the socialist candidate for the Presidential election that took place in 1918. His imprisonment served to prevent legitimate political debate (Head, 2024). Thirdly, a good legal approach needs to set out the core elements of the definition and not leave this to the courts to work out. This is significant in democratic systems, as it is the process of developing statute that involves processes of open deliberation and scrutiny. These should in turn lead to greater clarity and focus, but they are also central to achieving public acceptance. Most critically though, statute law is open to democratic accountability and challenge. In contrast, the development of case law is normally highly detailed and specific, with the thinking and balancing of considerations being largely opaque and unaccountable.

These three points highlight the inadequacy of current and recent approaches to legally defining terrorism. There has been a plethora of rushed and ill-considered responses, often driven by transitory media and increasingly social media pressures, rather than considered analysis. These largely reactive laws, particularly following the 9/11 and related attacks in Europe, gave rise of laws which have been seen as failing to match this outline of good laws. These have been progressively challenged and have needed revision over time, but this does not excuse the creation of rushed laws in the first place and the damage linked to them.

Other approaches to definition

The lack of an agreed definition of terrorism presents a series of challenges. These include how best to undertake research, develop policy and practice in the area. Here, a lack of agreed definition has undermined a normative moral stance in response to terrorism (Schmid, 2004). This has been further complicated by use of emotive, confused and often unhelpful language such as references to the 'war' on terrorism (Howard, 2002). There are multiple problems that stem from this but foremost amongst these, it has been suggested, is that such terminology gives terrorism an undue status. It suggests the presence of armed conflict that would be subject to the Geneva protocols that apply to war, when in fact these clearly do not apply. In fact, these are explicit in prohibiting terrorism as a legitimate means of warfare (O'Neil, 2004). The problems evident around such loose use of terminology in this area has led some to a counsel of despair, questioning whether a definition of terrorism is possible at all. A more limited version of this argument has questioned whether it is possible to conceive of and address terrorism as a unitary phenomenon (Laquer, 1987; Richardson, 2006).

Others have taken a more positive view of whether this can be achieved, stressing the important role of common definition of terrorism. This has included stress on at least five key roles here (Ganor, 1998):

(1) It is needed for the development of effective international strategy.
(2) For an effective international response.
(3) For effective international enforcement agreements.
(4) For reducing public legitimacy.
(5) For increasing the shift from terrorism to guerilla warfare.

A variety of approaches have been used to try to develop definitions of terrorism that would meet such goals and these often go well beyond the legal definitions outlined above. One method used here has involved various forms of what might loosely be seen as content analysis. An example of this kind of work used a sample of 73 academic journals to abstract a consistent definition. This methodology yielded a very broad definition, which suggested acts that were politically motivated, tactical, involved the threat or use of force or violence and were in pursuit of publicity (Weinberg, Pedahzur and Hirsch-Hoefler, 2004). This definition though shares many of the problems already discussed for legal definitions. It appears much too broad to be of practical use, capturing as it does a wide range of behaviours generally seen as entirely legitimate. A more detailed definition using a similar methodological approach was suggested by Schmid (2004) and involved multiple 'elements' of terrorism. Here, the aim was to develop a consensus definition, rather than achieve some form of lowest common denominator of agreement definition. This suggested that terrorism could be defined as:

(1)   A method intended to inspire anxiety.
(2)   Which involves repeated violence.
(3)   That involved clandestine or semi-clandestine actors.
(4)   Where the motivation was idiosyncratic, criminal or political and direct targets of violence are not the main targets.
(5)   Where people were the victims of violence.
(6)   Where immediate victims were generally chosen randomly.
(7)   Where immediate victims were not chosen randomly, they were chosen as being representative or symbolic, serving to generate a message.
(8)   Where acts involved violence or threat of violence.
(9)   Where a communication processes between terrorist and potential victims was involved.
(10) Where acts are used to manipulate a target audience(s).

Such definitions of terrorism conceive it primarily as a method of communication based on violence. Here, the goal is seen as generating terror or severe anxiety in a large group to manipulate or coerce others, in pursuit of some broadly political objective.

An alternative approach to these kinds of content analytic approaches have involved efforts to situate terrorism within existing models of conflict. Within these models, terrorism would be seen as being part of a continuum of political violence ranging from conventional wars, through various forms of unconventional warfare, such as guerilla and hybrid war, through to insurgency and terrorism at the other end of this continuum (Merari, 1993). Here, rather than analysing terrorism as a form of violent communication, it is seen as one form of violent conflict. This leads to it being analysed and compared in terms of other characteristics involved in conflict. These would include such things as the extent and nature of the organisational structure used, the kind of tactics used, the targeting involved, weapons used, territorial aims involved and so on. Within this general approach, the similarities between terrorism, insurgency and guerilla war tend to be stressed, rather than these being seen as clearly distinct forms of politically motivated violence.

Criminological approaches

Another model for analysis might broadly be termed a criminal justice or criminological approach to terrorism. These typically see terrorism as an extreme form of crime, with an illustrative example here seeing terrorism as a form of hate crime, motivated by some form of political ideology. This kind of definition serves to stress the similarities between terrorism other forms of criminal and anti-social behaviour. Those adopting this approach have often been critical of traditional definitions of terrorism, seeing these as being inconsistent and unduly narrow. An illustration of this would be the tendency to treat apparently unplanned violent attacks, motivated by some kind of political ideology, as hate crime rather than terrorism (Freilich and Chermak, 2009). Similarly, it might be argued that non-violent but ideologically motivated offences, such as money laundering or the use of some forms of cyber-attack, may often not treated as terrorism but would be captured as other forms of crime. Additionally, it has been noted that a great deal of the ideologically motivated violence that occurs within nation states, such as far-right extremism, is often treated as crime rather than being defined as domestic terrorism (Freilich, Chermak, Arietti et al., 2024).

The critique of traditional approaches to definition also sees much of the work in the area as being unduly narrow, serving to exclude a great deal of relevant information from acts that are not prosecuted as specifically terrorist offences. In turn, this is argued to have led to a loss of important insights. This is illustrated by the results of the American Terrorism Study (ATS) which was conducted using a wide range of data drawn from the Federal Bureau of Investigation (FBI) in the US, which captured a wide range of politically motivated violence (Smith, 1994). This work led in turn to analyses of the prosecution and sentencing for such offences (Smith and Damphousse, 1998). This was followed by the development of qualitative case analyses (Hamm, 2007, Hamm and Spaaij, 2017) and the tracking of the processes involved in 'radicalisation' and the outcomes over time (Gruenewald, Klein, Drawve et al., 2019). Here, changes to definition were reported to be associated with the application of a variety of methodologies commonly seen in the social sciences.

Stressing commonalities with other areas of crime has also supported inclusion of studies that use offender self-report methods, victim surveys and the use of open-source data to analyse patterns of terrorism. These methods are not without problems and the significant challenges present when using these has been noted (Clemmow, Schumann, Salman et al., 2020; Rottweiler, Gill and Bouhana, 2022). Two main advantages have though been suggested for treating terrorism within the broader framework of criminology. Firstly, that it allows for the consideration and analysis of a wider range of data than traditional approaches to terrorism. Secondly, that it allows for the application of a greater range of theory, drawn from across criminology and related fields of research such as criminological psychology.

Applying criminological theories

As noted above, defining terrorism as a form of criminal behaviour has been argued to allow the application of theoretical models deriving from this area. This is suggested to provide a means of addressing the largely descriptive and atheoretical approach of much of the existing work into terrorism (Freilich, Chermak, Arietti et al., 2024). An early example of this was the application of Routine Activity Theory (Cohen and Felson, 1979). This theory posits characteristics which interact to explain the development of motivated offenders, the presence of suitable targets and the convergence of both in a context where there is a lack of capable guardians. Within this model, the explanation of terror offences would not be fundamentally different from that for any other forms of violent criminality, other than for the initial motivations of the offenders. Here, there has been some support for this view of terrorism, as a form of extremist crime. This is based on the study of ideological and non-ideologically motivated homicides associated with far-right political views (Parkin and Freilich, 2015). There has also been some support in relation to the occurrence of suicide bombings (Canetti-Nisin, Mesch and Pedahzur, 2006), hate crimes (Waldner and Berg, 2008) and online hate crimes (Turner, Holt, Brewer et al., 2023).

Other theoretical models have stressed the role of situational or environmental 'criminogenic' factors in terrorism, referring to the social and environmental factors correlated with crime, whilst others have stressed the roles of structural inequalities and labelling (Anthony and Cuneen, 2008; Appleby, 2010). Such work has suggested that, in common with various forms of crime, terrorism offences appear to be highly concentrated, both in geographic terms and within specific populations. Taking research from the US as an example of this, one study reported that only 0.002% of counties accounted for 16% of domestic terror attacks (LaFree and Bersani, 2014). Other work has identified significant correlations between variables such as the level of population heterogeneity, residential instability and terrorism (Adamczyk, Gruenewald, Chermak et al., 2014; LaFree and Bresani, 2014). Results like this appear consistent with some findings from research into non-terrorist violent crime (Mills, 2021). This has led to debates around whether the distinction between acts such as hate crimes and terrorism is legitimate, with differing views around whether these are better be seen as overlapping forms of crime, a continuum or as having marked qualitative differences (Herek, Cogan and Gillis, 2002; Deloughery, King and Asal, 2012).

At the other end of the spectrum, some theoretical approaches have stressed the role of the individual and their characteristics, applying these as a means of developing and building criminological definitions of terrorism. For example, micro-level control theories have been suggested as an explanation for terrorism in terms of individuals showing poor self-control and low levels of social bonds. This idea has been supported by significant correlations reported between low levels of self-control and political and violent extremism (Perry, Wikström and Roman, 2018; Rottweiler, Gill and Bouhana, 2022). Thrill seeking and hate crime have also been reported to commonly co-occur in reported crimes (McDevitt, Levin and Bennett, 2002). These kinds of associations with individual characteristics do though appear to be strongly mediated by the environment, as well as the presence of social strains, grievances and contested areas of belief. All of these appear important to the occurrence of terrorist acts.

Developed from a rather different basis, ideas of social control and social learning theory have also been applied to this area. This builds largely on a fusion of work in behavioural and social psychology and more recently cognitive psychology. Terrorism and extremism are often seen as forming part of a continuum of similarly generated behaviours. The occurrence of these is seen as largely determined by various processes of reinforcement and modelling of behaviour (Bandura, 1962) with later recognition of the role of cognition in shaping this. In this context, this would typically involve contact with peer groups that diverge from mainstream views, associated with a reduction in social controls over behaviour and increasing acceptance and internalising of views consistent with other group members.

Theories of social control relate to the factors which serve to check or moderate individual behaviour, stressing restraining and limiting influences over anti-social acts. These would include such things as family, peer groups and institutional checks on behaviour (Hirschi, 2002). Social learning theories analyse behaviour in terms of common learning mechanisms, with these assumed to be the same for terrorism as for other forms of social learning, resting on various processes of reinforcement, imitation and punishment.

Critiques of such approaches to terrorism have been offered. Most fundamentally perhaps, some have argued that there is in fact often a clear distinction between terrorism and other forms of criminality, with these only being distantly related (Deloughery, King and Asal, 2012). This does not mean that social control and social learning theory are inapplicable, but it would mean that such analysis cannot be the same as for other criminal behaviours. Indeed, suggestions of a simple continuity between acts such as hate crime and terrorism can be criticised as being unduly simplistic. Additionally, social learning approaches, even in updated form, can be criticised for failing to adequately reflect the role of beliefs shaping behaviour. In common with theoretical approaches that have sought to define terrorism in terms of various forms of individual pathology, such models can be criticised for seeking to locate problems within individuals, rather than in broader social, economic and political relationships. Also, in common with studies looking at individual pathology, they have often received limited if any empirical support. Ideas of low self-control being important, for example, run counter to the reality that for some forms of terrorism very high levels of self-control are both evident and necessary (Hirschi and Gottfredson, 2000).

Summary and conclusions

The modern use of the term terrorism is generally traced back to the French Revolution of 1789 where it referred to the use of legalised violence conducted by the state, with the aim of generating terror in the wider populace. This early example of terrorism has echoes with the present, emerging largely because of a lack of functional political structures that addressed political views in a constructive way, with a state that had moved from a repressive absolute Monarchy to abstract principles rhetoric.

A variety of other terms have emerged subsequently including insurgency, guerrilla war and hybrid war. All involve forms of politically motivated violence but beyond this agreement over definition has been limited. Insurgency has normally been defined in ways that recognise it as an asymmetrical contest with an existing state or authority but one that has some justification, as for instance in anti-colonial or anti-apartheid movements. Guerrilla warfare is typically defined as a form of 'irregular' warfare typically against more powerful opponents with military or armed police targets. Hybrid warfare is a more recent term which places stress on use of multiple methods of violence and intimidation, blending the lethality of state actors directly or through proxies with tools such as information technology.

The term 'terrorism' is a contentious one and so has been defined in many ways across different disciplines and applications. There is wide agreement that it shares some core characteristics, including perceived illegitimacy. Most approaches to terrorism have focussed on action-based rather than conceptual definitions, primarily being concerned with form and purpose. This has led to a variety of legal definitions of terrorism relying on descriptive approaches. These often appear to serve political purposes for states, are excessively broad and rely on considerable self-restrain from agents of the state and legal systems to avoid abuses. Other approaches to definition have included the use of formal methods to draw out common themes conceptually underpinning terrorism. These have led to definitions stressing the role of terrorism as a form of communication to generate terror to coerce others for political objectives. Terrorism may also be seen as being part of a continuum of politically motivated violence ranging across conventional, guerilla and hybrid war through to terrorism.

In contrast, psychological and criminological approaches have often stressed individual or social pathology and similarities to other criminality, such as hate crimes. This has allowed for the application of existing models to balance the emphasis on descriptive studies of terrorism. These have included 'criminogenic,' structural inequality, labelling, social control and social learning theories.

The approach adopted here is that, whilst there is no universally agreed definition of terrorism, it can usefully be seen as forming part of a continuum of politically motivated violence. As such, it is not assumed to be fundamentally different from other forms of violence or to simply be a result of psychopathology or criminality. As a result, a wide range of methods and models appear relevant to a better understanding of terrorism.

References

Adamczyk, A., Gruenewald, J., Chermak, S. M., and Freilich, J. D. (2014). The relationship between hate groups and far-right ideological violence. *Journal of Contemporary Criminal Justice, 30*(3), 310–332.

Aninat, E., Hardy, D., and Johnston, R. B. (2002). Combating money laundering and the financing of terrorism. *Finance and Development, 39*(3), 44–47.

Anthony, T. and Cunneen, C. (2008). *The Critical Criminology Companion.* Toronto: Hawkins Press.

Appleby, N. (2010). Labelling the innocent: how government counter-terrorism advice creates labels that contribute to the problem. *Critical Studies on Terrorism, 3*(3), 421–436.

Bandura, A. (1962). Social Learning through Imitation. In M. R. Jones (Ed). *Nebraska Symposium on Motivation.* Lincoln: University of Nebraska Press.

Barber, B. R. (2007). Terror is inescapably contestable. *World Policy Journal, 24*(1), 55–56.

Belge, C. (2011). State building and the limits of legibility: kinship networks and Kurdish resistance in Turkey. *International Journal of Middle East Studies, 43*(01), 95–114.

Boyle, J. (1985). The anatomy of a torts class. *American University Law Review, 34*(5), 1003–1063.

Buchhandler-Raphael, M. (2011). What's terrorism got to do with it? The Perils of prosecutorial misuse of terrorism offenses. *Florida State University Law Review, 39*, 807–868.

Canetti-Nisim, D., Mesch, G., and Pedahzur, A. (2006). Victimization from terrorist attacks: randomness or routine activities? *Terrorism and Political Violence, 18*(4), 485–501.

Clemmow, C., Schumann, S., Salman, N. L., and Gill, P. (2020). The base rate study: developing base rates for risk factors and indicators for engagement in violent extremism. *Journal of Forensic Sciences, 65*(3), 865–881.

Cohen, L. E. and Felson, M. (1979). Social change and crime rate trends: a routine activity approach. *American Sociological Review, 44*(4), 588–608.

Crenshaw, M. (Ed.) (2010). *Terrorism in Context.* Pennsylvania: Pennsylvania State University Press.

Crenshaw, M. (2011). *Explaining Terrorism, Causes, Processes and Consequences.* London: Routledge.

Crenshaw-Hutchinson, M. (1972). The concept of revolutionary terrorism. *Journal of Conflict Resolution, 16*(3), 383–396.

Deloughery, K., King, R. D,. and Asal, V. (2012). Close cousins or distant relatives? The relationship between terrorism and hate crime. *Crime and Delinquency, 58*(5), 663–688.

Dworkin, R. (2002). The threat to patriotism. *New York Review of Books, 49*(3), 44–49.

Ferstman, C. (2024). *Conceptualising Arbitrary Detention Power, Punishment and Control.* Bristol: Bristol University Press.

Findley, M. G. and Young, J. K. (2012). Terrorism and civil war: a spatial and temporal approach to a conceptual problem. *Perspectives on Politics, 10*(2), 285–305.

Freilich, J. D. and Chermak, S. M. (2009). Preventing deadly encounters between law enforcement and American far-rightists. *Crime Prevention Studies, 25*, 141–72.

Freilich, J. D., Chermak, S. M., Arietti, R. A., and Turner, N. D. (2024). Terrorism, political extremism, and crime and criminal justice. *Annual Review of Criminology, 7*(1), 187–209.

Frisch, E. (2012). Insurgencies are organizations too: organizational structure and the effectiveness of insurgent strategy. *The Peace and Conflict Review, 6*, 1–23

Galeotti, M. (2015). Hybrid war and 'little green men': How it works, and how it doesn't. Ukraine and Russia: people, politics, propaganda and perspectives. *E International Relations, 156.* www.e-ir.info/2015/04/16/hybrid-war-and-little-green-men-how-it-works-and-how-it-doesnt/

Galeotti, M. (2016). Hybrid, ambiguous, and non-linear? How new is Russia's 'new way of war'? *Small Wars & Insurgencies, 27*(2), 282–301.

Ganor, B. (1998). *Defining Terrorism: Is One Man's Terrorist Another Man's Freedom Fighter?* Herzliya: International Institute for Counter-Terrorism.

Ganor, B. (2002). Defining terrorism: is one man's terrorist another man's freedom fighter? *Police Practice and Research, 3*(4), 287–304.

Gerhardt, M. J. (2011). *The Power of Precedent*. Oxford: Oxford University Press.

Gibbs, J. P. (1989). Conceptualization of terrorism. *American Sociological Review, 54*(3), 329–340.

Golder, B. and Williams, G. (2004). What is 'Terrorism'? Problems of legal definition. *University of NSW Law Journal, 27*(2), 270–295.

Goodwin, J. (2006). A theory of categorical terrorism. *Social Forces, 84*(4), 2027–2046.

Green, K. (2020). Does war ever change? A Clausewitzian critique of hybrid warfare. *E-International Relations*. Available at www.e-ir.info/2020/09/28/does-war-ever-change-a-clausewitzian-critique-of-hybrid-warfare/. Retrieved July 23, 2024.

Gruenewald, J., Klein, B. R., Drawve, G., Smith, B. L., and Ratcliff, K. (2019). Suspicious preoperational activities and law enforcement interdiction of terrorist plots. *Policing: An International Journal, 41*(1), 89–107.

Haggard, S. and Tiede, L. (2024). Judicial backsliding: a guide to collapsing the separation of powers. *Democratization*, 1–25. https://doi.org/10.1080/13510347.2024.2381092

Hamm, M. S. (2007). *Terrorism as Crime: From Oklahoma City to Al Qaeda and Beyond.* New York: NYU Press.

Hamm, M. S. and Spaaij, R. (2017). *The Age of Lone Wolf Terrorism*. New York: Columbia University Press.

Harmon, C. C. (2001). Five strategies of terrorism. *Small Wars and Insurgencies, 12*(3), 39–66.

Head, M. (2024). *Democracy, Protest and the Law: Defending a Democratic Right.* London: Taylor and Francis.

Herek, G. M., Cogan, J. C., and Gillis, J. R. (2002). Victim experiences in hate crimes based on sexual orientation. *Journal of Social Issues, 58*(2), 319–339.

Hoffman, F. G. (2007). *Conflict in the 21st Century: The Rise of Hybrid Wars.* Arlington: Potomac Institute for Policy Studies.

Higgins, R. and Flory, M. (Eds.) (1997). *Terrorism and International Law*. London: Routledge.

Hirschi, T. (2002). *Causes of Delinquency* (1st ed.). New York: Routledge.

Hirschi, T. and Gottfredson, M. R. (2000). In defense of self-control. *Theoretical Criminology, 4*(1), 55–69.

Howard, M. (2002). What's in a name? How to fight terrorism. *Foreign Affairs, 81*(1), 8–13.

Joes, A. J. (2006). *Resisting Rebellion: The History and Politics of Counterinsurgency.* Lexington: University Press of Kentucky.

Johnson, R. (2018). Hybrid war and its countermeasures: a critique of the literature. *Small Wars and Insurgencies, 29*(1), 141–163.

Jones, C. and Pedahzur, A. (Eds.) (2013). *Between Terrorism and Civil War: The Al-Aqsa Intifada.* London: Routledge.

Kalyvas, S. N. (2004). The paradox of terrorism in civil war. *The Journal of Ethics, 8*(1), 97–138.

Kydd, A. H. and Walter, B. F. (2006). The strategies of terrorism. *International Security, 31*(1), 49–80.

LaFree, G. and Bersani, B. E. (2014). County-level correlates of terrorist attacks in the United States. *Criminology and Public Policy, 13*(3), 455–481.

Laquer, W. (1987). *The Age of Terrorism.* Boston, MA: Little Brown and Co.

Linton, M. (2012). Friends, enemies, and the role of the individual. In P. McPhee (Ed.), *A Companion to the French Revolution.* Oxford: Blackwell.

McCormick, G. H. and Giordano, F. (2007). Things come together: symbolic violence and guerrilla mobilisation. *Third World Quarterly, 28*(2), 295–320.

McDevitt, J., Levin, J., and Bennett, S. (2002). Hate crime offenders: an expanded typology. *Journal of Social Issues, 58*(2), 303–317.

Merari, A. (1993). Terrorism as a strategy of insurgency. *Terrorism and Political Violence, 5*(4), 213–251.

Mills, C. E. (2021). Gay visibility and disorganized and strained communities: a community-level analysis of anti-gay hate crime in New York City. *Journal of Interpersonal Violence, 36*(17–18), 8070–8091.

Moses, L. B. (2003). Adapting the law to technological change: a comparison of common law and legislation. *University of New South Wales Law Journal, 26*(2), 394–417.

Nagl, J. A., Amos, J. F., Sewall, S., and Petraeus, D. H. (2008). *The US Army/Marine Corps Counterinsurgency Field Manual.* Chicago: University of Chicago Press.

O'Neil, M. M. (2004). Crawford v. Washington: Implications for the war on terrorism. *Catholic University Law Review, 54*(3), 1077–1111.

Parkin, W. S. and Freilich, J. D. (2015). Routine activities and right-wing extremists: an empirical comparison of the victims of ideologically- and non-ideologically-motivated homicides committed by American far-rightists. *Terrorism and Political Violence, 27*(1), 182–203.

Perry, G., Wikström, P. O. H., and Roman, G. D. (2018). Differentiating right-wing extremism from potential for violent extremism: the role of criminogenic exposure. *International Journal of Developmental Science, 12*(1–2), 103–113.

Ramraj, V. V. (2006). Counter-terrorism policy and minority alienation: some lessons from Northern Ireland. *Singapore Journal of Legal Studies, December*, 385–404. www.jstor.org/stable/24869086.

Rich, P. (1984). Insurgency, terrorism and the apartheid system in South Africa. *Political Studies, 32*(1), 68–85.

Richardson, L. (2006). *The Roots of Terrorism: An Overview.* London: Routledge.

Roberts III, M. E. (2018). *The Psychological War for Vietnam, 1960–1968.* Lawrence: University Press of Kansas.

Rottweiler, B., Gill, P., and Bouhana, N. (2022). Individual and environmental explanations for violent extremist intentions: a German nationally representative survey study. *Justice Quarterly, 39*(4), 825–846.

Sambanis, N. (2008). Terrorism and civil war. In P. Keefer and Loayza, N. (Ed.), *Terrorism, Economic Development, and Political Openness.* Cambridge: Cambridge University Press.

Sánchez-Cuenca, I. and De la Calle, L. (2009). Domestic terrorism: the hidden side of political violence. *Annual Review of Political Science, 12,* 31–49.

Saul, B. (2005). Definition of 'terrorism' in the UN Security Council: 1985–2004. *Chinese Journal of International Law, 4*(1), 141–166.

Schmid, A. (2004). Terrorism-the definitional problem. *Case Western Reserve Journal of International Law, 36,* 375–382.

Smith, B. L. (1994). *Terrorism in America: Pipe Bombs and Pipe Dreams.* New York: SUNY Press.

Smith, B. L. and Damphousse, K. R. (1998). Terrorism, politics and punishment: a test of structural-contextual theory and the "liberation hypothesis." *Criminology, 36*(1), 67–92.

Sorel, J. M. (2003). Some questions about the definition of terrorism and the fight against its financing. *European Journal of International Law, 14*(2), 365–378.

Stepanova, E. A. (2008). *Terrorism in Asymmetrical Conflict: Ideological and Structural Aspects.* Oxford: Oxford University Press.

Taber, R. (1970). *The War of The Flea: A Study of Guerrilla Warfare Theory and Practice.* London: Paladin.

Turner, N., Holt, T. J., Brewer, R., Cale, J., and Goldsmith, A. (2023). Exploring the relationship between opportunity and self-control in youth exposure to and sharing of online hate content. *Terrorism and Political Violence, 35*(7), 1604–1619.

Ünal, M. C. (2014). Strategist or pragmatist: a challenging look at Ocalan's retrospective classification and definition of PKK's strategic periods between 1973 and 2012. *Terrorism and Political Violence, 26*(3), 419–448.

Ünal, M. C. (2016a). Terrorism versus insurgency: a conceptual analysis. *Crime, Law and Social Change, 66*(1), 21–57.

Ünal, M. C. (2016b). Is it ripe yet? Resolving Turkey's 30 years of conflict with the PKK. *Turkish Studies, 17*(1), 91–125.

Waldner, L. K. and Berg, J. (2008). Explaining antigay violence using target congruence: an application of revised routine activities theory. *Violence and Victims, 23*(3), 267–287.

Walker, C. (2004). Terrorism and criminal justice: past, present and future. *Criminal Law Review, 311,* 55–71.

Walker, C. (2011). *Terrorism and the Law.* Oxford: Oxford University Press.

Weinberg, L., Pedahzur, A., and Hirsch-Hoefler, S. (2004). The challenges of conceptualizing terrorism. *Terrorism and Political Violence, 16*(4), 777–794.

Williams, D. (2003). Terrorism and the Law in the United Kingdom. *University of New South Wales Law Journal, 179,* 179–183.

Wilson, M. A. (2000). Toward a model of terrorist behavior in hostage-taking incidents. *Journal of Conflict Resolution, 44*(4), 403-424.

Zartman, I. W. (2006). Negotiating internal, ethnic and identity conflicts in a globalized world. *International Negotiation, 11*(2), 253–272.

3 State violence and terrorism

Questions of how to define state violence and when and indeed if this should be described as 'terrorism' remain a complex and contested area. A classical tradition of defining the state can be seen to have emerged in Western Europe following a period of marked social, economic and political change, now termed the Renaissance. This involved a rediscovery and growth in rational and positivist approaches to knowledge and its impacts spread, with some differences, to other parts of the world. This tradition has developed over time and has increasingly come to see the state as a depersonalised process, where public power could be seen as vested in a fictive 'person' or 'deliberative agent' which is called the state. Within this tradition, the state is seen as being different from ruler and ruled and being more than these. Such views of the state have been heavily influenced by the thinking of the English philosopher Thomas Hobbes and his published work, the Leviathan (Hobbes, 1996). This sees the state as an ordered whole, based on the interconnections between community, legal authority and political power. Concepts of state are seen here as integrating and legitimising a social order, in pursuit of an overall view of the 'public good.' In turn, this is founded on the idea of shared identity, with this acting to defuse competing individual and group interests (Kelman, 2006). Essentially, within this view of the state, distinctions between public and private interests become blurred, with the importance of social solidarity being stressed. It has been suggested that this traditional view of the state involves five characteristics: presence of legal order; institutionalisation of a specialised political system; self-authorisation; societal integrations and reflexivity (Walker, 2006).

The presence of a legal order is perhaps the most obvious of these suggested characteristics, acting as the bedrock for the state. The idea of legal order does though assume the existence of certain common features, with states needing to have a distinct identity or some degree of continuity. It also assumes the presence of autonomy, self-definition and self-enforcement: where the legal system does not require other approvals to act.

The idea that conceptions of the state require the presence of a specialised political system has a long history, traceable back to antiquity. Classical concepts of the state though can be seen to stem largely from the great instability and violence seen during the 17th and 18th centuries across Europe. This gave rise, eventually,

DOI: 10.4324/9781003429579-3

to new forms of political domination. These were based on ideas of the autonomy of states, replacing earlier notions of the state that had been based on military occupation and dominance (Walker, 2006). In line with this authority had come to be increasingly vested in the idea of a dedicated political domain, which served as a means of resolving conflicts through collective decision making. This replaced notions of divinely ordered rule and absolute monarchies. In turn, this can be seen to link to the idea of self-authorisation. This implies that a logic of a political process of decision making should prevail. In the absence of this, creation of political systems is essentially a form of window dressing that is of little value. At this point, it is perhaps worth noting the important point that the ideas of a dedicated political domain and of self-authorisation are not synonymous with democracy. These aspects of state creation have been and indeed remain entirely compatible with very different political systems.

The ideas of social integration and reflexivity are perhaps less obvious aspects of the state, when compared to self-authorising legal and political institutions. They are though no less important. Societal integration can be broadly seen as the assumption of a degree of social integration or cohesion, across those who the state claims to act for. There is a clear need for there to be a degree of sufficient common cause, if any state is to hold together. In turn, this requires a level of assent and affirmation from those who constitute a state. Without this, any state is likely to quickly fracture and fail. Many states can be identified which provide examples of this, having been sustained over time. It is though striking just how fluid this can be, with many states having shifted and changed over time. Such apparent instability may in turn be linked to the idea of reflexivity, referring to the extent to which states can adapt and change over time. Adaptability is an important capacity of states in addressing emerging and changing collective problems over time, and it has therefore been described as the glue which holds modern constitutions together (Walker, 2006). If social integration and reflexivity are absent, then the existence of state constitutions, whether they be written or informal, carries little force or value in sustaining that state.

The term 'social integration' appears to have first been coined by the French sociologist Emile Durheim in discussing suicide (Alpert, 1939). Here, the term was used to refer to one way in which society exerts powerful forces on individuals. Societal norms and shared values act as a shared way of interpreting events and acting. Here, a form of 'collective consciousness' was seen as binding individuals together, leading in turn to social integration. Durkheim saw this as resulting from individual actions and interactions, which led to people developing individual awareness of others as social beings. Here, the term 'social integration' is used to broadly refer to the extent individuals from different groups feel a sense of belonging to a society and how far they interact with one another on equal terms. Reflexivity is used here to refer to individual's examination of their own beliefs, judgements and practices and how they question assumptions (Giddens, 2014). Here, information gathering serves to give individuality to people, as a result of gaining more information and so being able to make more informed choices. Rapid technological development has raised this to an unprecedented level. There is though another side to this process of reflexivity, involving information gathering by states to identify 'enemies' suspected of acting against the current social contract. Now, information accessed by individuals can be collated by state and increasingly private companies.

The aspects of states outlined above are perhaps the major driver of state failures where, in the absence of overwhelming force, a lack of social integration, or deteriorating social integration, makes the maintenance of a common legal and political framework untenable. There are multiple examples from history, of this process of failure. Possibly the most vivid examples though come from the post-war era of decolonisation in Africa and Asia. Many colonial and post-colonial states were created with little thought of making these stable and sustainable, with many being formed on a largely arbitrary basis by external powers. This was often done by drawing arbitrary lines on maps and maintaining these by force, with little thought of social cohesion, tradition or pre-existing political systems. In some cases, colonial powers acted to exploit or even exacerbate existing tensions. On withdrawal, these external powers often sought to impose legal systems and written constitutions. Many of these artificial creations though lacked a sense of common cause or continuity and many quickly degenerating into violence between different groups, with some seeing abuse of minorities and genocides. Perhaps the most extreme examples of this can be drawn from central Africa. In Burundi, the German and Belgian colonial powers froze a weak and failing state in place, leading ultimately to genocide. Similarly, in Uganda, the British colonial power created a state with little regard to historical and tribal ties, resulting in an unstable creation riven by internal tensions and subsequent violence (Scott, 2019).

Where present though such characteristics mean that it is possible to meaningfully talk of the existence of a state, involving the depersonalisation of power by the creation of public institutions with a high level of acceptance. Such institutions involve a monopoly on legitimate public power and as such can be seen as addressing the central problem of maintaining social and economic viability of the state. This has been achieved through notions of law permeating the operation of the state and in turn by the state coming to permeate law. Notably, such ideas of the nature of the state emerged following periods of enormous instability and violence. They can be traced back to the ideas of Hobbes, whose thinking was in turn greatly influenced by the 17th-century Civil War that took place across the British Isles and Ireland. Later, ideas developed following the upheavals that followed from the 18th-century French Revolution. The state came to be increasingly seen as the locus of power, acting to deny any claims by other groups to be a continuing locus for exercising power, including Governments and public opinion (Dunn, 1984). This is achieved, somewhat paradoxically, by privileging some actors as representatives of 'the state' to express public power in both its symbolic and concrete forms. Essentially, this is achieved by giving state institutions such as the military, police and paramilitary police a monopoly on the legitimate use of public power including the use of violence, with this in turn subject to various constraints. This process can be seen, in some states, to result in such institutions developing something of a life of their own, with notions such as 'moral purpose' and 'public service' ethos, acting to protect the state against growing self-interest and social fracturing.

As such, the state has been described as both an ongoing problem-solving concept and a problem-creating one (Dyson, 2010). The problem-creating aspect of the state relates to inherent tensions that inevitably emerge. These include the tension between the institutions given power and created as part of the state. Fundamental tensions also arise between the ideals of democratic society and the exercise of public power to balance and limit the expression of popular sentiments. Equally, there are tensions here between institutions and elites which claim to embody the state. Emergent tensions have also been seen between concepts of the state and 'welfare state' ideas which see the state as being limited to the sum of activities undertaken for citizens. Linked to this, there has also been the re-emergence and growth of tensions, increasingly marked since the 1980s, between classical concepts of the state and managerialist ideas stressing 'efficiency' and instrumental views of government (Galbraith, 2001).

Classical views of how states are created have generally seen it as emerging from two main processes (Dyson, 2010). The first of these involves the actions of elites, where these successfully determine their self-interests and increasingly identify these with the concept of the state. This involves the state being imbued with special properties as well as it being given privileged status and authority to exercise public power (Runciman, 2003, 2023). The second process of state development has been seen as involving the association of this first process, with the self-interest of those elites who educate and train elite groups serving to privilege themselves intergenerationally (Bourdieu, 1998; Dyson, 2010; Dyson and Quaglia, 2010). Different political models are seen here as leading to the creation of distinct types of state, based on the same processes. A key distinction sometimes drawn here has been between 'strong' and 'weak' states. In this context, the terms are used to refer to political structure, rather than to aspects such as military or economic capacity. Strong states can be seen as being highly centralised and focussed on public power and weak ones can be seen as being more decentralised with more stress on private power. In the context of Europe, the archetypal example of the former is often given as France and the later form, at least historically, as Britain. It is perhaps worth stressing here that 'weak' states can, in practice, act very much like 'strong' ones, through the convergence of public and private power. The classical division between 'strong' and 'weak' states also has little to do with the stability of these states or their efficacy or legitimacy. Very different political systems can result in states where overall functioning appears similar. An example of this would be the convergence between the French state, with its highly centralised dirigiste political system and that of the Federal Republic of Germany, with its federal system of Government based on a social market economy (Dyson, 2010; Dyson and Quaglia, 2010). Although politically very different, these states can be seen as sharing some core characteristics, with both forming a unitary construction that is based on a rational ordering of power. Both also appear to have a core role of market-making and market-modifying, with these markets being socially embedded (Polanyi, 2001; Dyson and Quaglia, 2010).

Long-term tensions in the idea of the state

Several long-term stresses have been put forward in relation to the classical conceptions of the state outlined above. Perhaps one of the most salient of these currently is the role of the state as a counterweight to polarisation, political instability and populism. Here, the ability of states to do this effectively has, for varied reasons, appeared to be increasingly challenged. Likewise, the separation of the state from governments and governed has been questioned. The issue of which elite interests the state is serving has also been raised as a problem with classical views of the state. It is often unclear whose 'best interests' or 'general interests' a state is in fact acting in. Similarly, some have questioned where the state acting in an 'authoritative' manner become 'authoritarian' or even 'totalitarian.' Revolutionary change in public media and particularly the growth of social media has had major impacts here and will continue to do so. In many respects, this has created the kind of situation feared by Aristotle of rule by the demos (Kraut, 2002). Here, leading politicians act in ways that constantly seek positive affirmation through social media, which carries serious risks. These would include driving an ever-increasing short-termism, growing populism in decision making and maybe somewhat paradoxically, leading to lower levels of trust in central authority.

Tensions have also emerged from broader social and economic policy, where notions of the state have increasingly conflicted with growing globalisation, marketisation and managerialism. The creation of globalised markets can be seen to reduce the extent of public power that a state can exercise, with this being increasingly circumscribed by international law and more recently international economic agreements. Such agreements have grown rapidly and have weakened traditional notions of the state as exercising public power. These economic and trade agreements in particular have been criticised as being outside any political control. This has been made more serious by the often damaging social and economic impacts seen within states (Burfisher, Robinson and Thierfelder, 2001).

A growing marketisation and managerialism within states has been described by the term 'New Public Management (NPM).' This too has challenged traditional concepts of the state. No longer a new idea, NPM stressed ideas of 'efficiency' and 'performance' in state institutions and functions (Towl, 2021). It did this by drawing on the model of an increasingly globalised private sector. The changes that NPM brought were also often associated with ideas of 'modernity' and notions that the private sector was 'good' and the public sector 'bad.' This has led to a decline in the centrality of public power, allowing a growth in alternative and privately controlled locations of power. In classical terms this can be seen as promoting the creation of 'weaker' states. Compounding this has been some of the effects linked to economic globalisation, where states have increasingly been faced with autonomous and disembedded markets and non-state actors that have appeared largely beyond their control (Polanyi, 2001; Gray, 2023).

Misunderstanding the state

A major error in this area is the routine conflation of the state with the government. As touched on above, the state is in fact a far broader notion than government. Conflation of state and government therefore leads to a much weaker understanding of the nature of the state and public power (McLean, 2003; Skinner, 2009). Views of this kind have been evident in some schools of thought, within what can be seen as a broadly Anglo-American tradition of the 19th and 20th centuries. These had grown to largely neglect or indeed reject the work of Hobbes and others, which stressed analogies between the state and a notional 'person.' Alternative views of this kind placed great stress on the primacy of the economic role of the state, as a creator and maintainer of autonomous markets, in turn allowing for the operation of rational choice economic models. This conception of the state serves to disaggregate it primarily into a series of economic structures and functions.

Claims that the concept of the state is reducible in such a way, into essentially a particular form of business operation, have recurred over time. Concerns about such ideas and their adverse effects were though evident throughout the 19th and early 20th centuries, and these have emerged again in recent decades (Dyson, 2012). During both periods, there had been a marked shift from the state having a monopoly on public power, to views which stressed its role in managing this power. Ideas such as 'self-regulation' and 'co-regulation' were variously described and stressed here. Terms such as 'deregulation,' 'privatisation' and ideas of the 'lean,' 'enabling' or 'preventative' state emerged. Such changes clearly altered the operation of the state but in doing so it can convincingly be argued that they have not displaced the core concepts that underpin it (Dyson, 2009, 2012; Sandel, 2012). Contemporary managerialist ideas, stressing the efficiency of the private sector can be seen largely as a repeat of the debates between statism and neoliberalism of the early 20th century. There are important parallels here with the early years of the 20th century seeing a peak in economic 'globalisation.' Then, it led to dramatic political and economic effects including the Great Depression and global warfare. The history of that time is well documented and many of the current tensions around notions of the state have strong historical echoes of the last time the world was so 'globalised' and so unequal. Responses to these tensions have again seen reassertions of more traditional views of the state and statism. A contemporary example of this growing assertiveness of traditional statist views comes from the German Constitutional Court. Here, the court acted to stress the 'statehood' of the of Federal Republic of Germany, in response to the growing power and influence of supra-National institutions. These have included the European Union and also supra-National economic agreements where the court has acted to limit the authority of such bodies and reinstate the traditional role of the state (Möllers, 2018). More widely, the growth of supra-National economic agreements can be seen to have acted as a major driver for the reassertion of the traditional role for the state (Stiglitz, 2010).

The growth in globalism and NPM models, from the 1980s onwards, have presented major challenges to traditional concepts of the state (Pollit, 2006). These have included reduced emphasis on hierarchy and formality of process in public service. In place of this, values from the private sphere have often displaced traditional statist values including legality, probity and predictability. Increasingly, these have been replaced by stress on 'efficiency,' 'business planning' and 'service delivery.' It has been eloquently observed that ideas of autonomy and distinctiveness in public power seemed to vanish in "…a vapour of performance management, multi-level 'governance' and policy 'networks.'" (Dyson, 2010: xxxi). Such intentional withering of the traditional state was seen for some time as a triumph of neoliberal philosophy over other competing views. Interestingly here, the growth of the European Union (EU) following its establishment of a common market can be criticised for driving this process, rather than acting to check or moderate it. The EU has been increasingly open to the criticism that it has increasingly privileged markets, over other considerations. Funding to poorer states within the EU was increasingly made conditional on application of the 'rule of law,' but the legal framework concerned came to be increasingly centralised. Little or no allowances were made for local needs and democratic accountability was weak or absent. Member states were also required to increasingly converge on centrally mandated economic criteria, which took little account of the economic conditions that existed in a diverse group of states. Supra-national economic agreements and treaties also appeared to increasingly take precedence over the interest of states, although this was not unique to the EU. This has been noted to be especially onerous for new entrant states to the EU but has been more broadly criticised for giving primacy to and entrenching a free market fundamentalism. At least until recently, with for example the decision in 2008 of the German Constitutional Court to impose limits, this appeared to increasingly have taken precedence over other social and political values and considerations (Dyson, 2010).

The future of the state

The effects outlined above and particularly the resurgence of globalisation and managerialist concepts of the state have clearly had a negative impact on traditional notions of the state. They have not though led to the demise of the state. In fact, there is recent evidence of a reaction against what are seen as damaging and undesirable effects from such change, through a strengthening of the role of nation state. Following the financial global collapse of 2008, it was primarily nation states, working in collaboration, that acted to preserve economic stability. Notably, the transnational companies, which had benefitted enormously from globalisation, appeared largely powerless to control, or indeed understand, the financial instruments and markets they had created. As a result, some have argued, compellingly, that it is much too early to write off traditional concepts of the state, even if this is likely to be modified to some extent (Dyson, 2010, 2012; Self, 2021). Drawing on Europe as an illustrative example, the European Court of Justice (ECJ) has adopted a teleological rather than textual approach to its judgements: in turn often using European Court of Human Rights (ECHR) rulings as a basis for this. In doing this, the ECJ approach has been seen to be acting to construct a European civil society rather than just a larger free market, trading through more supranational economic treaties. This fits more closely with traditional concepts of the state and has increasingly been delivered through incorporation into domestic laws, strengthening broader and non-managerialist aspects of the state.

Concepts of the state have also proved central to efforts to understand national politics, and here, the distinction between the state and transitory governments has been critical. Ideas around the state have often served as a strong check to democratic excesses, short-term expediency and populism. A capacity to frustrate government action where this is judged to be subversive or damaging has been evident here, where for example this may be couched in terms of national interest. Such governments may threaten the legitimacy of the state or its long-term viability, stability and cohesion. There are though clear limits to this, as illustrated by Europe in the 1920s and 1930s where such checks proved incapable of stopping the authoritarian governments from capturing states. A contemporary example here would be events or acts that impact across state borders, impact on future generations or both. Governments clearly struggle to address these kinds of problems, with the most pressing example being global climate change. Here, notions of the state can provide a motive to address such global and cross-generational questions which is often lacking in governments concerned with short-term political advantage. Here, the state provides a mechanism to consider the needs of future generations, refocussing thinking on concepts such as public service, solidarity and justice (Denhardt and Denhardt, 2000).

Despite this importance, the state has suffered a period of deterioration stretching from at least the late 1970s and the UK provides a good illustration of this. This trend has been accelerated by the relative decline of two key pillars of the state and associated 'machinery of government': the Civil Service and public law. As already noted, this has been driven in part by growing economic globalisation and the related ideas that focus the role of the state on making and managing markets for private actors. This has led some to question whether the state has now become a ghostly presence (Dyson, 2010). Recent trends though suggest a reaction against these ideas, often driven by necessity. There has been something of a rejuvenation of more traditional concepts of the state. Efforts to compel ever greater social and political convergence in Europe, particularly though not exclusively for new entrant states, is an illustration of such a response in both in legal and political terms. Here, German courts have begun to draw a line, restricting the extent to which that state's laws can be impinged on by international treaties. Other nations, often from a weaker position, have been similarly resistant to social and political convergence. The 2008 financial crisis also showed, in a very costly and vivid manner, the dangers of globalised free markets that appeared to lack accountability and be beyond control, having been actively deregulated. Here, it was states which were required to step in and restore some economic order.

International law and state terrorism

International law draws on concepts of the state as the basis for defining and prohibiting a wide range of acts of violence. This would include the use of violence in civilian settings, such as prisons and policing, through to paramilitary and military use of violence. Even in the context of self-defensive war, states face limitations on how they can legitimately act. The concept of state terrorism though has no clear status in international law. For obvious reasons perhaps, states have been highly resistant to defining themselves as being capable of engaging in terrorism. Two bodies of international law are though relevant here: International Human Rights Law (IHRL) and International Humanitarian Law (IHL). Human rights deal primarily with the rights that people share in both peacetime and during war. These would include some of the most fundamental rights within international law such as: the right to life; prohibition of torture, cruel, inhuman or degrading treatment or punishment; prohibition of slavery or servitude and prohibition of retroactive laws (ICRC, 2003). However, targeting enemy combatants is an exemption to this and it is legal, in international law, to target and kill them. There are though limitations imposed here as well, which make some forms of state violence illegal. It is therefore illegal, for example, to kill or torture combatants who have surrendered and become prisoners of war (ICRC, 1949).

IHL deals with the area of non-combatants or civilians during war, and here, the targeting of non-combatants is illegal under IHL as well as breaching parts of IHRL. IHL recognises that harm to non-combatants may be a secondary effect of other actions, deemed legal during some armed conflicts. Such acts though need to be proportionate, with non-combatants being protected from harm as far as reasonably possible. Similarly, IHRL allows for some derogations, during times of public emergency. Some rights continue to be protected though, even under such extreme conditions. These would include the four key rights outlined above. State terrorism can therefore be seen as derogation from such 'core' rights in international law, with this being used as a means of invoking fear in a wider audience to some political end.

State terrorism and state violence

States clearly do routinely use their monopoly on public power to engage in violence, both internally and externally. The extent to which this is viewed as legitimate though is contentious and has changed significantly over time. Some aspects of state violence continue to receive broad acceptance through acquiescence, whilst others do not. The idea that states should maintain social order, using formal institutions such as the police, courts, prisons, security and intelligence services, typically enjoys a high degree of support. This is not inevitably the case though. Where a state is seen as illegitimate, or there is a lack of perceived 'common cause,' such acquiescence and acceptance may break down. This can lead to instability which can grow into resistance, insurgency and guerilla warfare against the state by non-state actors. An example of this, drawn from the United Kingdom, would be the state created by the partition of Ireland in 1921. Here, a new province which became part of the United Kingdom was formed, which resulted in political domination by one part of the population. A period of unbroken rule by one political party followed, lasting for around 50 years. By the 1960s though, conditions had come to be seen as increasingly oppressive by a religious minority population, leading in the first instance to calls for civil rights. Initially, these were seen through normal channels of political protest, but this was met with restrictions, counter demonstrations and force, leading to growing resistance and escalation into insurgency, direct conflict and ultimately campaigns of terrorism against the British state which lasted for decades (Kennedy-Pipe, 2014).

Whilst the use of violence by the state can be seen as essential to its existence, there has been less consensus over whether it is ever appropriate to describe this as 'terrorism' and if it is, when the term is applicable. There has been resistance within fields such as international relations to the notion that the actions of states can ever usefully be seen as terrorism, in a similar manner to non-state actors. Here, it has been argued that there are fundamental differences between state and non-state actors and that, in conflating these, important differences are neglected. Such viewpoints suggest that state and non-state actors have very different motives, with their actions serving quite different functions that have distinctive effects. On this basis, it can be suggested that 'oppression' by states, societies or religions, needs to be seen as something fundamentally different from 'political' terrorism (Lacquer, 1987, 1998). Equating these two forms of violence it is argued obliterates the differences, resulting in greater confusion rather than greater insights. Including state acts within the definition of terrorism, it is suggested, would result in an unduly broad definition, making effective study impossible. This is because the field of study would become unwieldy, encompassing a very wide range of disparate phenomena.

Such problems appear far from intractable, and there is little clear advantage gained by adopting terms such as 'state atrocities' or 'state repression' to describe actions that appear largely indistinguishable from the terrorism of non-state actors. Whilst states do take on a monopoly for the use of public power and violence, this does not extend to acts intended, for political purposes, to put wider society in fear. The use of state power as a means of 'terrorising' populations into compliance with the demands of a particular regime appears to fit well with the definitions of terrorism set out earlier. Here, the Soviet Union under Stalin and Nazi Germany perhaps provide the clearest and most extreme examples of this. In both cases, the application of state violence was exercised with the clear intention and effect of creating terror, within and between states, in pursuit of clearly articulated political goals. The focus on these two extreme examples though can be seen to have had a distorting study in this area, exaggerating the differences between state and non-state actors. Most forms of what can be seen as state terrorism have been rather different from these extremes. For example, some colonial regimes of the 19th and early 20th centuries routinely used violence as a means of generating terror in the wider population, to achieve political goals (Gearty, 1997; Wilkinson, 2006). These political goals were often to keep together states, which often enjoyed little sense of common cause and had weak infrastructural power (Orwell, 1957; Cogneau, Dupraz and Mesplé-Somps, 2021).

It has been noted that there are two fundamental problems with trying to distinguish between state and non-state terrorism. Firstly, this involves drawing a distinction based on the actor rather than the act. As a result, the same acts may end up being differently categorised. Secondly, it has been argued that the distinction appears to be based on a false assumption that monopoly coercive power enjoyed by states allows for the use of any form of coercive power (Blakely, 2012). Efforts to treat the acts of states differently here may serve to suggest and entrench the moral legitimacy of any state violence, or at least confer greater moral legitimacy on it. In response to such criticisms, it has been argued that states differ from non-state actors in that they are governed by legal frameworks and rules, limiting their actions (Hoffman, 1998). In contrast, non-state actors often do not recognise any such limitations on their actions. This distinction though is largely unconvincing. Governments may simply capture or control legal systems. Even where this does not happen, state actors do not always adhere to legal requirements and rules, even when the use of state violence is clearly lawful. For example, when the Geneva Conventions are breached during defensive wars in both serious and less serious ways (Medlong, 2012). In other areas, it has been evident, throughout history, that states have often not felt the need to act within the rules and have deliberately breached them or alternatively sub-contracted breaches to semi-official groups (Reynolds, 2019). As such, the presence of legal frameworks and rules does not appear to be a compelling basis for excluding states from being able to engage in terrorist acts.

The legal basis for state violence has also been suggested as a reason why state terrorism is not a useful concept. This does not seem convincing either, since having a legal basis does not mean that states can always legitimately use violence. As already touched on, states may use a range of violence for what are widely, though not universally, accepted as legitimate actions. These would include the use of violence in defensive wars, although importantly not in wars of aggression. They also include the use of violence as a means of maintaining social order, through the actions of for example the police and prison services. There are though limits to this in states that are subject to the rule of law. Here, the use of violence and acts may fall outside the scope of what is legitimate and therefore lawful (Stanley, 2004; Jefferson and Grimshaw, 2023). As a result of this, the state monopoly on legitimate violence does not appear to provide convincing grounds for rejecting the term state terrorism, any more than it justifies excluding states from other illegitimate uses of violence (Stohl, 2006; Blakeley, 2007).

Distinguishing state violence and state terrorism

As discussed above, functioning states hold a monopoly on the legitimate use of violence as a means of maintaining social order and preserving the state. This monopoly confers a significant degree of latitude in both policy and practice. It implies that states retain, for themselves, the right to use a broad range of violent acts that are not acceptable in non-state actors. Perhaps the most striking example here is the right of institutions of law enforcement to use violence against the population. Other examples would also include the right to limit civil rights and political freedoms such as public protests and to use violence to enforce such limits. Typically, there are clear limits imposed on what is legitimate state action, administered through formal structures such as independent legal systems. How well these kinds of formal check on state power work though can be seen to vary markedly across different states and indeed within single states over time. Even where such checks and balances are largely functional, it has been suggested that state violence can be and is routinely used to coerce the broader population to comply with the wishes of elite groups. The use of state violence can also be used as a means of creating fear in a wider audience, something which is often described in terms of general deterrence. The broader population of those tempted to engage in violent disorder, such as riots and violent protests, is likely to be deterred from this where they see others being met with a severe response from the state. There is a slippery slope here between using such deterrence exclusively to maintain social order and using it to achieve political goals and, largely for this reason, many states will have complex legal arrangements to try to protect public order and rights to political resistance and protest. How well order is maintained will vary between states and will be contentious but where the actions of states move from deterring social order breaches, to deterring expressions of civil rights through fear, then it can be seen as moving towards the threshold for definition as terrorism (Blakeley, 2007, 2012).

State actions may obviously be intended to achieve political goals and object-ives, which may include efforts to progressively reduce or eliminate political challenge and dissent (Kirk, 2010; Rogov, 2018). On this basis, the progression from legitimate state violence through repression and on to terrorism can be seen as a continuum. It is reasonable for states to claim the right to use violence in self-defence against its illegitimate use by others, or in the protection of social order. Such claims can be and are used as cover for illegitimate acts. It has therefore been suggested that non-state actors can reasonably make a similar argument, claiming a legitimate right to use violence. This would apply to specific circumstances, such as when they are acting to resist the illegitimate use of violence by the state through dissent, protest, insurgency, guerilla warfare or even civil war, or by helping others to do so (Finlay, 2010; Blakely, 2012).

A working definition of state terrorism has been suggested based on the presence of four core characteristics. This involves deliberate acts of violence against indi-viduals which the state has a duty to protect, or the threat of such violence when this happens within a wider 'climate of fear' established by previous violent acts. This involves acts that are perpetrated by or in conjunction with the state, so would include the acts of paramilitary and private security groups. These acts or threats of violence from the state are intended to induce extreme fear in the population or a sub-group of the population; on the basis, they will identify with the victim. Finally, the target audience will be forced to consider changing their behaviour as a result (Blakely, 2012).

A key theme of this definition is the instrumental use of violence but this of itself is insufficient. The importance of a having a target audience for the acts of violence is fundamental and an example here would be the torture of political opponents (Blakely, 2012). This clearly involves the illegitimate application of state violence. It would though only fall within the definition of state terrorism where it was used for its known, or anticipated, effects on a target audience. Where such acts occur without public knowledge, or without an intent to cause fear in a wider audience, then they would involve criminal violence but would not fall within the definition of state terrorism. An example here would be the use of torture by the Guatemalan government in the 1970s and 1980s, where this formed part of a counterinsurgency campaign. As part of its strategy, photographic evidence of dead torture victims was published, with the apparent intent of causing fear and changing the behaviour of both insurgents and the public, including potential supporters (Sullivan, 2014). As such, this would fall within the definition of state terrorism suggested by Blakely (2012). Equally, it can be suggested that the acts of the Argentine government during its 'Dirty War,' between 1976–1983 and the UK government during the industrial action taken by mine workers, between 1984 and 1985, both involved acts of state terrorism (Monaghan and Prideaux, 2016).

It is important to note here that psychology, both as a pure and applied discipline, has a very far from unblemished record in relation to illegitimate state violence and state terrorism. Despite a relatively brief history as a distinct subject area and profession, there have been repeated incidents of participation in the criminal state violence, including its most extreme forms (Wyatt and Teuber, 1944; Geuter, 1992; Etkind, 1996). A comparatively recent example of this would be the events that followed the invasion of Iraq by a military coalition in 2003. The then UK government participated in this action, based on claims that were subsequently observed to have been false (Herring and Robinson, 2014). In the prolonged occupation that followed from this, serious concerns emerged concerning the application of psychology in torture and other abuses of the human rights of prisoners. Linked to this, criticisms were also raised around the progressive social and cultural changes, which it was argued had gradually encouraged practitioners and professional bodies to participate in abuse without challenge. Most seriously, it was suggested that governmental and professional bodies had engaged in adjusting and blurring professional ethics, so potentially supporting acts of gross malpractice (Wilks, 2005).

Such concerns were initially met with very strong denials from the American Psychological Association (American Psychological Association, 2005a). These included reference to existing and prior ethical guidance to psychologists as protecting against such abuses (American Psychological Association, 2005b). Aspects of the guidance then in place though seemed, in reality, to support the criticisms. Subsequent investigation and reviews of the area also clearly demonstrated that psychology had a 'controversial' role in torture, in settings like Abu Ghraib prison, Bagram air base and Guantánamo Bay military prison. This was in marked contrast to the comforting rhetoric offered by the profession and led to revisions to ethical guidance. Serious concerns though have continued, with questions raised about whether the actions of psychologists and their organisations reflected 'professional ethics' or 'guild ethics' (Pope, 2016). The distinction here being that professional ethics aim to protect the public against abuse of power imbalances, holding individuals accountable to values beyond self-interest. Guild ethics, by contrast, involve a blurring between professional self-interest and protecting the public. In its response to the 9/11 attacks and the 'war on terror', psychology has not been seen as acquitting itself well in this and other respects (Halpern, Halpern and Doherty, 2008; Pope, 2016).

Difficulties identifying state terrorism

Developing a working definition of state terrorism is one challenge, but the identification of state terrorism is even more complex. In line with the discussion above, this fundamentally requires the presence of two distinct things: the use of illegitimate violence by the state and the intent to achieve a political goal through communicating fear to a wider audience. When seeking to analyse the behaviour of states, this generates significant challenges, since determination of the motives of state actors is often difficult. It may also be more complex or nuanced than in the case of non-state groups. Questions of agency are often hard to discern where it involves states. This may in turn be compounded by the way in which states typically have greater scope to conceal or disguise the actions they take, facilitated by the security apparatus of states. At a political level, states can also engage in false justifications, or propaganda, such as defining events as 'policing' or 'protective' actions (Snyder, 2022).

Defining acts as state terrorism also requires determination of whether effects intentionally generate high levels of fear and terror in a wider population. Here, the effects of state action may be multiple and the generation of such fear may be a secondary or an unintended effect. To take two specific examples, the Khmer Rouge in Cambodia engaged in the systematic destruction of sections of society: undoubtedly an act of genocide and as such clearly illegal in international law (Lambourne, 2008). This also generated widespread terror in broader society but here, the creation of terror, does not appear to have been the primary aim of the genocide but rather a secondary effect of it. By contrast, Operation Pheonix in the War between North and South Vietnam involved detentions, torture and assassinations of National Liberation Front members. Here, the primary aim was to increase fear in wider society, as part of a political objective of the United States to support the then South Vietnamese regime (Mitchell, Stohl, Carleton et al., 1986; Gabbe-Gross, 2012). This illustrates the difficulties that often arise in distinguishing between terrorism as a primary and secondary objective of an act. Indeed, such difficulties have led some to suggest that efforts at doing so are misplaced (Blakely, 2007, 2012).

In seeking to resolve this, an approach used to look at the legitimacy of acts during war might usefully be applied when looking at terrorism. Within war, it has been argued that acts are only legitimate where several conditions are met. Firstly, an act itself must be a legitimate act of war and its direct effect must, as such, be morally acceptable. In addition, the actors intentions must aim for an acceptable effect and they must also be proportionate (Walzer, 2000). Bombing a military installation used to launch attacks against another state would be permissible here, whereas bombing schools or hospitals would not. Applying this framework to the question of state terrorism suggests that an act should not be defined as state terrorism where it is an unintended secondary effect of a positive or indifferent act. An illustrative example here concerns the generation of terror as a secondary effect to what might otherwise be legitimate acts of state violence. The Gulf War I in 1991 involved a multi-national coalition, responding to an invasion and war of aggression by Iraq, which had occupied a militarily weaker neighbouring state. Within international law, a violent response by states, in the form of a defensive war, was entirely lawful. Here though, in pursuing this defensive war, this coalition of states targeted the electrical power grids within Iraq. This caused catastrophic effects on civilian infrastructure, and the extent of this bombing was notable. More bombing was reported in 1 day than during the 8-year war between Iraq and Iran (Arkin, Durrant and Cherni, 1991). Here, there was no evidence of efforts to minimise the effects of this on civilians, and the 'reduced morale' of civilians may shamefully have been seen as a positive effect by some military planners. Here, the actions of the coalition forces appear illegitimate, based on disproportionality and targeting civilian infrastructure, as well as this being intended at least in part to generate terror in the civilian population to speed the fall of the Iraqi government.

The problem of agency

The problem of agency refers to the need for acts to be part of the state exerting its power. It would therefore exclude isolated criminal acts by individuals from those of states. There is in addition the need to demonstrate presence of intent to cause fear to some wider audience. Even where these requirements are not present though, states still retain a degree of responsibility and issues of complicity may arise, where states have failed to prevent such acts. One example of this would be the series of events at Abu Ghraib prison near Baghdad, when under the control of the United States military. Here, it is clear that a series of criminal acts happened and that these were perpetrated, against detainees, by those employed by the United States. Analysis of these has largely turned on the question of whether they were largely isolated and criminal acts, committed by individuals, or whether they were in fact sanctioned and supported by the state. Early responses to the emerging evidence stressed individual criminality and failures to adhere to required and explicit standards. This would suggest no complicity by the state in events. The response of the state here was to impose measures to avoid recurrence and to swiftly punish individuals for their actions. A lack of evidence of state sanction of the behaviours reported was also stressed. Such claims in relation to Abu Ghraib became more difficult to sustain in the face of other evidence though. There were in fact few prosecutions for criminal behaviour and those that were taken forward focussed on junior staff from the lower military ranks. Of the small number who were prosecuted, the sentences were light. Senior military officers and administrators were largely unpunished. In addition, there were reports of evidence of policies being in place, for the treatment of those identified as insurgents, that were tantamount to the use of torture (Hersh, 2004; Greenberg and Dratel, 2005). Within the prison, it was also reported that no efforts were made to apply the Geneva Conventions to detainees, allowing the use of torture to extract information (Haynes, 2002). Such events are not unique or an isolated incident. Many other examples of such behaviour by states can be observed historically and in recent years, during what was unhelp-fully characterised as a 'war on terror.' Some of these can be seen as indicative of a wider pattern of applying state sanctioned violence as a means of generating fear in populations to achieve some broadly political goal.

The nature of state terrorism

The nature of state terrorism has been a relatively neglected area of study (Jackson, 2009, 2016). This is despite the suggestion that terrorism conducted by states, or sponsored by them, is more prevalent than non-state terrorism or insurgency (Martini, Ford and Jackson, 2020). Indeed, it has been suggested that non-state terrorism can be seen as happening on a 'retail' scale, whereas state or state-sponsored terrorism is conducted on a 'wholesale' scale (Chomsky, 1990). Such neglect is odd since, whilst the motives, functions and effects of these acts may differ, the core characteristics are often the same (Blakely, 2010).

This does though raise the question of whether anything is gained or lost by capturing acts of state and non-state actors under common terms. Most obviously, there is the fact of the similarity of the acts themselves and it is often difficult to see any clear difference. Both may involve apparently similar actions, with similar intent (Davenport and Inman, 2012). It has been argued that incorporating the notion of state terrorism greatly extends and indeed overextends the field of study. As a result of this, important distinctions between state and non-state actors are neglected or lost altogether, with little being gained in compensation by studying these together (Jackson, 2009, 2016). There would though seems to be no compel-ling case for the inevitability of these negative effects, with no *a priori* reason why differences between actors cannot be captured along with similarities. Excluding one type of actor from the field of study of terrorism also appears problematic, running the risk of an unduly limited or misleading understanding of similar acts. Creating new terminology and separate fields of study may appear to be an exces-sive reaction to the breadth of the field of study. Indeed, it has been suggested that extension of the field to address the relative neglect of state actors is overdue, as are efforts to study the interactions between state and non-state actors. The acts of both may often be linked and interacting in complex ways (Thaler, 2022). Here, the use of violence may occur in cycles and it is not clear that studying one side of such interactions is the most useful way forward. It has been stressed that state and non-state actors may develop a mutually shaping dialectic, involving cycles of violence, with state actors as prone to error as non-state (English, 2015). A useful illustra-tion of this from history is that of the Weimar Republic in Germany (1918–1933). Here, largely out of fear, the state engaged in unprecedented levels of 'warlike' vio-lence against its own civil population. This was undertaken in pursuit of real and imagined internal political enemies (Jones, 2016). In this example, it is difficult to see the difference in the behaviour of state and non-state actors.

It is perhaps worth reiterating at this point that the modern notion of 'terrorism' was seen to arise from the state first, emerging from the 18th-century French Revolution (Tackett, 2015). Since then, it has been argued that terrorism has remained part of the core business of states and so has been elemental to the modern world, forming a part of the monopoly use of violence fundamental to the state (Chomsky, 1990; Wilson, 2013). Such ideas echo the view of the modern state which saw it as a compulsory association enforced through a successful monopoly of intimidation within a sovereign territory (Weber, 1919). States work hard to disguise this foundational reality and effective states manage to convert this potentially overwhelming force into social legitimacy (Thorup, 2010). This would include such things as the formal and actual separation of powers, as a check against tyranny. It also includes acceptance of the 'rule of law' by the population, whatever the social and economic realities this enforces. The legitimacy of the state is aided here by publicly demonstrating restraint in response to the law. Alternatively, some states may seek to balance the effects of repressing populations through appeals to shared values, such as religious beliefs (Masters, 2013).

The use of methods associated with terrorism by states clearly carries significant risks. Most striking perhaps, it risks undermining many of the acts used to develop social legitimacy. It replaces observance of the rule of law with violence. It fails to demonstrate restraint and signals that 'might is right.' This perhaps accounts for the tendency for states to externalise notions of terror and to resist the idea of state terrorism, generally only accepting these in the most extreme cases, such as seen in Nazi Germany or the Soviet Union under Stalin. More critical approaches have though stressed the act and not the actor, so bringing in less extreme examples of state terrorism (Wilson, 2019). One approach to this has been to see the variation across states in the use of power as being dimensional, rather than binary. Here one end, the spectrum is seen as involving the full use of the 'infrastructural' power of the state to generate terror. The other end of such a spectrum concerns the actions of weak or fragile states and is characterised as localised, with acts occurring outside the full control of institutions or state. An example of this would be the Sharpeville massacre which took place in the Transvaal province of South Africa in 1960. Here, around 10,000 'Africans' had been forcibly relocated to Sharpeville, a township with high rates of unemployment, crime and disease. Protests from those forcibly located there were met with the use of violence by the local authorities, resulting in many deaths and serious injuries of adults and children (Lodge, 2011). In practice, most elites have aimed for the use of infrastructural public power. Some regimes though have, for varied reasons, been unable to achieve this going on to act in despotic ways. The reasons why the apartheid state of South Africa drew on this kind of despotic power, despite the presence of highly developed institutions, is perhaps obvious. It is not though unique. For example, the state in El Salvador in the 1990s used 'demonstrative atrocities' as a means of control (McClintock, 1985), and likewise, the Syrian state did so from 2011 (Lesch, 2012) until its fall in 2024.

The relationship between state and anti-state terrorism

The focus on the most extreme cases of state terrorism has led to marked bias of research in field. This has involved technologically advanced states with sophisticated bureaucracies, geared towards social engineering through mass human destruction, in pursuit of 'utopian' goals. Here, the analysis of this kind of state terrorism has been complicated by its combination with genocide. Regimes of this kind are also quite atypical in generally experiencing, in contrast to liberal states, low levels of anti-state terrorism. Most state terrorism though is quite different from this. They do not have the kind of overwhelming infrastructural power that characterised Germany and the Soviet Union. More typically, it has involved precarious regimes that depend on using despotic power. Examples of this would include the colonial regimes established by European powers and many of the post-colonial states that followed. Lacking in social legitimacy, changing conditions led to the growth of anti-state insurgencies and terrorism, which was often met with violent responses. Ultimately, states like this were seen to lack the will, rather than the capacity, to maintain such escalating violence. It has been noted that there has been a curious and sustained lack of reflection on this area (Wilson, 2019). This is particularly surprising given the extent and severity of these transitions (Elkins, 2005).

This historic pattern contrasts with the later 20th century and a series of what have been termed 'dirty wars' that took place. The term 'dirty war' here reflects the use of increasingly severe acts of violence by non-state and state actors alike, with little or no regard to questions of legality or morality. Here, stamina was not an issue in the same way as it was for post-World War II colonial regimes and escalating 'auctions' of violence were often seen between state and non-state actors. In these, states came to dominate completely. Examples of this kind of escalation would include Syria post-1976 (Hinnebusch, 2005; Lefèvre, 2013) or Argentina in the 1970s (Moyano, 1995). The 'stamina' for these acts of state and anti-state terrorism was often as result of external support, with many conflicts of this kind being conducted as proxy conflicts between contesting superpowers. It is notable here that many state acts were often highly opaque and many remained so. The involvement of civil society here was often present, favouring stability over change and contributing to such things as intelligence gathering in support of despotic governments. Indeed, such tendencies may account more widely for the durability of many authoritarian and repressive regimes and the reluctance to fully investigate these when they fail (Teets, 2014; Lewis, 2021).

There has been an often-naïve approach to the history of state terrorism and this has, at times, led to misleading ideas and conclusions. There has been a tendency in the research to see what exists now as what has always existed and also a bias towards analysis of contemporary western or global north states, when looking at state terrorism. Yet, the experience of such states appears highly atypical, both in terms of international comparisons and their own historical experiences (Wilson, 2019). In many societies, high levels of state violence and the generation of fear are expected. The question then becomes one of where and why some forms of violence are prevalent and others not. For example, why do some states in practice accept the use of death squads but see genocide as taboo. The basis for such decisions remains poorly studied and understood.

Efforts to better understand state terrorism have as noted above been handicapped by a perhaps understandable focus on the massive, centralised and institutionalised violence and terror, seen in 20th Germany and the Soviet Union, in pursuit of different political 'utopias.' These are not representative of most state terrorism though, which has often been a reaction of weak, failing or threatened states. There is a large field of study here of despotic power and the overlap of this with anti and pro-state activities (Wilson, 2019). Acts such as lynchings, pogroms, massacres and death squads would fall within this. All of these have been noted to look very much like politically motivated violence, intended to spread fear to a wider audience: in other words forms of state terrorism (Wilson, 2019).

Hybrid organisations

The term 'hybrid organisation' captures state use of shadow, quasi-official and unofficial groups in the expression of public power and use of violence. It has been argued that there was no real precedent for such groups before 1914 and that these emerged from the effects of World War I (Hobsbawm, 1999). The development of Freikorps in the German republic between 1918 and 1933 is given as the first example of the state acting in this manner. Freikorps were irregular paramilitary volunteers of German and European origin, often demobilised and unemployed soldiers, who were used by the state to fight against German communists. Similar practice spread to other states and have persisted, with examples such as the Black and Tans, the Belfast Police Death Squads and the Wagner Group (Campbell and Brenner, 2000; Leeson, 2011; Wilson, 2010; Marten, 2019).

These kinds of quasi-official and unofficial groups can be seen to emerge in Europe alongside the economic and social demands of 'total war' which, in turn, led to the creation of 'total states' during wartime (Winter, 2014). These states though faced strictly limited scope to act, at least where they respected notions such as the rule of law and separation of powers. The creation or emergence of such groups provides an entirely illegitimate way around such restrictions on the state, allowing deniability however implausible this might be. This in turn allows states to claim they continued to uphold the rule of law (Campbell and Brenner, 2000). This pattern has continued with the often apparently spontaneous development of groups such as death squads in Latin America (Chippendale and Harriman, 1978). It can also be argued that there has been a new growth in the use of such groups, in the form of private security contractors (Fitzsimmons, 2024). These can be used by states with varying degrees of control or 'influence' as an extension of state violence and terrorism (Sluka, 2000).

Research in this area is limited by the often-opaque nature of these relationships and organisations. They do though appear to be a hybrid of 'state' and 'civil' society based on perceived common interests (Mazzei, 2009). They often emerge at times of stress for the state, where demands are pulling between security concerns, devolution of power and provision of services. Current evidence may though have under estimated the importance of state weakness in this process, with such groups often emerging where the state is felt to be unable to meet emerging challenges to its monopoly of public power. Examples of the role of state weakness have certainly been evident in recent history, with the weakness of the state in Pakistan suggested as a cause for the growth of such hybrid groups (Lieven, 2011). Similarly, the weakness of the state in Iraq, mainly post-2003 and albeit for very different reasons, can be claimed to have had similar effects (al-Khafaji, 1991; Cockburn, 2008).

Possible impacts of human rights on state violence

Some analysis has drawn attention to possible links between the growth of hybrid groups and sub-contracting by states and the growing influence of human rights law. Intended to have purely positive effects, it is suggested that such legal frameworks also carry a clear moral hazard. The focus on human rights may, it is suggested, have served as a further incentive to use methods and groups based on deniability (Campbell and Brenner, 2008). Building on this, some important criticisms have arisen in relation to the growth of human rights internationally (Wilson, 2019). Some critics have stressed the apparently teleological nature of much of human rights thinking, whilst others have suggested it as an example of European universalism, linked in turn to historic mercantilism and colonialism. Concerns here include the process of rolling out human rights being seen as entirely positive and a one-way road, where good outcomes are inevitably followed by better ones. Better here being defined by norms set by European and North American elites. In this view of human rights, state terrorism will simply wither on the vine and in line with the teleological view the one-way road to progress allows for no exits or U-turns. This implicit view has been criticised as being unduly optimistic (Risse, Ropp and Sikkink, 2013; Langford, 2018).

There is in fact a paucity of good quality research looking at how states have adapted in response to the growth of human rights. There have though been some exceptions to this, with impressive research which has looked at the 'semi-democracies' in Israel and Serbia (Ron, 2003). This work distinguished between 'frontiers' and 'ghettos' in analysing some of the acts of these states. The distinction drawn here related to the extent of state control and responsibility that applies. Ghettos were seen to contain despised minorities, but they remained protected by substantial responsibility imposed on the state by international laws. Frontiers on the other hand existed as areas where no single state was in control and therefore responsible. In many respects, these appear like stateless zones (Snyder, 2010) as places where the state feels free to use elevated levels of violence and to have few if any obligations to respect international law. An example of this would be the fate of Gaza since its 'liberation' in 2005 (Chomsky, 2010).

There is also some evidence, suggesting the kind of modification of methods raised as a moral hazard emerging from human rights. Here, concern for human rights leads to changed methods, rather than any reduction in state violence and state terrorism. The British mandate in Palestine, for example, developed the use of 'waterboarding' between 1936 and 1939 apparently for these kinds of reasons (Rejali, 2007; Hughes, 2009). A concern here is that the effects of stronger human rights have frequently been to change the methodology, rather than abandon the methods of terrorism. Additionally, the use of torture and state terrorism may be more common in those states with a tradition of institutions which shun scrutiny and accountability. Such institutions are unlikely to feel meaningfully bound by concerns around human rights.

Research in this area can be criticised for its emphasis on western and later 'global north' states (George, 1991). This in turn has often involved an ahistorical approach to the subject, lacking consideration of the historical context and contingencies faced by states, whilst also neglecting other state traditions (Blakeley, 2009). This has meant that geopolitical changes across Asia, with the rise in economic power and the rise of China in particular, have often received scant attention. This has been noted to be a particularly surprising omission given China's role in the development and supply of equipment used in repression internationally (Moore, 2014).

Rather than face the considerable social, economic and political costs of invasions and wars, there has been a progressive shift by most states to the use of alternative means. This has included the use of various forms of hybrid warfare as well as the use of remote weapons such as unmanned aerial vehicles or 'drones' (Boyle, 2013). This can perhaps be seen as reflecting the executive branches of these states developing a growing awareness of public resistance to open use of military force, along with their citizens increased unwillingness to support and fund costly foreign wars in financial and human terms (Wilson, 2019). Such arm's length techniques though carry a clear moral hazard, and this has been increasingly noted. The very ease of use and the lack of apparent costs present states with a temptation to increasingly deploy them, carrying the risk of normalising such violence in the form of 'low intensity' conflicts with extended duration and harmful impacts (Weizman, 2007).

Summary and conclusions

Traditional views of the state see it as involving a distinct and sustained identity based on legal order and some form of political system. This is based on a monopoly of legitimate power and the use of violence to deal with a central problem of maintaining social order. Notions of state are sometimes erroneously conflated with transitory governments. In functional states, the use of public power and violence is moderated by efforts to increase legitimacy and balance the growing self-interest in elite groups.

Notions of the state have increasingly been in tension with the effects of increased globalisation and marketisation. These have reduced public state power through international legal and economic agreements. These have increasingly been criticised as unaccountable and harmful to the wider public good, replacing political accountability with autonomous and disembedded markets.

States use violence both internally and externally, and this may be acquiesced to as legitimate or challenged. The question of whether illegitimate state violence can be described as 'terrorism' has been contentious, with the suggestion of fundamental differences between state and non-state actors. The use of terms such as 'state atrocities' or 'state repression' though often appears to refer to acts indistinguishable from the terrorism by non-state actors and add little to understanding. The use of state power in such acts is therefore described here as state terrorism.

This includes the increasing state use of shadow or semi-official groups in such acts. These hybrid organisations can be seen as a form of public–private partnership, allowing states some deniability. This has been suggested to be partly a result of growth of international and human rights laws, applicable to illegitimate uses of violence. Psychology has a poor record in this regard and on occasions has contributed to this kind of violence, engaging in such practices in support of states and state actors. There is considerable scope to learn from experience here, with greater reflection on ethical practice across psychology. The development of better institutional memory for the history of the discipline seems critical to this and to the teaching and training of future generations of psychologists: particularly for those who work in settings where the state routinely uses violence.

References

Al-Khafaji, I. (1991). State terror and the degradation of politics in Iraq. *Middle East Report*, *176*, 15–21.

Alpert, H. (1939). *Emile Durkheim and His Sociology*. New York: Columbia University Press.

American Psychological Association. (2005a). *Response from the American Psychological Association to "A stain on medical ethics" The Lancet, Volume 366, Issue 9484, August 6, 2005*. Washington: American Psychological Association.

American Psychological Association. (2005b). *Report of the APA Presidential Task Force on Psychological Ethics and National Security*. Washington: American Psychological Association.

Arkin, W., Durrant, D., and Cherni, M. (1991). *On Impact: Modern Warfare and the Environment – A Case Study of the Gulf War*. Denver: Greenpeace USA.

Blakeley, R. (2007). Bringing the state back into terrorism studies. *European Political Science, 6*, 228–235.

Blakeley, R. (2009). *State Terrorism and Neoliberalism: The North in the South*. London: Routledge.

Blakeley, R. (2010). State terrorism in the social sciences: theories, methods and concepts. In R. Jackson, Murphy, E., and Poynting, S. (Eds.), *Contemporary State Terrorism*. London: Routledge.

Blakeley, R. (2012). State violence as state terrorism. In: M. Breen-Smyth (Ed.), *The Ashgate Research Companion to Political Violence*. London: Ashgate.

Bourdieu, P. (1998). *The State Nobility: Elite Schools in the Field of Power*. Stanford: Stanford University Press.

Boyle, M. J. (2013). The costs and consequences of drone warfare. *International Affairs, 89*(1), 1–29.

Burfisher, M. E., Robinson, S., and Thierfelder, K. (2001). The impact of NAFTA on the United States. *Journal of Economic Perspectives, 15*(1), 125–144.

Campbell, B. and Brenner, A. (Eds.) (2000). *Death Squads in Global Perspective: Murder with Deniability*. New York: Palgrave Macmillan.

Chippendale, P. and Harriman, E. (1978). *Juntas United!* London: Quartet Books.

Chomsky, N. (1990). *Pirates and Emperors: International Terrorism in the Real World*. Brattleboro: Amana Books.

Chomsky, N. (2010). Exterminate all the Brutes: Gaza 2009. In P. Ilan (Ed.), *Gaza in crisis: reflections on Israel's war against the Palestinians*. Chicago: Haymarket Books.

Cockburn, P. (2008). *Muqtada al-Sadr and the Fall of Iraq*. London: Faber and Faber.

Cogneau, D., Dupraz, Y., and Mesplé-Somps, S. (2021). Fiscal capacity and dualism in colonial states: the French empire 1830–1962. *The Journal of Economic History, 81*(2), 441–480.

Crandall, R. (2014). *America's Dirty Wars: Irregular Warfare from 1776 to the War on Terror*. New York: Cambridge University Press.

Davenport, C. and Inman, M. (2012). The state of state repression research since the 1990s. *Terrorism and Political Violence, 24*(4), 619–634.

Denhardt, R. B. and Denhardt, J. V. (2000). The new public service: serving rather than steering. *Public Administration Review, 60*(6), 549–559.

Dunn, J. (1984). The concept of trust in the politics of John Locke. In R. Rorty, Schneewind, J. B., and Skinner, Q. (Eds.), *Philosophy in History: Essays on the Historiography of Philosophy*. New York: Cambridge University Press.

Dyson, K. (2009). The evolving timescapes of European economic governance: contesting and using time. *Journal of European Public Policy, 16*(2), 286–306.

Dyson, K. (2010). *The State Tradition in Western Europe: A Study of an Idea and Institution*. Colchester: ECPR Press.

Dyson, K. (2012). 'Maastricht Plus': managing the logic of inherent imperfections. *Journal of European Integration, 34*(7), 791–808.

Dyson, K. H. and Quaglia, L. (2010). *European Economic Governance and Policies, Vol. 2: Commentary on Key Policy Documents*. Oxford: OUP Catalogue.

Elkins, C. (2005). *Britain's Gulag: The Brutal End of Empire in Kenya*. London: Pimlico.

English, R. (Ed.) (2015). *Illusions of Terrorism and Counter-Terrorism*. Oxford: Oxford University Press.

Etkind, A. M. (1996). Psychological culture. In D. N. Shalin (Ed.), *Russian Culture at the Crossroads*. London: Routledge.

Finlay, C. J. (2010). Legitimacy and non-state political violence. *Journal of Political Philosophy, 18*(3), 287–312.

Fitzsimmons, S. (2024). Contracting blowback?: The use of violence by private security companies and insurgents during the Iraq war. *Studies in Conflict and Terrorism, 47*(1), 78–97.

Gabbe-Gross, M. (2012). A dirty, inglorious affair: the Phoenix program in Vietnam. Unpublished Master's thesis, California State University.

Galbraith, J. K. (2001). The essential Galbraith. Selected and edited by A.D. Williams. New York: Houghton Mifflin.

Gearty, C. (1997). *Terror*. London: Faber and Faber.

George, A. (Ed.) (1991). *Western State Terrorism*. Cambridge: Polity Press.

Geuter, U. (1992). *The Professionalization of Psychology in Nazi Germany*. Cambridge: Cambridge University Press.

Giddens, A. (2014). Information, reflexivity and surveillance. In F. Webster (Ed.), *Theories of the Information Society* (4th ed). London: Routledge.

Gray, J. (2023). *The New Leviathans: Thoughts After Liberalism*. New York: Random House.

Greenberg, K. and Dratel, J. (Eds.) (2005). *The Torture Papers. The Road to Abu Ghraib*. Cambridge: Cambridge University Press.

Halpern, A. L., Halpern, J. H., and Doherty, S. B. (2008). " Enhanced" interrogation of detainees: do psychologists and psychiatrists participate?. *Philosophy, Ethics, and Humanities in Medicine, 3*, 1–11.

Haynes, J. (2002). Counter-Resistance Techniques (Action Memo from William J Haynes, General Counsel, to Secretary of State for Defense Donald Rumsfeld), 27 November, https://nsarchive2.gwu.edu/NSAEBB/NSAEBB127/02.12.02.pdf. Accessed September 15, 2024.

Herring, E. and Robinson, P. (2014). Deception and Britain's Road to War in Iraq. *International Journal of Contemporary Iraqi Studies, 8*(2), 213–232.

Hersh, S. (2004). *Chain of Command. The Road from 9/11 to Abu Ghraib.* London: Penguin Books.

Hinnebusch, R. (2005). *Syria: Revolution from Above.* London: Routledge.

Hobbes, T. (1996). *Leviathan: Revised Student Edition* (R. Tuck Ed.), Cambridge: Cambridge University Press.

Hobsbawm, E. (1999). *On History.* London: Abacus.

Hoffman, B. (1998). *Inside Terrorism.* New York: Columbia University Press.

Hughes, M. (2009). The banality of brutality: British armed forces and the repression of the Arab revolt in Palestine, 1936–39. *The English Historical Review, 124*(507), 313–354.

ICRC. (1949). *The Geneva Conventions of 12 August 1949.* Geneva: ICRC.

ICRC. (2003). International Humanitarian Law and the Challenges of Contemporary Armed Conflicts. Report prepared for the 28th International Conference of the Red Cross and Red Crescent, Geneva, 2–6 December 2003.

Jackson, R. (2009). Knowledge, power and politics in the study of political terrorism. In R. Jackson, Smyth, M. B., and Gunning, J. (Eds.), *Critical Terrorism Studies: A New Research Agenda.* London: Routledge.

Jackson, R. (2016). Introduction: a decade of critical terrorism studies. In R. Jackson (Ed.), *Routledge Handbook of Critical Terrorism Studies.* London: Routledge.

Jefferson, T. and Grimshaw, R. (2023). *Controlling the Constable: Police Accountability in England and Wales.* London: Routledge.

Jones, M. (2016). *Founding Weimar: Violence and the German Revolution of 1918–1919.* Cambridge: Cambridge University Press.

Kelman, H. C. (2006). Interests, relationships, identities: three central issues for individuals and groups in negotiating their social environment. *Annual Review of Psychology, 57*(1), 1–26.

Kennedy-Pipe, C. (2014). *The Origins of the Present Troubles in Northern Ireland.* London: Routledge.

Kirk, A. (2010). Political Repression and Islam in Iran. Human Rights and Human Welfare: Vol. 10: Issue. 1. Available at: https://digitalcommons.du.edu/hrhw/vol10/iss1/23/. Retrieved September 19, 2024.

Kraut, R. (2002). *Aristotle: Political Philosophy.* New York: Oxford University Press.

Lambourne, W. (2008). The Khmer Rouge Tribunal: Justice for Genocide in Cambodia?. Law and Society Association Australia and New Zealand (LSAANZ) Conference, W(h)ither Human Rights, 10-12 December, University of Sydney. Available at https://ses.library.usyd.edu.au/handle/2123/4042. Retrieved September 17, 2024.

Landis, E. (2002). The furies: violence and terror in the French and Russian revolutions. *Kritika: Explorations in Russian and Eurasian History, 3*(1), 152–163.

Langford, M. (2018). Critiques of human rights. *Annual Review of Law and Social Science, 14*(1), 69–89.

Lacquer, W. Z. (1987). *The Age of Terrorism.* Boston: Little Brown.

Lacquer, W. Z. (1998). Terror's new face: the radicalization and escalation of modern terrorism. *Harvard International Review, 20*, 48–51.

Leeson, D. M. (2011). *The Black and Tans: British Police and Auxiliaries in the Irish War of Independence, 1920-1921*. New York: Oxford University Press.

Lefèvre, R. (2013). *Ashes of Hama: The Muslim Brotherhood in Syria*. London: Hurst and Co.

Lesch, D. (2012). *Syria: The Fall of the House of Assad*. New Haven: Yale University Press.

Lewis, A. (2021). *A State of Secrecy: Stasi Informers and the Culture of Surveillance*. Lincoln: University of Nebraska Press.

Lieven, A. (2011). *Pakistan: A Hard Country*. London: Allen Lane.

Lodge, T. (2011). *Sharpeville: An Apartheid Massacre and Its Consequences*. New York: Oxford University Press.

Marten, K. (2019). Russia's use of semi-state security forces: the case of the Wagner Group. *Post-Soviet Affairs*, *35*(3), 181–204.

Martini, A., Ford, K., and Jackson, R. (Eds.) (2020). *Encountering Extremism*. Manchester: Manchester University Press.

Masters, B. (2013). *The Arabs of the Ottoman Empire, 1516–1918: A Social and Cultural History*. Cambridge: Cambridge University Press.

Mazzei, J. (2009). *Death Squads or Self-Defence Forces? How Paramilitary Groups Emerge and Challenge Democracy in Latin America*. Chapel Hill: University of North Carolina Press.

McClintock, M. (1985). *The American Connection: Volume One: State Terror and Popular Resistance in El Salvador*. London: Zed Books.

McLean, J. (2003). Government to state: globalization, regulation, and governments as legal persons. *Indiana Journal of Global Legal Studies*, *10*, 173–197.

Medlong, J. (2012). All other breaches: state practice and the Geneva conventions' nebulous class of less discussed prohibitions. *Michigan Journal of International Law*, *34*, 829–856.

Mitchell, C., Stohl, M., Carleton, D., and Lopez, G. (1986). State terrorism: issues of concept and measurement. In M. Stohl and Lopez, G. (Eds.), *Government Violence and Repression: An Agenda for Research*. Westport: Greenwood Press.

Möllers, C. (2018). Constitutional state of the European Union. In R. Schütze (Ed.), *Globalisation and Governance: International Problems, European Solutions*. Cambridge: Cambridge University Press.

Monaghan, M. and Prideaux, S. (2016). Fighting 'the enemy within': internal state terrorism, Argentina's 'Dirty War' (1976–83) and the UK miners' strike (1984–85). State Crime and Immorality: The *Corrupting Influence* of the *Powerful*. Bristol, 2016; online edn, Policy Press Scholarship Online, 22 Sept. 2016, Available online https://doi.org/10.1332/poli cypress/9781447316749.003.0008. Accessed January 31, 2025.

Moore, M. (2014). China exports its expertise in torture. *Daily Telegraph*, 23rd September.

Moyano, M. J. (1995). *Argentina's Lost Patrol: Armed Struggle, 1969–1979*. London: Yale University Press.

Orwell, G. (1957). *Selected Essays*. London: Penguin.

Polanyi, K. (2001). *The Great Transformation*. Boston: Beacon Press.

Pollit, C. (2006). Changing European states, changing public administration: Antistatist reforms and new administrative directions: public administration in the United Kingdom. In E. E. Otenyo and Lind, N. S. (Eds.), *Comparative Public Administration* (*Research in Public Policy Analysis and Management, Vol. 15)*. Leeds: Emerald Group Publishing Limited.

Pope, K. S. (2016). The code not taken: the path from guild ethics to torture and our continuing choices. *Canadian Psychology/Psychologie Canadienne*, *57*(1), 51–59.

Rejali, D. (2007). *Torture and Democracy*. Princeton: Princeton University Press.

Reynolds, N. (2019). *Putin's not-so-secret mercenaries: Patronage, geopolitics, and the Wagner group (Vol. 8)*. Washington: Carnegie Endowment for International Peace.

Risse, T., Ropp, S., and Sikkink, K. (Eds.) (2013). *The Persistent Power of Human Rights: From Commitment to Compliance*. Cambridge: Cambridge University Press.

Rogov, K. (2018). The art of coercion: repressions and repressiveness in Putin's Russia. *Russian Politics, 3*(2), 151–174.

Ron, J. (2003). *Frontiers and Ghettos: State Violence in Serbia and Israel*. Berkeley: University of California Press.

Runciman, D. (2003). Moral responsibility and the problem of representing the state. In T. Erskine (Ed.), *Can Institutions Have Responsibilities? Global Issues Series*. London: Palgrave Macmillan.

Runciman, D. (2023). *The Handover: How We Gave Control of Our Lives to Corporations, States and AIs*. London: Profile Books.

Sandel, M. (2012). *Liberalism and the Limits of Justice* (2nd ed.). Cambridge: Cambridge University Press.

Scott, C. (2019). *State failure in Sub-Saharan Africa: The Crisis of Post-Colonial Order*. London: Bloomsbury Publishing.

Self, P. (2021). *Government by the Market?: The Politics of Public Choice*. London: Routledge.

Skinner, Q. (2009). A genealogy of the modern state. *Proceedings of the British Academy, 162*, 325–370.

Sluka, J. (2000). *Death Squad: The Anthropology of State Terror*. Philadelphia: University of Pennsylvania Press.

Snyder, T. (2010). *Bloodlands: Europe between Hitler and Stalin*. London: Bodley Head.

Snyder, T. (2022). Ukraine holds the future: the war between democracy and nihilism. *Foreign Affairs, 101*(124), 1–21.

Stanley, R. (2004). Everyday forms of illegal coercion: explaining abuse of police powers in Argentina. *Journal of Third World Studies, 21*(2), 83–105.

Stiglitz, J. E. (2010). Lessons from the global financial crisis of 2008. *Seoul Journal of Economics, 23*(3), 321–339.

Stohl, M. (2006). The state as terrorist: insights and implications. *Democracy and Security, 2*, 1–25.

Sullivan, C. M. (2014). The (in) effectiveness of torture for combating insurgency. *Journal of Peace Research, 51*(3), 388–404.

Tackett, T. (2015). *The Coming of the Terror in the French Revolution*. Cambridge: Harvard University Press.

Teets, J. (2014). *Civil Society under Authoritarianism: The China Model*. New York: Cambridge University Press.

Thaler, K. M. (2022). Delegation, sponsorship, and autonomy: an integrated framework for understanding armed group–state relationships. *Journal of Global Security Studies, 7*(1), 1–19.

Thorup, M. (2010). *An Intellectual History of Terror: War, Violence and the State*. London: Routledge.

Thurnher, J. S. (2008). Drowning in Blackwater: how weak accountability over private security contractors significantly undermines counterinsurgency efforts. *Army Lawyer, 64* (July 2008), Available at SSRN: https://ssrn.com/abstract=2296362

Towl, G. J. (2021). The politics of forensic psychological research, policy and practice. In D. Crighton and Towl, G. (Eds.), *Forensic Psychology*. Chichester: John Wiley.

Walker, N. (2006). Constitutionalism and New Governance in the European Union: Rethinking the Boundaries. EUI Law Working Paper No. 2005/15. Available at http://dx.doi.org/10.2139/ssrn.891027. Retrieved September 11, 2024.

Walzer, M. (2000). *Just and Unjust Wars* (3rd ed.). New York: Basic Books.

Weber, M. (1919). *Politics as a Vocation.* Munich: Duncker and Humboldt.

Weizman, E. (2007). *Hollow Land: Israel's Architecture of Occupation.* London: Verso.

Wilkinson, P. (2006). *Terrorism Versus Democracy: The Liberal State Response.* London: Routledge.

Wilson, T. (2010). The most terrible assassination that has yet stained the name of Belfast: the McMahon murders in context. *Irish Historical Studies, 37*(145): 83–106.

Wilson, T. (2013). State terrorism: an historical overview. In G. Duncan, Lynch, O., Ramsay, G., and Watson, A. (Eds.), *State Terrorism and Human Rights: International Responses since the End of the Cold War.* London: Routledge.

Wilks, M. (2005). A stain on medical ethics. *The Lancet, 366,* 429–431.

Wilson, T. (2019). State terrorism. In E. Chenoweth, English, R., Gofas, A., and Kalyvas, S. N. (Eds.), *The Oxford Handbook of Terrorism.* Oxford: Oxford University Press.

Winter, J. (Ed.) (2014). *The Cambridge History of the First World War: Volume 2, The State.* Cambridge: Cambridge University Press.

Wyatt, F. and Teuber, H. L. (1944). German psychology under the Nazi system: 1933–1940. *Psychological Review, 51*(4), 229–247.

4   Responses to politically motivated violence – the UK example

To have a continuing existence states and other entities, such as international political bodies, need to be able to respond effectively to the threats that arise to their integrity and also be willing to do so. Threats may emerge in many ways, including increasing political instability, increasing polarisation and political extremism, civil disorder, insurgency, guerilla warfare, terrorism or civil war. The primary focus here is on the challenges that arise from various forms of politically motivated violence and particularly those which are identified as terrorism. The approach adopted here is to focus in some detail on how a single state, the United Kingdon (UK), has responded to these kinds of threat. An alternative to this would have been to try and review multiple states, or multiple states and international political bodies. This would though have inevitably resulted in superficial coverage of both the responses involved and the critiques of these. Focus on a single state, as an illustrative example, of reactions to maintain integrity, provides scope for a more in-depth analysis and discussion of the issues involved and the main critiques that have emerged.

The UK is comprised of a union of three separate nations, England, Scotland and Wales which together form Great Britain. In addition to this, the UK includes the province of Northern Ireland. Some regions of the UK also have devolved powers and at present examples of this include Greater Manchester and London regions. Each of the nations and Northern Ireland has their own distinctive legislative assemblies, with differing powers and areas of political responsibility, including areas such as health, education and transport. More limited powers and responsibility are devolved to the regions. Ultimate authority and some areas are reserved to the UK Parliament which remains the sovereign political body, with legal safeguards in place to ensure this is preserved. Areas reserved to the UK include economic, foreign and defence policy, as well as security and intelligence.

The UK has a long history of responding to politically motivated violence and as such provides a good illustrative example (Childs, 2014). The nations that make up the UK have had wide ranging experience of this, linked to its history of religious conflicts, imperial expansion and colonisation. More recently, the UK has experienced a withdrawal from empire, progressively leaving many former colonial states. This often involved violence including civil protests, insurgencies,

DOI: 10.4324/9781003429579-4

guerilla wars and terrorism (Evans, 2014). Much of this conflict took place across Asia, the Middle East and Africa. Examples of this include withdrawals from India (Wolpert, 2009), Palestine (Ovendale, 1980), Kenya (Olson, 2008) and Malaysia (Pwarham, 2010). All these examples involved considerable levels of politically motivated violence, with some resulting in ongoing conflict as a result of the solutions adopted. Indeed, many political conflicts current in the world today can only be adequately understood with reference to past actions and policies of the British Empire. Many of the responses to political violence in the UK have also been strongly influenced by this history.

A review of the UK's imperial history is not attempted here, and the focus has been limited to aspects of counter-terrorism policy in the period since the late 1960s. This arbitrary starting point has been chosen simply as a convenient one, since it provides a relatively clear starting point for a prolonged period of civil disorder, insurgency and later terrorism within the UK. This began in Northern Ireland (then commonly referred to as Ulster) and followed civil rights protests. These were organised by civil rights groups which represented the minority Catholic population, and the start of this period is often cited as being a planned protest march on 5 October 1968. This was supported by the Northern Ireland Civil Rights Association and was focused on claims of unfair allocation of housing and jobs, as well as limitations on the electoral franchise in local government elections. Following the announcement of the planned march the Apprentice Boys, a group with opposing views drawn from the majority Protestant population, announced a 'parade' on the same day. On the 3rd October, the Northern Ireland (Stormont) government, fearing disorder, banned these events. The following day though, the organisations behind the civil rights protest all decided to go ahead and this ended in violence, when the police blocked the route and dispersed the marchers. This was extensively televised, with images of the high levels of violence broadcast around the world. A period of escalating tensions followed this, with increasing sectarianism and subsequently insurgent violence and then campaigns of terrorism (Power, 1972).

Rapidly escalating levels of violence resulted in the British armed forces being deployed to the province in August 1969 under 'Operation Banner.' This was initially intended as a short-term action, where the military would act in support of the civilian authorities and civilian police force, the Royal Ulster Constabulary (RUC). The British military was to be used as impartial peace keepers for a relatively short time. This impartiality was only achieved in the short term, and the British military soon came to be associated with the majority community and the RUC. Notions of a quick withdrawal once civilian authorities restored control were never achieved and the military remained until final withdrawal in 2007. The 1970s saw an escalating campaign of violence, led initially by the Provisional Irish Republican Army (PIRA) but which later involved other groups, from both minority and majority communities.

Within UK government, this is generally referred to as Northern Ireland Related Terrorism (NIRT). Broadly speaking, this represents a re-emergence of a much longer history of political violence in Ireland and influence of this on the UK mainland. Responses to NIRT evolved over time, involving distinct legislative and policy responses by the UK government. This was certainly the dominant concern within the UK, in relation to counter-terrorism, until the violence in Northern Ireland largely abated during the 1990s. A formal peace agreement, partly brokered by the US, was reached in 1998 called the 'Good Friday' agreement (Fenton, 2018).

The other main driver of terrorism policy in the UK has been the emergence of politically motivated violence, insurgencies and terrorism arising primarily from the Middle East, parts of Asia and more recently Africa. These involved the emergence of campaigns of violence largely from the 1980s, undertaken by groups working across international borders. These groups typically engaged in attacks against multiple states and as such can be seen as distinct from anti-colonial groups which engaged in political violence. Initially, these attacks were focused on the Middle East but later extended into Africa, Asia, Europe and North America. An example of this was a suicide bombing attack on a United States Marines Corp (USMC) base in Beirut. Here, a USMC contingent had been deployed as part of a multinational peacekeeping force and were subject to a suicide bombing attack in 1983, using an explosive device in a truck which was driven into their barracks. This resulted in the deaths of 220 US marines, 18 sailors and 3 soldiers (Carr and Scott, 2024). Other examples included the Aden Hotel bombings in Yemen in 1992 (Kohler and Findlay, 2011), the 1993 bomb attack on the World Trade Centre in New York (Murphy, 2002) and attacks against the Paris Metro in 1995 (Jenkins, 1997). The most severe of these attacks, in terms of deaths, serious injuries and political impacts, was on 11th September 2001 (9/11) in the US. This involved the coordination of four simultaneous attacks, using an approach not seen previously, with suicidal attacks using hijacked commercial aircraft. This resulted in thousands of deaths and severe injuries and was the most serious attack to take place on the US mainland (National Commission on Terrorist Attacks, 2011). This was followed by a series of smaller-scale attacks, which predominantly took place in Muslim countries and countries with significant Muslim populations. This included attacks in Pakistan, Tunisia, Morocco, Qatar, Jordan, Indonesia, Turkey, Egypt, Saudi Arabia, India and Yemen (HM Government, 2006). Attacks were also seen in Europe, on the Madrid train network in 2004 (Reinares, 2017) and in the UK in 2005 which involved explosions on the London Underground rail network and bus services (Hoffman, 2014). These attacks caused mass casualties and disruption and were conducted by groups including al-Qa'ida (AQ), Islamic State (IS), Boko Haram (BH) and others. These groups drew on interpretations of Islamic religious beliefs, with political aims that were in turn based on these interpretations (Howells, 2009; Nesser, 2018). Initially, this was often misleadingly referred to, by governments and others, as 'Islamic' terrorism (Antúnez and Tellidis, 2016). More recently, it has generally been described by governments as 'Islamist terrorism' and 'Islamist extremism.' The term 'Islamist' here being used to describe a totalitarian ideology with sectarian variants (Sunni, Shi'a and Wahhabi) which includes global and national forms. These various Islamist strands can be seen to share a common aim of establishing Islamic 'might' in the world, including the use of violence as a means of achieving this (Mozaffari, 2007).

In recent years, the UK government response to terrorism, at political and policy levels, can be seen as having been driven by these two distinct threats. The first of these, concerned with responses to NIRT, has decreased in importance. Terrorism and politically motivated violence in Northern Ireland have reduced following the Good Friday agreement. This threat has continued but has increasingly been focussed in small splinter groups. In contrast, the growth of Islamist terrorism and more recently other forms of trans-national terrorism has become increasingly important in UK government counter-terrorism policy and practice.

Politically motivated violence and political accountability

The UK has a defined system for managing threats and ensuring political account-ability in this area. At UK level, this involves a National Security Council (NSC) and Secretariat, led by the Prime Minister of the UK. The Prime Minister should in turn be advised by a National Security Adviser (NSA). Below this are structures at the level of central government departments, led by Ministers and supported by Permanent Secretaries, who are the most senior civil servants in government departments. Key departments involved in this area include the Home Office, which has responsibility for areas including counter-terrorism policing, domestic security, immigration and borders: the Foreign Office, which has responsibility for areas including intelligence services and Government Communications Headquarters (GCHQ): Defence, with responsibility for the military and the Ministry of Justice, with responsibilities including courts, prisons and probation.

The political and administrative structures concerned, both directly and indir-ectly, are all ultimately accountable to the UK Parliament. In constitutional terms, this is the sovereign political body and scrutiny and accountability by Parliament are largely delivered through specialist Parliamentary Committees. These committee are made up of Members of Parliament appointed on a cross-party basis and elected by secret ballot by all members of the legislature. These committees have wide-ranging powers to call witnesses and scrutinise the work of government. Central to this work are the Intelligence and Security Committee (ISC) and Home Affairs Committee (HAC). In addition, the government also appoints an Independent Reviewer of Terrorism Legislation and an Investigatory Powers Commissioner and Investigatory Powers Tribunal.

At a departmental level, NIRT is led by the Northern Ireland Office (NIO) which forms part of the UK governments administration, based in Belfast and London. For threats from other forms of terrorism, lead responsibility rests with the Home Office, although some areas such as cyber threats have been moved to other departments. Within this department, work is currently led by the Homeland Security Group (HSG) which is responsible for working with other agencies with interests and responsibilities in this area, including bodies such as the Health Protection Agency (HPA), the Borders and Immigration Service, the Nations and Regions of the UK, Local Authorities, and so on.

Addressing politically motivated violence that does not emerge from Northern Ireland is covered by a policy framework called Contest (HM Government, 2023a).

This framework was introduced in 2003 and most recently updated in response to the UK government Integrated Review of Security, Defence, Development and Foreign Policy in March 2023 (HM Government, 2023b). The initial 2003 version of Contest was produced as a classified document but was revised and partly declassified in 2009. Major revisions were seen in 2011, 2018 and 2023. From its inception, Contest, in many respects, closely mirrored the wider European Union (EU) strategy. It has a structure based on four 'pillars' or 'themes' called: Prevent, Pursue, Protect and Prepare, and this has been continued across its multiple revisions and updates (Gregory, 2009; HM Government, 2023a). Contest also appears to have changed in significant ways, and the current version appears very different from the earliest versions. This includes a marked increase in the number and breath of 'factors' suggested as being linked to or involved in threats of politically motivated violence. There has also been a reduction in the unhelpful emphasis given to specifically named groups, as the flexibility of these groupings and emergent nature of threats has become increasingly evident. The rationale given for the policy framework has also been expanded and clarified, introducing greater consistency. An example here would be the move away from overly broad notions of 'right wing violence.' These have increasingly been replaced with a focus on 'extremism' and 'right-wing terrorism' as a growing threat. Recognition of the extent and severity of cyber threats has also developed markedly, including the threat of hybrid warfare by state and state backed actors, although arguably this has still been too inflexible and slow.

Some legislative milestones

NIRT and other terrorist threats have been kept largely separate and is largely addressed through legislation that pre-dates the Contest framework. It has continued to be largely treated as a separate area of counter terrorism in the UK (Pantazis and Pemberton, 2009). As touched on above, the responses to NIRT are traceable back to the 1960s and a period that came to be called, somewhat euphemistically, 'the Troubles.' This prolonged era involved serious politically motivated violence, campaigns of terror within Northern Ireland and the mainland UK and political assassinations. Violence still continues in the form of now relatively small groups which reject the political settlement reached in 1998 (Lelourec, 2016).

The response to 'the Troubles' involved multiple legislative changes, with perhaps the most significant of these being the Prevention of Terrorism (Temporary Provisions) Act of 1974 (PTA). This followed a series of terrorist bomb attacks on pubs on the British mainland, including the most serious of these in the city of Birmingham in November 1974. This killed 21 people and injured 180 fuelling public anger and leading to a swift and arguably hasty and ill-considered legislative response. Even at the time, this was recognised as being novel in introducing 'draconian' measures to the UK mainland, mirroring some of what was already present in Northern Ireland. This law explicitly referred to the provisions being temporary, although in fact most went on to become permanent. Despite obvious concerns about some of the provisions, the act went through the UK parliament with little or no concern being recorded. Not for the first time, or the last, strong public sentiment seems to have driven legislators into short-term reactions. This was also associated with serious miscarriages of justice in relation to terrorist attacks in Guildford and Birmingham (Walker and Starmer, 1999). The 1974 PTA went on to be subsequently amended and ultimately replaced, with important changes coming in 1984, when legislation was extended to bring international terrorism within scope. This was in response to the emerging threats that were becoming evident internationally, with a later Criminal Justice (Terrorism and Conspiracy) Act 1998 further extending coverage to include conspiracy to engage in terrorism, within the scope of legislation.

Another major legislative milestone for the UK was the Terrorism Act 2000. This wide-ranging act sought to draw together what had increasingly become an incoherent patchwork of legislation. This brought much of this into a single place, giving a definition of 'terrorism' that continues to be used capturing acts and threats. The kind of activities that fall within scope were summarised and included the need for these being designed to influence the government or an international governmental organisation, or to intimidate the public or a section of the public. Additionally, the 2000 act stressed the need for actions or threats to have the purpose of advancing some political, religious or ideological cause. The act also defined proscribed organisations, 'terrorist property,' investigations and counter terrorism powers. A government list of proscribed organisations was established. Later extensions to the act brought in other offences, including the encouragement of terrorism, glorification of terrorism, dissemination of terrorist publications and engaging in preparation and training. Furthermore, 'temporary provisions' initially made for Northern Ireland were subsequently added to by later legislation, including the Security Act of 2001 (ATCSA), the Terrorism Act 2006 (TA 2006) and the Counter Terrorism and Security Act of 2015 (CTSA) 2015.

These legislative changes have been subject to significant criticism. They have been noted to have extended police powers, beyond those seen in the criminal law. For example, by allowing detention for up to 48 hours, based on suspicion of being a terrorist. The police and Home Secretary (the elected politician heading the UK Home Office) were also empowered to define areas of the country where searches could be carried out, without a need for reasonable suspicion. This can be criticised as breaking down the operational independence of the police in the UK from political interference, itself an important check against abuse. The definition of 'terrorism' has also been problematic, shifting the focus away from some forms of politically motivated violence. At the same time, it has been criticised for excessive breadth, potentially capturing legitimate political activities. Partly in response to such concerns amendments, as well as extensions of power related to areas such as possession of information or materials related to terrorism have followed. Aspects of legislation in this area though have at times been found by the courts to be incompatible with the European Convention on Human Rights (ECHR). As a result, many of the powers given by the UK Parliament have subsequently been struck down by the courts or subject to significant amendment.

Broadly speaking, current UK legislation in this area has been described as having developed four central characteristics. First, the current legal provisions appear designed to be relatively permanent, with references to temporary provisions seen in earlier legislation now generally absent. The legislation also seeks to cover the whole of the UK, including Northern Ireland. However here, there does appear to be a recognition of the unique circumstances and ongoing concerns around NIRT, with the continuation of some special provisions. Current legislation also appears to have retained almost all the draconian powers around politically motivated violence that so seriously concerned previous legislators. Indeed, these powers can be seen to have been added to, with new offences and powers being applied to a much wider range of actions and groups than previously. This has included splinter groups involved in NIRT, who opposed the peace process and current settlement, as well as international terrorists and domestic politically motivated violence based on religious or political ideals (Fenwick, 2002).

Current UK policy responses

The approach taken to NIRT by the UK government has been characterised by some as a generally 'hard' one, meaning this appeared to be primarily based on detection, policing, defence and security responses (Pantazis and Pemberton, 2009). The stress here seems to have been on areas such as detection and deterrence, using a variety of techniques including infiltration and intelligence gathering. These extended, at points, to serious and counter-productive errors in approach, such as the suspension of normal civil and political rights in Northern Ireland. These included 'Operation Demetrius' which introduced internment without trial and mass arrests and detention. This was based on intelligence information which subsequently proved to be seriously compromised and faulty (McCleery, 2015). A further example here was the removal of the right to a jury trial in some circumstances, with the creation of what were called Diplock Courts (Rasnic, 1999). The approach adopted also required a prolonged period where large numbers of military, security and intelligence personnel were deployed to or focussed on Northern Ireland. The 'troubles' though ended through political agreement and the Good Friday Agreement in 1998 (Cox, Guelke and Stephen, 2006; Tonge, 2006).

Despite this 'hard' response being deployed for a long period of time and this formal political settlement, politically motivated violence and terrorist activity has still not been eliminated though. There has been a continuation of this by small groups, which have remained committed to violent means of achieving political objectives. As a result, the level of threat in this area, as estimated by the UK government, has usually remained either 'substantial' or 'severe.' Primary targets for these groups have tended to be police, prison staff and military personnel in Northern Ireland, although some evidence of targeting of other parts of the UK has also been reported (McGlinchey, 2021).

The UK's response to the developments that followed the new emergent forms of politically motivated violence and terrorism operating trans-nationally can be contrasted in several ways to those seen in NIRT. Most obviously, there has been the development and later publication of the Contest policy. This framework set out what has been seen as a 'soft' or softer approach than used in Northern Ireland. This has included a focus on broad based 'preventative' efforts involving 'assessment' and 'treatment' responses to politically motivated violence and terrorism. Broadly speaking, this can be seen as drawing on public health ideas. In line with this, in addition to policing and security responses, there is emphasis within Contest on tackling the causes of constructs such as 'extremism' and 'radicalisation.' This is to be achieved through prevention efforts and treatment interventions. Contest therefore stresses psycho-social intervention with those judged at risk of engaging, along with provision of 'treatment programmes' claimed to address risk in those who have already engaged in politically motivated violence.

As touched on above, the use of terminology in Contest has been controversial and has generated strong, often polarised, views. The National Association of Muslim Police (NAMP), for example, has argued against using the terms 'Islamist' and 'Islamism' to describe those defining themselves as acting violently, based on 'Muslim' ideologies. In written evidence to a UK Parliamentary Committee, the NAMP noted that the actions and ideologies by these groups are far from being Islamic. Accepting such a linkage means that negative stereotypes of minority groups may be strengthened, increasing community division and fuelling discrimination. In this respect, the NAMP appear to see little difference between the use of terms 'Islamic' and 'Islamist.' Additionally, it has been argued that creating this kind of link has clear potential to offer support for 'Extreme Right-Wing Terrorism' (ERWT) groups. The use of language also appears quite different here from that used for other groups and individuals engaged in politically motivated violence. For example, ERWT actors who have claimed to be acting based on 'Christian' ideologies have not been identified on a religious basis. Terms such as 'Christianism' have not been created to identify them. On this basis, the NAMP went on to suggest that it would be better to avoid references to religion completely (National Association of Muslim Police, 2019). Others have strongly contested this view, arguing that such a link needs to be maintained and is essential to properly capture and understand the threat. Suggestions that such actions would better be described as 'anti-Islamic' have also been rejected by some, who have argued this would mean the UK state taking a theological position. Similarly, it has been suggested that the use of 'evasive' or 'convoluted' language is itself unhelpful, making analysis and discussion of potential root causes more difficult than it needs to be. Terms such as 'faith-claimed terrorism' have been rejected on this basis, as being both unduly vague and ineffective in separating religion from acts of violence.

Early iterations of Contest did in fact recognise that Muslims were equally at risk from such terrorism and many had died as a result of attacks, including the Muslim victims of the 7 July 2005 attacks in London (HM Government, 2011). The 'distorted' and 'unrepresentative' interpretations of Islamic faith involved have also been noted within Contest, with later iterations also broadening coverage to take in other ideological motivations. It has though been suggested that this has largely been 'window dressing' for a policy that, in many respects, remains 'Islamophobic' (Allen, 2020).

Extremism

The softer approach that forms part of Contest has also included a focus on 'extremism' and 'radicalisation' in recent policy. Use of these constructs in this area of policy appear largely or wholly absent before Contest. Both though have become increasingly central in later policy. Both constructs have been criticised for being far from straightforward, either to understand or to apply in practice (Backes, 2010). The notion of an extreme clearly involves a sense of the mainstream. How the extent and nature of deviations from this needed to constitute 'extremism' are arrived at is unclear, involving as it does a focus on beliefs rather than acts. Perhaps unsurprisingly efforts at definition have proved highly problematic. The 2011 revision of Contest, for example, provided a definition of 'extremism' as: "…vocal or active opposition to fundamental 'British values,' including democracy, the rule of law, individual liberty and mutual respect and tolerance of different faiths and beliefs" (HM Government, 2011). There are many problems with this but two problems perhaps stand out. First is the remarkable breadth of the definition, potentially capturing many areas of political activity and debate. Second is the use of the even vaguer term 'fundamental British values.' This drew extensive criticism as being vague, divisive and unhelpful (Hodkinson, 2020). Indeed, the current version of Contest omitted this term, including only a passing reference to 'British values,' a phrase so marginal, vague and open to interpretation that few have bothered to challenge its inclusion. The current version of Contest has though made efforts to more clearly define 'extremism,' defining this as the promotion or advancement of an ideology that is based on violence, hatred or intolerance, that aims to: (1) negate or destroy the fundamental rights and freedoms of others; or (2) undermine, overturn or replace the UK's system of liberal parliamentary democracy and democratic rights; or (3) intentionally create a permissive environment for others to achieve the results in (1) or (2) (HM Government, 2023c). This appears to be a slight improvement but still fails to address the criticisms outlined above. Clear potential to capture a great deal of entirely legitimate political activity remains.

Radicalisation

The term 'radical' is a comparatively recent one in this context, traceable back to the 18th century when, for example, it was used in reference to French and American revolutionaries. The term became more widely used during the 19th century, where it was used to refer to political agendas advocating extensive social and political reform. The term 'radical' also came to increasingly be used to identify those supporting the more extreme section of a political party or grouping. This clearly involves a significant degree of judgement about values, further complicated by the fact that people are not all consistently 'moderate' or 'traditional' in their views and may differ across topics (Schmid, 2013). Equally, there is no reference point of 'moderation' from which to measure the distance from views that are deemed acceptable, common sense or politically mainstream, along some political axis. The term 'radical' has also shifted meaning over time. The 19th century advocates of 'radical' views typically held republican rather than royalist views, advocated for universal suffrage and electoral reform, rather than revolution. Recently, the term has been largely co-opted to refer to those engaged in 'radical Islamism,' by adopting anti-liberal, religiously fundamentalist and anti-democratic views (Rogers, 2008; Schmid, 2013).

Alongside this shift has been the apparent construction of 'radicalisation.' This presumably refers to a developmental psychological and social process leading to 'extremism.' This seems to assume a process of becoming more radical in relation to broadly political views and also that there will be observable indicators of this. Various means are seen as contributing to this process, including the use of various means to access content expounding or contributing to the development of 'extremist' views. Concern has grown progressively around the use of information technology and digital communications, although other more traditional media also remain a serious concern. Other observable indicators of 'radicalisation' are suggested, such as the justification of violent action as a means of solving social and political issues, visible alterations in dress or appearance and unwillingness to engage with people viewed as different. The use of symbols associated with terrorist organisations has also identified as a specific indicator of 'radicalisation.' Definition in this way has been noted to present significant problems, not least of which is that it is over-inclusive (Jarvis, 2019).

A widened range of threats

Later iterations of Contest have also broadened the focus here, from radicalisation linked to religious ideas and ideologies to other previously neglected or discounted forms of ideology. Most obvious has been the increased emphasis on right-wing ideologies. Here, the focus appears to be on ultra-nationalist anti-democratic views. This has grown quickly as an area of concern, with ERWT accounting for 22% of attacks since 2018, 'around a quarter' of the caseload of the UK's internal security service and 28% of those detained in prison custody (HM Government, 2023a). Contest can be seen to have been adapted to better recognise such threats and transnational influences associated with them. The area of Left Wing, Anarchist and Single-Issue Terrorism (LASIT) is addressed in the current version of Contest but is not viewed as a major or emerging threat.

As well as broadening the range of threats, Contest has introduced greater flexibility of response, although how successful this has been in practice remains unclear (Baker-Beall, Miles, Leach et al., 2024). As noted above, policy here can be seen as something of a break from historic practice. A 'softer' approach might be seen as UK governments response to previous policy failures, where already difficult situations were inflamed, precipitating and escalating the use of violence. In Northern Ireland for example, the actions of UK governments often appeared largely counter-productive, impairing counter-terrorism work and recruiting support to NIRT groups (Pantazis and Pemberton, 2009).

Contest also appears to have been adapted in efforts to better anticipate developing threats. Recent revisions have increasingly recognised an increasingly challenging national and international security environment. This has involved an increasingly complex mix of state, state-sponsored and non-state threats, along with a greater variety of organisational structures and the growth of 'leaderless' approaches in politically motivated violence (Kaplan, 1997; Sageman, 2011; Michael, 2012). This would include trans-national influences on lone-actors, money laundering or the use of criminal groups. Early versions of Contest were seen as being notably inadequate in this respect, focussing on the domestic context and threats from a small number of Islamist groups. Stress on specific groups, added to this narrow view, even as responses to these groups meant they were being increasingly replaced by other new and emerging groupings (Herrington, 2015).

Prevent

The stated aims of Contest are to reduce the level of threat to the UK, whilst simultaneously avoiding damaging legal and democratic rights. It is evidently the case that in a democracy, as opposed to an authoritarian state, the way such threats can be reduced or managed are more limited. As a result, higher levels of uncertainty may need to be lived with, because actions by the state need to be legal and to be judged in proportion to the threats. This is clearly a difficult balance to achieve requiring a degree of flexibility and judgement in practice.

The currently stated aim of Prevent aspect of Contest is to stop people from becoming involved in politically motivated violence and terrorism in the first place and where they have getting them to disengage and desist from involvement. A number of objectives are set out as flowing from this. These are given as: tackling the ideological causes of terrorism; intervening early to support people susceptible to radicalisation and enabling people who have already engaged in terrorism to disengage and rehabilitate (HM Government, 2023a). In turn, Prevent seems to rest on two key assumptions. First that extreme beliefs and ideology are major drivers and second, that it is possible to effectively intervene using psycho-social methods, to change beliefs and ideology in ways that will lead to disengagement and desistance.

At a practice level, this has involved encouraging and compelling public bodies to raise concerns about individuals and organisations, with a broad emphasis on interventions thought likely to reduce the associated risks. Many changes have been made to Prevent over time, and the version currently in force has evolved markedly across its major iterations. As noted, this has included efforts to respond to some of the criticism raised around language and presentation. More substantively, efforts have been made to try and achieve more consistent use of thresholds across the UK and more proportionate application, although there is a lack of adequate data to evaluate of how effective this has been. Other substantive concerns though appear to have been less effectively addressed. These have included concerns over the dominant terminology of 'extremism' and 'radicalisation' discussed above. The invention and reliance on this seem to suggest a rather better understanding of the processes involved in engagement, progression, disengagement and desistance than actually exists. Prevent has also largely failed to address criticisms that it has rendered some communities as suspicious, whilst simultaneously needing to engage with them. This initially applied to the Muslim community in the UK. With the increasing focus on ERWT, this can also be seen as increasingly true of some working-class communities, being portrayed as reactionary, racist and xenophobic. Such framing of communities and individuals within them as both 'vulnerable' to 'radicalisation' and 'extremism' and therefore also dangerous has been criticised as lacking coherence and damaging the effectiveness of efforts to respond (Heath-Kelly, 2013).

The processes currently involved in Prevent impose statutory obligations across a range of public and private sector bodies including a 'Prevent duty' which was introduced in 2015. This required mandatory reporting of significant concerns about individuals from many agencies and practitioners: in addition to the duty to report terrorist acts already captured in pre-existing anti-terrorism legislation. Within Prevent, this is framed in terms of a need to support prevention, disengagement and 'rehabilitative' work. Delivery of this is described as involving a 'multi-level' approach. This is founded on broad efforts to tackle ideological drivers. Where this has not worked the next level involves early intervention work, with the next level focussed on efforts to actively 'rehabilitate' those who have already become engaged with terrorist activity.

Pursue

Pursue aims to stop terrorist attacks happening in the UK or against its overseas interests. Objectives here are listed as being to: detect and understand terrorist activity, investigate terrorist activity and disrupt terrorist activity (HM Government, 2023a). The concern with detection and disruption can be seen as more closely akin to the methods used in Northern Ireland in the past. As such, this reflects a very different philosophy to that seen in the Prevent strand of policy. Changes over time have occurred in this area as well and these have included major changes to central organisational arrangements. These changes perhaps give clues to past failings that have often remained hidden from public view. In the forefront of these, current policy can be seen to place great stress on realising the potential of a recently established Counter Terrorism Operations Centre (CTOC). CTOC was designed to integrate practice across different agencies. Potential gains from this process are seen as central to delivering more effective working across areas such as data gathering, data analysis and the delivery of specialist technical capabilities. This closely links to work aimed at better understanding 'threat indicators,' with increased focus on better data gathering in terms of areas such as profiling, risk assessment and risk management.

Some of the other changes here appear to have been rather more generic in nature or to be mentioned in passing. They can nevertheless be seen as reflecting wider failings in UK state. This includes the intention to reduce what has been called 'silo' working, which can be summarised as the tendency for different departments and agencies of the UK state to focus on their own interests or targets, rather than achieving aims and objectives that involve working with others in strategic partnerships. This has been an enduring problem linked to the organisational structure of many state institutions. In many respects though, this has been made more severe and more acute as a result of applying New Public Management (NPM) models of state administration. This increases the likelihood of creating multiple points of failure. It also acts in opposition to notions of overall 'public good' or state interests and the foundations of shared identity that may act to defuse competing interests (Kelman, 2006). The intention to end, or at least significantly reduce this tendency, appears as a recurrent and failed aspiration of successive UK governments, not limited to the area of politically motivated violence. One way of addressing this might be for Permanent Secretaries, as the administrative heads of government departments, to be primarily rewarded for their effectiveness in cross-departmental and partnership working, rather than simply the delivery of the goals of individual departments. Making such delivery secondary to broader goals, which it surely must be relative to the needs of the whole of the machinery of the state, remains aspirational though.

Protect

The aim of Protect is to strengthen various barriers and checks against attacks. The objectives here are currently listed as being to: reduce the physical risk to people as they go about their lives; reduce the vulnerability of public venues, transport, and Critical National Infrastructure; reduce the ability of terrorists to access and use materials and technology of concern; and identify and manage individuals and goods of terrorist concern through the migration and border system (HM Government, 2023a).

As such, this area can be seen to be largely focussed on risk management in general and perhaps risk assessment and resilience in particular. To work effectively, efforts here obviously require governmental and non-governmental actors to work effectively together. Many of the areas that present the most critical risks will be in the private sector, or will be part public and part private. For example, the infrastructure supporting clean water and sewage disposal was moved to the private sector, as a matter of ideological commitment to the ability of the private sector to inevitably deliver more efficient and effective public services. Involvement of such a broad range of agencies though generates considerable challenges in the face of changing and adapting threats, with an additional need for continuous improvement and updating of responses.

Work in this area suggests a somewhat mixed picture in practice, with reality often being very different from the policy described in Contest. For example, a review of preparedness was undertaken looking at London. This suggested vulnerabilities to attack and a need for significant improvements in the face of increased referrals to Prevent for ERWT increases in individuals 'self-radicalising' and learning techniques online and a greater likelihood of hostile state-sponsored acts (Harris, 2016). Whilst the recommendations identified for improvement were quickly implemented, they also suggested multiple areas of serious historic neglect, ranging across all parts of the state. This vulnerability is all the more remarkable, given the economic and political importance of London to the UK state.

Prepare

The aim of Prepare is given as being to minimise the impact of an attack and reduce the likelihood of further attacks. The objectives are set out as being to: build proportionate responses to a range of attack methodologies, wherever they might occur; in response to an attack, deploy a systemised, effective and co-ordinated multiagency response, using specialist and non-specialist capabilities, to save lives, mitigate harm, and prevent further attacks and to enable recovery, including the long-term care of victims and survivors; the mitigation of any ongoing hazard; adapt and improve by identifying and sharing learning from research, training, testing, exercising and previous incidents (HM Government, 2023a).

There appears to be a significant overlap here with the Protect aspect of Contest, with a clear stress on aspects of risk management, although perhaps with a greater emphasis on risk robustness and organisational learning. As with the other pillars of Contest outlined above, several areas of evolution and development can be seen here. These have included the recognition of a need for more and much better research in the area, with the need for this to be focussed on applied questions that can directly inform and improve practice. Much of the work in this area seems to have failed in this respect. Needs for the improvement of preparation and training have also seen greater emphasis. The need for this to involve realistic testing and meaningful structured exercises, drawing on previous incidents, has been increasingly recognised. A suicidal bomb attack on a large public arena in the city of Manchester in May 2017 is illustrative of some of the problems seen here. The responses to this attack at the Manchester Arena were seen as both inconsistent and poorly coordinated across different emergency services and other agencies (Pettinger, 2023). Possibly linked to this, the current version of Contest stresses the importance of the Joint Emergency Services Interoperability Principles (JESIP). These cover the need for emergency services to maintain core skills and organisational arrangements in working effectively together (JESIP, 2023).

Criticisms of UK policy

UK responses to the threat of politically motivated forms of violence have been criticised for their impacts on fundamental legal and political rights. This has included concerns over provisions that have impaired the normal operation of the legal system, undermining its independence. The wider negative effects of this on communities, social cohesion and the nature of the state have been noted as important negative effects. Legislation here has also raised significant concerns around the taking and keeping of draconian powers by governments (Honeywood, 2016). These have often drawn on historic aspects of the UK constitution, stemming from a time of rule by monarchy and giving recourse to largely unchecked powers. Such legal provision has typically been framed as a temporary response to an emergency situation, only to go on to become permanent, ratcheting up the power of government and the scope for abuses. Concerns around this kind of conversion of temporary powers into permanent ones continue to be a serious cause for concern. This has often been exacerbated by a lack of transparency, candour and accountability from relevant organisations. Concerns have been raised, particularly in relation to early versions of Contest, around failures to distinguish between legitimate differences of view and illegitimate views advocating political violence. Here, use of very broad and vague definitions meant that expressing unpopular views, or engaging in non-violent protests, could be captured under draconian legislative provisions.

Criticisms of Contest have also included concerns that stem generally from human rights perspectives. These include anxieties around current policy representing dramatic extension of areas such as state surveillance, as well as the capacity for spying on the population in general and some communities in particular (Kaleem, 2022). This is greatly exacerbated by the growth of information technology and the extent to which routine and essential activities are increasingly conducted through digital media. Application of 'data mining' techniques to information of this kind carries with it serious risks, including adverse impacts on rights to privacy and a family life. Criticisms of this kind have been strongly rejected by others, who have argued there is a lack of empirical or other evidence to support these claims (Jenkins, Perry and Stott, 2022).

Concerns have also been raised around discrimination against particular communities and groups, as well as racial discrimination. This has been a recurrent theme in the history of the UK and its nations, including legal discrimination based on Christian sectarianism. More currently, there have been concerns over systematic discrimination and the creation of a specific Irish 'suspect community' (Hillyard, 1993). This claim received limited attention at the time but in retrospect can be seen to have created significant antagonisms, as well as potentially being counterproductive. Contemporary criticisms of the Contest framework show some parallels here, with the approach taken being criticised for creating a new 'suspect community' of Muslims (Modood, 2003; Pantazis and Pemberton, 2009). Others have argued there is no convincing evidence for this, with the evidence in fact pointing in the opposite direction (Greer, 2010).

The idea of a 'suspect community' was not explicitly defined by Hillyard (1993), but Pantazis and Pemberton (2009) subsequently defined this as:

> a sub-group of the population that is singled out for state attention as being 'problematic.' Specifically in terms of policing, individuals may be targeted, not necessarily as a result of suspected wrong doing, but simply because of their presumed membership to (sic) that sub-group. Race, ethnicity, religion, class, gender, language, accent, dress, political ideology or any combination of these factors may serve to delineate the sub-group.
>
> (Pantazis and Pemberton, 2009: 649)

The creation of Contest as a public framework can be seen as an attempt to change practice here. It has though been criticised, especially in its earlier iterations, for the level of focus on some forms of terrorism and for encouraging discrimination on this basis. Here, the focus on Islamism has been challenged as disproportionate to the threats (Rehman, 2007). As a result, it has been suggested that policy was excessively reactive to events such as 9/11 and the attacks in London in 2007. For a long time, other serious and emerging threats were neglected in favour of this focus. Various community-based groups have also voiced these kinds of concerns about current UK policy. These have included organisations such as the Muslim Council of Britain (MCB), the Islamic Human Rights Commission (IHRC) the Federation of Islamic Student Societies (FOSIS) and the National Association of Muslim Police (NAMP). Some have argued that the approach taken has served to criminalise 'conservative' Muslim beliefs, whilst also creating suspicions based on simplistic notions of Islam and group membership (Sabir, 2014; Gould, 2020). There appears to have been recognition of these concerns in later versions of the Contest framework, where other threats have received more attention. Some critics though have argued that this has been too little too late, arguing that putting right failings in the recognition of other areas, such as the growth of ERWT threats, does little to redress the pre-existing inherent biases (Gregory, 2009).

The revisions made to Contest have been criticised for building on a badly flawed model, rather than making an entirely fresh start. Contest has also been strongly criticised from other perspectives, which see it as lacking in focus. Here, concerns have been expressed that it has progressively backed away from a focus on Islamist terrorism and extremism, following critical reactions from others. Here, it has been argued that references to the size of the Muslim population in the UK are misleading when looking at questions of proportionality and levels of referral. In common with previous responses to NIRT, it is suggested that the proportion of threats that come from groups within specific communities is the relevant statistic and that other considerations should not determine the focus here (Jenkins, Perry and Stott, 2022). Having been created in the wake of the 9/11 attacks on the US and later attacks in the UK and Europe, it is argued that the focus on Islamist terrorism was both reasonable and proportionate, even if changes in focus may be required over time.

Other concerns with Contest have involved its apparent construction of recent events as a 'new terrorism' and this being 'unprecedented,' rather than it reflecting an extension and adaptation of existing historic trends. This naïve approach also involved a swift and seemingly uncritical adoption of the language of 'war' and the idea of a 'war on terror.' This idea appears to have come largely from a small number of academic settings and a few private think tanks in the US (Burnett and Whyte, 2005). The notion of 'new' terrorism carried with it the idea of a fundamental change, in terms of things such as motivation, methods and tactics, based in turn on religiously motivated 'extremism' and ethnic separatism. Assumptions that this form of terrorism was 'new' and qualitatively different in nature have been strongly criticised as being poorly founded and misleading (Kurtulus, 2011). Whilst some of the tactics used in the 9/11 attacks and subsequently did appear novel, there was certainly nothing new in religious motivations to engage in politically motivated violence and terrorism. Nor was there anything new in the use of suicidal attacks (Lewis, 2012). Later, iterations of UK policy have shown a somewhat belated recognition of this. Such oversights are even more surprising in a state like the UK, which has such a long history of contact with these kinds of political violence across its former Empire.

The critique that the focus on some Islamist threats led to a neglect of other areas also appears to carry some force. This has been evidenced by the growing recognition of a wider range of threats over time (Home Office, 2021). Suggestions that the focus on Islamist terrorism is currently associated with a neglect of other threats is contradicted by the changing emphasis in policy. The most obvious change in policy here, has been the growing recognition of ERWT and single-issue threats, including those which involve trans-national links (HM Government, 2011, 2023a). By 2021, the proportion of referrals for ERWT to specialist Prevent panels had increased to 57% (Home Office, 2021). Of 186 arrests, half of these were Islamist in nature and 41% ERWT.

The idea that counter-terrorism policy represents an attack on 'conservative' interpretations of Islam has also been pushed back on strongly, with it being stressed that 'conservative' views are not synonymous with 'extremism' (Jenkins, Perry and Stott, 2022). The distinction here being that there are clearly some beliefs and views which lie outside the bounds of acceptability in the UK, many of which are illegal. Such views it is argued should be defined as 'extremist.' A good example of this is perhaps the 'Trojan Horse' letter sent to the local authority for Birmingham and the events that surrounded this, which were later the subject of a detailed review (Clarke, 2014). In essence, this involved a small number of actors, who were reported to have a coordinated agenda to gain control and impose a particular strand of Salafism within state schools in parts of Birmingham, without regard to the rights and views of others. This included efforts to change the curriculum, limiting the teaching of some areas such as modern languages and Sex and Relationships Education (SRE) (Clarke, 2014). Another example put forward here has been views expressed around homosexuality and conflicting religious and other opinions. Here, it has be argued that opposition to same sex marriage can be legitimately questioned and opposed on 'conservative' religious grounds, noting that such views include a range of different faith groups, although the focus here often appears to have largely been on Muslims. Where critical views extend though to calls for homosexuality to be subject to violent punishments and even execution, then this can legitimately be described as 'extremist' (Jenkins, Perry and Stott, 2022).

Contest has also generated specific criticisms from within the education sector. These have included anxiety around the erosion of human rights and freedom of expression. Such concerns have not been limited to the role of Contest but the role of this in policing of academic debate, discussion and freedoms more generally has been one focus of concern here. Negative effects of Contest have been stressed in relation to contentious areas involving political and religious beliefs, with the 'Prevent duty' to report concerns being seen as a mechanism of control and restriction. This view has been supported by reference to some high-profile cases, where Student Unions and others in some higher education settings have expressed a lack of confidence in the policy and have urged non-cooperation. This in fact cuts across a range of UK legislation in this area, which imposes a duty to inform the police of concerns (Greer and Bell, 2018).

Critics have also suggested a lack of public trust as a significant problem in this area of policy in the UK, linked to excessive secrecy and lack of transparency. The first version of Contest is illustrative of this, initially being a classified document that the public could not see. Yet, a few years later in 2006 a public version was made available, with a version of the 2003 document also becoming available. This can be seen as a shift in approach, with a recognition that more detail and rationale for policy in this area can appropriately, and usefully, be made public. Concerns have continued to be aired though around a general a lack of transparency and public accountability, especially given the duration of policies often presented as short-term expedients.

The final criticism of Contest touched on here is focussed on bureaucracy. The response to the threats presented here has involved the establishment of an extensive and complex bureaucratic structure. This has imposed considerable administrative demands, primarily on local government structures in the UK. Oversight of this has been criticised as being overly bureaucratic. Here, concern has been strongly focussed, in line with NPM approaches, on measures and 'metrics.' Estimation of performance standards, compliance and centralised administrative control often seems to have taken priority at the expense of genuine political and legal oversight and accountability (Coaffee, 2023). To date, there appears to have been little serious effort to address these concerns or to tackle the bureaucracy involved.

Specific concerns around Prevent

The Prevent aspect of the UK government approach to terrorism has attracted and continues to attract particular attention and some of the most serious criticisms, this despite having undergone a great deal of amendment and change since its inception. It was significantly impacted by the Counter Terrorism and Security Act 2015, which introduced a statutory duty for specific authorities to report concerns about individuals, in order that they could be assessed under Prevent. This duty added to pre-existing legal requirements to inform the authorities of terrorist activity and seems to represent a significant widening of the net. As part of the 2018 version of Contest, a role in the 'rehabilitation' of convicted terrorists was also added to the scope of the policy.

Perhaps the most serious and general criticism made of Prevent is that it has increased the drift away from the core function of Contest in addressing politically motivated violence and as a counter-terrorism framework. In its later iterations, critics have observed a shift away from focussing on a core of serious threats (Jenkins, Perry and Stott, 2022). It has also been suggested that the increasing stress within Prevent on individual 'vulnerability,' rather than beliefs and ideologies may be harmful, drawing in large numbers of referrals more in need of mental health and social care support. The operation and cost-effectiveness of the idea of working further 'upstream' to steer individuals away from political violence and 'radicalisation' has been strongly criticised, as indeed has been the growth of emphasis on ERWT threats.

As already observed, effective working across different agencies and levels of the state in the UK has been a recurrent problem and one that has been notably resistant to change. Prevent has certainly not been immune to this criticism, suffering from recurring problems with communication and inter-agency working. Similarly, the ambition set out in Prevent to improve 'upstream' prevention work, with problems being addressed as early as possible, has been a common ambition across government administration. So too has been the need for better and deeper international collaboration and the need for more effective working across private industry and service sectors. Whilst these may seem entirely reasonable ambitions, they also appear to run against the grain of some other areas of UK policy, such as the recurring focus on within department numerical performance indicators or 'metrics' and target setting. These inevitably become the focus and things that are difficult to quantify, such as effective collaborative working and public engagement, have increasingly been neglected.

Of marked relevance to forensic practice, Prevent has also been subject to significant criticisms in relation to its intervention and 'treatment' work. Work with and management of those convicted of terrorism related offences provides a stark illustration of this, with a review of this in prisons, probation and youth justice undertaken in 2015–2016 (Acheson, 2016). Much of the review remains classified but a guarded summary of findings has been published by the UK government. This makes clear a pressing need for very much better training in this area, along with needs for better research, development and delivery of work in this area. The management of those released from prison custody was identified as an area of particular weakness, with poor inter-agency working, especially marked in joint working across counter-terrorism police, prisons and probation and security services. The concerns identified in this review went on to prove well founded, with later events showing serious management failings across prisons and under community supervision. The most vivid example of this are perhaps the events which culminated in the deaths of two young volunteers, attending an event at Fishmongers Hall in London in 2019 (Basu, 2021; Nash and Williams, 2024). Here, assessment and 'rehabilitative' work undertaken in custody and the community by the Prison and Probation Service seemed at best remarkably naïve. More broadly prison, probation and youth justice services seem to have been remarkably poor at recognising and responding to the nature of the challenge posed (Acheson and Paul, 2021).

Part of the efforts to move work 'upstream' mean Prevent has increasingly adopted a 'dragnet' approach to collecting referrals, which can in fact be made by anyone or any organisation. Within Prevent, it is stressed that referrals should be made where any concerns arise, as identifying risk where none exists is greatly preferred to missing genuine cases of radicalisation (HM Government, 2023a). Once made, referrals enter a complicated administrative process involving initial checks, conducted by the local Police Service. This should include checking for any immediate security threats and 'risk of radicalisation.' Where neither are felt to apply then no further action is taken. Where an immediate risk is identified, then this would be addressed through interventions, potentially including referral to counterterrorism policing, to assess and respond to any acute threats in a proportionate way. Where no immediate security risk appears to be present but a risk of 'radicalisation' is identified, then a referral should be made to a multi-agency panel, led by the local government authority. This may in turn lead to offers of support and intervention, with these made on a voluntary basis. This approach though is open to a variety of criticisms. By design, it leads to many individuals being drawn into the scope of the policy without reason and it is far from clear that the over-inclusive approach is the correct one. This clearly serves a function in terms of serving some professional interests, as well as expanding bureaucratic reach and funding. In doing this though, it also creates and amplifies the real risk of missing some of those of most concern, simply as a function of processing growing numbers of 'false-positive' cases.

The nature of interventions within Prevent has also raised serious concerns. For those not felt to reach the threshold for Prevent, this typically involves efforts to refer individuals to mainstream services, such as adult mental health or social care services. The reality of this is often adding to the weight of referrals facing already stretched services that are either inappropriate, or that are ill equipped, to deal with the kinds of problems involved. For those reaching the threshold, the main forms of what are called specialist interventions can be divided between those led by prisons and probation and those led from the Home Office. Examples of the former include the 'Motivational and Engagement Intervention' (MEI) and the 'Healthy Identities Intervention' (HII). The later involves the 'Desistance and Disengagement Programme' (DDP). All of these are generally described as 'bespoke' interventions and are claimed to be based on established approaches to rehabilitation, grounded in sound theories.

The MEI and HII interventions appear to have been developed as complimentary 'programmes' for use in prisons and probation settings. The MEI is described as having the aims of developing and strengthening motivation of participants, as well as dispelling myths and reducing 'fears' around undertaking more intensive intervention work in the form of the HII. This includes efforts to address 'extremist offenders' distrust of authority (Dean, Lloyd, Keane et al., 2018). As such, the MEI can be seen as a common form of psycho-social intervention, designed to increase motivation to engage in 'treatment.' The HII is described as building on the motivation achieved and as not being ideologically focused or intended to 're-educate' beliefs or doctrine. Rather, it is described as having the aims of encouraging some reassessment of beliefs and values that are judged to underpin terrorism, as well as supporting 're-examination' of commitments to extremist groups or causes (HM Prison and Probation Service, 2018). There is little public detail on the Desistance and Disengagement Programme (DDP) led from the Home Office, but it is described as part of efforts at risk reduction, linking to public protection arrangements, for those involved in terrorism or related activities. This is intended to reduce risk, through rehabilitative efforts aimed at desistance, disengagement and ultimately reintegration in the community. Unlike most other Prevent interventions, this includes efforts to address theological and ideological areas and participation is a compulsory aspect of community supervision (Elshimi, 2020; HM Inspectorate of Probation, 2024; Home Office, 2024).

The basis of the psycho-social interventions has been questioned. A major criticism raised here is the apparently uncritical adoption and application of psycho-social interventions to the area of politically motivated violence. The MEI and HII seem to have been taken from what has been described as the 'programmes industry,' which has grown in prisons and probation since the 1980s (Towl and Podmore, 2019). This has also included the adoption of 'risk–needs–responsivity' (RNR) principles and the 'better lives' model from work with criminal offenders. In combination, these are claimed to provide the strong theoretical basis for these types of intervention alluded to above. In reality though, both RNR and 'better lives' are nowhere near as compelling as suggested. Interventions of this kind appear to be lightly modified and repackaged forms of psycho-social treatments, based on cognitive–behavioural theory (CBT). These have been transferred over from the clinical settings where they were developed. This has happened, even though the results of CBT interventions in addressing better understood areas such as anxiety or depression, had for many years been raising increasing and serious concerns (Beidel and Turner, 1986). This repackaged CBT was first applied in relation to what were felt to be better understood forms of criminality, going on to include interventions for those convicted of sexual and non-sexual violent crimes. Although the extent of understanding of these areas was and remains the subject of debate, strong early claims around effectiveness were made with further extension to areas such as family and intimate partner violence. There has in fact always been limited evidence that these 'programmes' were having the positive effects claimed for them (Crighton and Towl, 2007; Dennis, Khan, Ferriter et al., 2012; Towl and Crighton, 2016; Towl, 2021).

Despite such concerns, the same approach seems to have been extended directly to politically motivated violence. There are good reasons to be anxious about this based on findings from other areas. Not least of these is that CBT approaches are fundamentally based on a collaborative process. The method is therefore not suited to those who are either unable or unwilling to work in this manner. It seems totally unsuited to those motivated to present a false or misleading picture of improvement in the direction therapists are aiming for, having been developed for settings where such considerations are largely irrelevant. As a result, the extension and repackaging of this to forensic settings already raises significant concerns. These are amplified when trying to apply this to those convicted for offences involving politically motivated violence and terrorism, where there is little evidence on the effects.

This lack of evidence means that current practice in this area rests on the wider evidence base. Perhaps the closest analogue here, where there is good evidence on effects, are those convicted of sexual offences. As a group, these offenders tend to be distinct from other offenders. They may also be motivated to engage in misdirection and the demonstration of false engagement, compliance and desistance.

Some will have a high level of skill in doing so. There are adequate evaluations of the effects of using these kinds of 'programmes' with this broad group, and here, the results have been concerning. These findings are not new, with initial expression of concerns that work of this kind was not showing any significant positive effects in terms of desistance or reconvictions (Crighton and Towl, 2007; Dennis, Khan, Ferriter et al., 2012). This led to concerns around unnecessary costs and waste and in economic terms the effect of reducing the productivity of the staff involved. More recent evidence suggests these interventions when undertaken in prisons and secure hospitals are in fact actively harmful, serving to significantly increase reconviction. Worryingly, this effect seems to be significantly worse as the extent and intensity of the 'programmes' increased (Marques, Wiederanders, Day et al., 2005; Towl and Crighton, 2016; Mews, DiBella and Purver, 2017).

The widescale adoption and expansion of the areas covered by these kinds of CBT 'programmes' has also been strongly criticised for its linkage to strong professional self-interests (Towl, 2021). Growth in this area of practice seems intrinsically linked to this and persuasive arguments have been made that there needs to be far greater transparency around this, along with the nature of and findings from evaluation work (Towl and Podmore, 2019). This seems critical in application of this approach to politically motivated forms of violence and terrorism. The idea that such 'programmes' are helpful or indeed essential appears to be based on faith and professional interest and not credible evidence.

Summary and conclusions

The UK has been chosen here as providing a useful case study of responses to politically motivated forms of violence. As a result of its history, the UK and its constituent parts have a lengthy history of facing and responding to threats of this kind. From 1969 to the 1980s, this primarily involved responding to threats arising from Northern Ireland Related Terrorism (NIRT). From the 1980s, this was added to be emergent and growing threats coming from groups motivated by 'Islamist' ideologies, working across national borders and often linked to states and hybrid forms of warfare. More recently, there has been a growth in Extreme Right-Wing Terrorism (ERWT). Some of this also appears to involve trans-national links to states, non-state groups and hybrid warfare.

Current UK policy and practice in this area is captured with a framework called Contest, which is built around four themes: Prevent, Pursue, Protect and Prepare. This approach differs from that taken towards NIRT and has been characterised as 'softer' approach with a greater emphasis on tackling 'upstream' threats and winning community support. In line with this, the Prevent strand of policy has increasingly emphasised efforts to tackle constructs of 'extremism' and 'radicalisation,' which are seen as causal.

Contest has been controversial from its inception in 2003 and has been extensively criticised from a range of very different and often opposing viewpoints. It has been subject to ongoing changes and several major revisions. Some of this change appears to have been in an effort to respond to criticism, but others have come from a recognition of a broadening range of threats. Over time, Contest has become more transparent and flexible in its responses. Organisational changes have also been implemented which perhaps give clues to past failings. This has included an emphasis on reducing 'silo' working, which appears as a recurrent ambition across the UK state. Practice changes to deliver this include a stress on more effective data gathering, analysis and research, as well as better integration of practice across different state bodies and private sector organisations.

The Prevent aspect of Contest represents the adoption of a more 'public health' approach into this area of practice, and as such, it has perhaps come in for particular criticism. Serious concerns have been raised about the appropriateness of taking a population-based screening or 'dragnet' approach. Concerns here have included the effects of and costs of this, given the already highly bureaucratic structure put in place. There has also been around the overloading of those trying to manage risk, in the absence of effective means to screen and assess referrals. The leadership of this area at local government level has also been criticised. Here, responsibility has been transferred to already hard-pressed bodies, whilst specialist expertise and resources have not.

A central plank of Prevent has been the use of psychological assessments of risk and the use of psycho-social interventions to increase disengagement and desistance from politically motivated forms of violence. This has involved the apparently uncritical use and application of approaches used to address varied forms of criminality to politically motivated violence. This has involved adopting what appear to be lightly modified and repackaged checklist-based assessments and 'programmes' of psycho-social treatment. The evidence in support of these in forensic practice has been unconvincing, with evidence of serious adverse effects reported. Given the lack of credible evidence in support, the adoption of the same approach to politically motivated violence and terrorism seems at best inappropriate and ethically questionable.

References

Acheson, I. (2016). Summary of the main findings of the review of Islamist extremism in prisons, probation and youth justice Published 22 August 2016. www.gov.uk/government/publications/islamist-extremism-in-prisons-probation-and-youth-justice/summary-of-the-main-findings-of-the-review-of-islamist-extremism-in-prisons-probation-and-youth-justice. Retrieved February 9, 2025.

Acheson, I. and Paul, A. (2021). *Hiding in Plain Sight? Disguised Compliance by Terrorist Offenders*. Brussels: European Policy Centre.

Allen, C. (2020). That which must not be named: Islamophobia and new labour. In C. Allen (Ed.), *Reconfiguring Islamophobia*. London: Palgrave Pivot Cham.

Antúnez, J. C. and Tellidis, I. (2016). The power of words: the deficient terminology surrounding Islam-related terrorism. In I. Tellidis and Toros, H. (Eds.), *Terrorism: Bridging the Gap with Peace and Conflict Studies*. London: Routledge.

Backes, U. (2010). Political extremes. In R. Eatwell and Goodwin, M. J. (Eds.), *The New Extremism in 21st Century Britain*. London: Routledge.

Baker-Beall, C., Miles, L., Leach, N., and Reed, E. (2024). From prevent to protect and prepare: the Manchester arena attack and shifting priorities in the United Kingdom's counter-terrorism strategy (CONTEST). *Studies in Conflict and Terrorism*. https://doi.org/10.1080/1057610X.2024.2327664

Basu, N. (2021). Learning lessons from countering terrorism: the UK experience 2017–2020. *Cambridge Journal of Evidence-Based Policing*, *5*, 134–145.

Beidel, D. C. and Turner, S. M. (1986). A critique of the theoretical bases of cognitive behavioral theories and therapy. *Clinical Psychology Review*, *6*(2), 177–197.

Brooks, S. K. and Greenberg, N. (2021). *Mental Health, Complex Needs and Vulnerability to Radicalisation*. London: Department of Health and Social Care.

Burnett, J. and Whyte, D. (2005). Embedded expertise and the new terrorism. *Journal for Crime, Conflict and the Media*, *1*, 1–18.

Carr, J. and Scott, J. M. (2024). *Targeted: Beirut: The 1983 Marine Barracks Bombing and the Untold Origin Story of the War on Terror*. New York: Simon and Schuster.

Childs, J. (2014). *God's Traitors: Terror and Faith in Elizabethan England*. Oxford: Oxford University Press.

Clarke, P. (2014). *Report into Allegations Concerning Birmingham Schools Arising From the 'Trojan Horse' Letter. HC576*. London: OGL.

Coaffee, J. (2023). Discipline, morality and the façade of localism in action: the war on terror and the regulation of UK community resilience. *International Journal of Law, Crime and Justice*. https://doi.org/10.1016/j.ijlcj.2019.100372

Copeland, S. and Marsden, S. (2020). *Right-Wing Terrorism: Pathways and Protective Factors*. Lancaster: Centre for Research and Evidence on Security Threats (CREST).

Cox, M., Guelke, A., and Stephen, F. (Eds.) (2006). *A Farewell to Arms? Beyond the Good Friday Agreement*. Manchester: Manchester University Press.

Crighton, D. and Towl, G. (2007). Experimental interventions with sex offenders: a brief review of their efficacy. *Evidence Based Mental Health*, *10*(2), 35–37.

Dean, C., Lloyd, M., Keane, C., Powis, B., and Randhawa, K. (2018). *Intervening with Extremist Offenders – A Pilot Study*. London: HM Prison and Probation Service.

Dennis, J. A., Khan, O., Ferriter, M., Huband, N., Powney, M. J., and Duggan, C. (2012). Psychological interventions for adults who have sexually offended or are at risk of offending. *Cochrane Database of Systematic Reviews*, *2012*(12), Art. No.: CD007507. https://doi.org/10.1002/14651858.CD007507.pub2

Dickson, B. (1989). The prevention of terrorism (temporary provisions) act 1989. *Northern Ireland Legal Quarterly*, *40*, 250–252.

Dodd, V. and Syal, R. (2023). *Former Counter-Terror Chief Hits out at 'Insulting' Findings or Prevent Review*. The Guardian (8 February).

Elshimi, M. S. (2020). Desistance and disengagement programme in the UK Prevent strategy: a public health analysis. In S. J. Hansen and Lid, S. (Eds.), *Routledge Handbook of Deradicalisation and Disengagement*. London: Routledge.

Evans, E. (2014). *The Shaping of Modern Britain: Identity, Industry and Empire 1780-1914*. London: Routledge.

Fenton, S. (2018). *The Good Friday Agreement*. London: Biteback Publishing.

Fenwick, H. (2002). The anti-terrorism, crime and security act 2001: a proportionate response to 11 September? *The Modern Law Review*, *65*(5), 724–762.

Garrett, R. K. (2009). Echo chambers online? Politically motivated selective exposure among Internet news users. *Journal of Computer-Mediated Communication*, *14*(2), 265–285.

Gould, R. R. (2020). The limits of liberal inclusivity: how defining Islamophobia normalizes anti-Muslim racism. *Journal of Law and Religion*, *35*(2), 250–269.

Greer, S. (2010). Anti-terrorist laws and the United Kingdom's 'suspect Muslim community': a reply to Pantazis and Pemberton. *The British Journal of Criminology*, *50*(6), 1171–1190.

Greer, S. and Bell, L. C. (2018). Counter-terrorist law in British universities: a review of the" Prevent" debate. *Public Law*, January, 84–104. www.bristol.ac.uk/media-library/sites/law/GreerBell%20PREVENT%20final%20article.pdf

Gregory, F. (2009). *CONTEST (2009): An Evaluation of Revisions to the UK Counter-Terrorism Strategy with a Special Focus on the CBRNE Threat (ARI)*. Madrid: Real Institute Elcano.

Haddon, C. (2020). *COBR (COBRA)*. London: Institute for Government. Available online www.instituteforgovernment.org.uk/explainer/cobr-cobra. Accessed October 10, 2024.

Harris, T. (2016). *An Independent Review of London's Preparedness to Respond to a Major Terrorist Incident*. London: Mayor of London.

Heath-Kelly, C. (2013). Counter-terrorism and the counterfactual: producing the 'radicalisation' discourse and the UK PREVENT strategy. *The British Journal of Politics and International Relations*, *15*(3), 394–415.

Herrington, L. (2015). British Islamic extremist terrorism: the declining significance of Al–Qaeda and Pakistan. *International Affairs*, *91*(1), 17–35.

HM Government. (2006). *Countering International Terrorism: The United Kingdom's Strategy Cm 6888*. London: HMSO.

HM Government. (2011). *Prevent Strategy*. London: The Stationery Office.

HM Government. (2023a). *CONTEST The United Kingdom's Strategy for Countering Terrorism 2023. CP 903*. London: OGL.

HM Government. (2023b). *Integrated Review Refresh 2023: Responding to a More Contested and Volatile World*. London: OGL.

HM Government. (2023c). New definition of extremism 2023. www.gov.uk/government/publications/new-definition-of-extremism-2024/new-definition-of-extremism-2024. Retrieved February 9, 2025.

HM Inspectorate of Probation. (2024). Extremism and terrorism. Available online www.justiceinspectorates.gov.uk/hmiprobation/research/the-evidence-base-probation/specific-sub-groups/extremism-and-terrorism/. RetrievedFebruary 9, 2025.

HM Prison and Probation Service. (2018). *The Healthy Identity Intervention (HII) Theory Manual*. London: HM Prison and Probation Service.

Hillyard, P. (1993). *Suspect Community: People's Experience of the Prevention of Terrorism Acts in Britain*. London: Pluto Press/Liberty.

Hodkinson, A. (2020). Fundamental British values: radicalizing British children into a manufactured them and us narrative concept of Britishness? *International Review of Qualitative Research*, *13*(1), 23–40.

Hoffman, B. (2014). The 7 July 2005 London Bombings. In B. Hoffman and Reinares, F. (Eds.), *The Evolution of the Global Terrorist Threat: From 9/11 to Osama bin Laden's Death*. New York: Columbia University Press.

Holmwood, J. and Aitlhadj, L. (2022). *The People's Review of Prevent: Full Report*. Manchester: Prevent Watch.

Home Office. (2021). *Individuals Referred to and Supported Through the Prevent Programme, England and Wales, April 2020 to March 2021*. London: OGL.

Home Office. (2024). *Factsheet: Desistance and Disengagement Programme*. London: Home Office. https://homeofficemedia.blog.gov.uk/2019/11/05/fact-sheet-desistance-and-disengagement-programme/. Accessed January 27, 2025.

Honeywood, C. A. (2016). Britain's approach to balancing counter-terrorism laws with human rights. *Journal of Strategic Security, 9*(3), 28–48.

Howells, K. (2009). *Could 7/7 Have Been Prevented? Review of the Intelligence on the London Terrorist Attacks on 7 July 2005*. London: OGL.

Jarvis, L. (2019). Terrorism, counter-terrorism, and critique: opportunities, examples, and implications. *Critical Studies on Terrorism, 12*(2), 339–358.

Jenkins, B. M. (1997). *Protecting Surface Transportation Systems and Patrons from Terrorist Activities: Case Studies of Best Security Practices and a Chronology of Attacks [1997] (No. CA/R-96/26)*. San Jose: Norman Y. Mineta International Institute for Surface Transportation Policy Studies.

Jenkins, J., Perry, D., and Stott, P. (2022). *Delegitimising Counter-Terrorism*. London: Policy Exchange.

JESIP. (2023). *Joint Doctrine: The Interoperability Framework*. Welwyn Garden City: Author.

Kaleem, A. (2022). Citizen-led intelligence gathering under UK's prevent duty. In H. Ben Jaffel and Larsson, S. (Eds.), *Problematising Intelligence Studies: Towards A New Research Agenda (1st ed)*. London: Routledge.

Kaplan, J. (1997). Leaderless resistance. *Terrorism and Political Violence, 9*(3), 80–95.

Kelly, C. (2013). Counter-terrorism and the counterfactual: producing the 'radicalisation' discourse and the UK PREVENT strategy. *The British Journal of Politics and International Relations, 15*(3), 394–415.

Kelman, H. C. (2006). Interests, relationships, identities: three central issues for individuals and groups in negotiating their social environment. *Annual Review of Psychology, 57*(1), 1–26.

Kohler, N. and Findlay, S. (2011). Bin Laden's ruinous legacy: how a series of terror attacks totally changed the Western way of life. *Maclean's, 124*(18), 161–167.

Kurtulus, E. N. (2011). The "new terrorism" and its critics. *Studies in Conflict & Terrorism, 34*(6), 476–500.

Lelourec, L. (2016). Responding to the IRA bombing campaign in mainland Britain: The case of Warrington. In G. Dawson, Dover, J., and Hopkins, S. (Eds.), *The Northern Ireland Troubles in Britain: Impacts, Engagements, Legacies and Memories*. Manchester: Manchester University Press.

Lewis, J. W. (2012). *The Business of Martyrdom: A History of Suicide Bombing*. Annapolis: Naval Institute Press.

Macdonald, S., Whiting, A., and Jarvis, L. (2024). Evidence and ideology in the independent review of Prevent. *Journal for Deradicalization,, 39*, 40–76.

Marques, J. K., Wiederanders, M., Day, D. M., Nelson, C., and Van Ommeren, A. (2005). Effects of a relapse prevention program on sexual recidivism: final results from California's Sex Offender Treatment and Evaluation Project (SOTEP). *Sexual Abuse: A Journal of Research and Treatment,, 17*, 79–107.

McCleery, M. J. (2015). *Operation Demetrius and Its Aftermath: A New History of the Use of Internment Without Trial in Northern Ireland, 1971–75*. Manchester, UK: Manchester University Press.

McGlinchey, M. (2021). The unfinished revolution of 'dissident' Irish republicans: divergent views in a fragmented base. *Small Wars & Insurgencies, 32*(4–5), 714–746.

Mews, A., Di Bella, L., and Purver, M. (2017). *Impact Evaluation of the Prison-Based Core Sex Offender Treatment Programme*. London: Ministry of Justice.

Michael, G. (2012). Leaderless resistance: the new face of terrorism. *Defence Studies, 12*(2), 257–282.

Modood, T. (2003). Muslims and the politics of difference. *Political Quarterly, 74*, 100–115.

Mozaffari, M. (2007). What is Islamism? History and definition of a concept. *Totalitarian Movements and Political Religions, 8*(1), 17–33.

Murphy, S. D. (2002). Terrorist attacks on world trade center and pentagon. *American Journal of International Law, 96*(1), 237–254.

Nash, M. and Williams, A. (2024). *Politics and Public Protection.* Leeds: Emerald Publishing Limited.

National Association of Muslim Police. (2019). Written evidence submission from NAMP (HCL0062), UK Parliament, October 2019. Available at: https://committees.parliament.uk/writtenevidence/105884/pdf/. Retrieved February 9, 2025.

National Commission on Terrorist Attacks. (2011). *The 9/11 Commission Report: Final Report of the National Commission on Terrorist Attacks Upon the United States (Authorized Edition).* New York: WW Norton & Company.

Nesser, P. (2018). *Islamist Terrorism in Europe.* Oxford: Oxford University Press.

Olson, B. S. (2008). Withdrawal from Empire: Britain's Decolonization of Egypt, Aden, and Kenya in the Mid-Twentieth Century. Unpublished MA dissertation, School of Advanced Military Studies, United States Army Command and General Staff College Fort Leavenworth, Kansas.

Ovendale, R. (1980). The Palestine policy of the British Labour Government 1947: the decision to withdraw. *International Affairs (Royal Institute of International Affairs 1944-), 56*(1), 73–93.

Pantazis, C. and Pemberton, S. (2009). From the 'old' to the 'new' suspect community: examining the impacts of recent UK counter-terrorist legislation. *The British Journal of Criminology, 49*(5), 646–666.

Pettinger, T. (2023). Embodying the inquiry: disaster, affectivity, and the localized politics of security. *Environment and Planning C: Politics and Space, 41*(7), 1282–1300.

Pham, P. L. (2010). *Ending 'East of Suez': The British Decision to Withdraw from Malaysia and Singapore 1964-1968.* Oxford: Oxford University Press.

Power, P. F. (1972). Civil protest in Northern Ireland. *Journal of Peace Research, 9*(3), 223–236.

Rasnic, C. D. (1999). Northern Ireland's criminal trials without jury: the Diplock experiment. *Annual Survey of International & Comparative Law, 5*, 239–257.

Rehman, J. (2007). Islam, "War on Terror" and the future of Muslim minorities in the United Kingdom: dilemmas of multiculturalism. *Human Rights Quarterly, 29*(4), 831–878.

Reinares, F. (2017). *Al-Qaeda's Revenge: The 2004 Madrid Train Bombings.* New York: Columbia University Press.

Rogers, P. (2008). Contesting and preventing terrorism: on the development of UK strategic policy on radicalisation and community resilience. *Journal of Policing, Intelligence and Counter Terrorism, 3*(2), 38–61.

Sabir, R. (2014). Understanding Counter-Terrorism Policy and Practice in the UK since 9/11. Unpublished PhD dissertation, University of Bath.

Sageman, M. (2011). *Leaderless Jihad: Terror Networks in the Twenty-First Century.* Philadelphia: University of Pennsylvania Press.

Schmid, A. P. (2013). *Radicalisation, De-Radicalisation, Counter-Radicalisation: A Conceptual Discussion and Literature Review. ICCT Research Paper.* The Hague: International Centre for Counter-Terrorism.

Thomas, P. (2017). Changing experiences of responsibilisation and contestation within counter terrorism policies: the British prevent experience. *Policy and Politics, 45*(3), 305–321.

Tonge, J. (2006). *Northern Ireland*. Cambridge: Polity Press.

Towl, G. (2021). The politics of forensic psychological research, policy and practice. In D. A. Crighton and Towl, G. J. (Eds.), *Forensic Psychology (3rd ed.)*. Chichester: John Wiley.

Towl, G. and Crighton, D. (2016). The emperor's new clothes. The Psychologist, *8th February*. Available online www.bps.org.uk/psychologist/emperors-new-clothes-0. Retrieved on February 8, 2025.

Towl, G. and Podmore, J. (2019). Still in denial? The sex offender treatment industry. *The Justice Gap*, 2nd August. www.thejusticegap.com/still-in-denial-the-sex-offender-treatment-industry/. Retrieved on February 9, 2025.

Walker, C. and Starmer, K. (Eds.) (1999). *Miscarriages of Justice: A Review of Justice in Error*. London: Blackstone.

Wolpert, S. (2009). *Shameful Flight: The Last Years of the British Empire in India*. Oxford: Oxford University Press.

5   Psychological profiling

Psychological profiling can be broadly defined as the use of scientific method to identify probable characteristics. This can be applied at any stage from investigation through apprehension of perpetrators to prosecution. The field does though have a somewhat chequered history (Crighton, 2021). Profiling rests on the active gathering of relevant information, followed in turn by the generation of descriptive 'profiles' and offender or psychological profiling of this kind has roots that are traceable back to at least the 19th century. This development and use of early forms of profiling formed part of a more general optimism and enthusiastic embrace of 'science', stemming from the European enlightenment (Lively, 1981). This had seen a shift away from religious authority and revelation towards a growing reliance on rational and empirical approaches to the development of knowledge. The use of these methods to develop profiles has taken two main forms: one to develop better insights into known individuals and secondly to identify likely actors or offenders. Both of these are quite recent development, with modest initial efforts seen in the late 19th and early 20th centuries. This was followed by a period of rapid development, with the advent of systematic approaches from the 1940s onwards. Pioneered in North America, the development of profiling went on to expand internationally, going on to become an intrinsic part of the forensic and intelligence practice.

The initial focus of this work was on high profile individuals and on crimes that proved to be particularly intractable and resistant to existing forensic and detection methods. This in large part accounts for an initial focus on highly unusual political actors and very rare high-profile crimes, such as serial sexual homicides. This was followed by a broadening of interest, with efforts to apply a variety of profiling methods to a wider range of individuals and criminality, including efforts to profile terrorists. This has thrown up methodological and practical challenges, although these have not proved to be insuperable, with profiling of at least some areas of terrorism showing significant promise.

A brief history

Systematic profiling has long been popular in crime fiction, with the stories of Sherlock Holmes providing an archetype of the application of the scientific method,

DOI: 10.4324/9781003429579-5

involving the testing of common-sense deductions, to profile likely perpetrators of crime (Conan Doyle, 1897/2001). The later stories about Hercule Poirot, the fictional Belgian detective, can be seen to follow a similar pattern of adopting systematic and scientific methods around the collection, integration, testing and interpretation of available information, to develop profiles that can aid in detection (Christie, 1936). Notably, both Agatha Christie and Arthur Conan Doyle had significant scientific backgrounds.

The earliest attempt at developing such profiles in Europe, outside the world of fiction, has been widely attributed to the work of Thomas Bond: a physician and a Police Surgeon working in London during the 19th century. In this role, he was asked by the Police to develop a profile of the perpetrator of what were felt to be linked homicides in the East end of London. These took place between 1888 and 1891 and involved five murders of women in the Whitechapel and Spitalfields area. At the time, these were amongst the most overcrowded and deprived parts of London. As a result of the high levels of violence towards women in these areas, the true number of crimes that may have been linked is not known. Four later murders of women in the same area were judged by the Police not to be linked or to be 'copycat' killings. These murders in the East end of London were the subject of lurid and frequently inaccurate coverage in the popular press of the time and went on to be called the 'Jack the Ripper' murders. They have continued to attract both popular and academic interest, with recurring efforts at applying modern methods of detection and analysis to identifying likely perpetrators.

In the 19th century, the Police would have had very limited means of detection open to them. They also appeared largely unmotivated, at least initially, to actively investigate these violent crimes against impoverished women. Forensic science would then have been in its infancy limiting investigation to the questioning of witnesses and 'likely' perpetrators, with few lines of inquiry being available. In the case of homicides committed by a stranger to the women, these methods were unlikely to be productive and the identification of suspects was frequently based on tenuous grounds. It is perhaps unsurprising then that Bond was asked to provide a scientific profile of the perpetrator. The fact that the killer, or killers, were never identified though, means that the accuracy of this profile cannot now be adequately evaluated. The approach though is open to such a review, and given the constraints of the time, this appears to have involved the clear application of scientific thinking and method. In that respect, current approaches to profiling can be seen as building Bond's early work.

Despite the absence of almost all the forensic evidence that would now be routinely gathered, Bond was able to draw some inferences and produce a limited profile of the likely perpetrator. These included the inference that the five murders were linked and had been committed by the same person, which was based on examination of the crime scenes and post-mortem assessment of the injuries the women had suffered. Based on the extreme violence used, the profile developed stressed the role of rage. As a drive for this level of rage, Bond hypothesised that the perpetrator would show a strong hatred of women. Using this information, Bond also made clear efforts to construct a profile, grounded in logical analysis, using this to predict likely characteristics of the perpetrator that might aid detection. Contrary to many of the popular accounts at the time and subsequently, Bond rejected the idea that the offender would have any specialist anatomical knowledge, either as a surgeon or a butcher (Petherick, 2005).

Further progress in profiling was largely absent until the 1930s when new work in this area began to emerge largely from North America. This involved two distinct efforts at psychological profiling which acted to drive later progress (Crighton, 2021). Global war had generated a very practical demand for better and more systematic understanding of key political actors. Driven largely by government, military and civilian intelligence services, the aim was to develop better understanding and more accurately predict the likely actions of these individuals. The United States Office of Strategic Services (OSS) in the United States provides an early example of this, commissioning detailed psychological profiles of foreign leaders. The most widely known of these profiles is perhaps that developed by Dr Walter Langer of the German Nazi leader Adolf Hitler. Typically for that era, Langer had been trained as a psychoanalyst and the profile he developed rested heavily on psychodynamic thinking. In many respects, these kinds of profile of political leaders and other key actors show marked similarities to offender profiling. They do though differ in some important respects, the most obvious of these perhaps being the richness of the data often available to profilers. Additionally, they will know who they are profiling and will have, to a greater or lesser extent, the opportunity to directly observe samples of behaviour, as well as written information.

The other major development of profiling emerged from New York and involved the production of offender profiles as part of the process of criminal investigation. This followed a series of explosions between 1940 and 1956, which appeared to the police to have been undertaken by one offender. These bombings were seen as forming part of a terror campaign and had involved placing explosive devices in public settings, such as cinemas, telephone boxes and railway stations. These attacks had proved resistant to the conventional investigation and detection methods then available and no progress had been made in identifying the perpetrator. As a result, the New York police sought expert advice, from James Brussel, who was asked to develop a psychological profile of the likely offender. Brussel was a psychiatrist and is reported to have had a prior background developing profiles for government and intelligence services. In completing his offender profile for the New York police, he used an approach which involved multiple suggestions about likely characteristics. These included a mix of very general and very specific characteristics. Examples of these included hypothesising that the offender would be a heavily built middle-aged man, that he was likely to be single, that he may be living with a sibling, that he would have some basic mechanical skills, and that he would come from Connecticut, be a Roman Catholic and foreign born. In line with his use of psychodynamic models of behaviour, it was suggested that the perpetrator would harbour an obsessional love for his mother and hatred of his father. The offender profile developed also included a common-sense observation that the offender may have a grudge against the city power company. This was apparently made on the basis that the first bomb attack had targeted the company headquarters, and it remains surprising that detectives had apparently not pursued such an obvious line of inquiry.

This profile became famous and also notorious, largely as a result of intensive press coverage at the time. Some of the very specific predictions made in the offender profile and the apparent accuracy of these were highlighted. For example, the prediction that the offender would be wearing a buttoned double-breasted suit when arrested was noted (Brussel, 1968). This focus perhaps explains the mythic status that has at times attached to the area of psychological profiling.

Drawing on this profile though, the New York police had adopted the very practical line of inquiry of tracing and questioning disgruntled former employees of the power company. It was this routine detective work, rather than the detailed profile, which led to the identification of George Metesky as the perpetrator of the terror attacks. Subsequently, it was possible to compare the offender profile developed with the perpetrator and this suggested that many of the predictions were in fact accurate. In line with the profile, he did in fact live in Connecticut and was heavily built, single, Roman Catholic and foreign-born. These results are though less impressive than they first appear, with the methods used by Brussel being criticised for being less scientific and of lower utility than the earlier work of Bond. The kinds of offender profiles that were developed by Brussel and others who followed him have gone on to be extensively criticised as being unscientific and showing little genuine understanding of perpetrators or their psychology. Critics have observed that the methodology used here involved the generation of a large number of varied predictions. In itself, this makes it more probable that some will prove to be accurate. Linked to this, the predictions seemed to involve a mixture of predictions that can be seen as common sense or even obvious and those with high base rates. So, for example, the idea that a violent offender may have a grudge seems common sense and the prediction that they are likely to be male or aged 15 to 30 will both have high base rates. In turn, high base rate and perhaps common-sense predictions are more likely to be confirmed, with these confirmed predictions being more likely to be recalled than those proving to be inaccurate. Such biasing in recall may act to suggest more positive evidence of accuracy than more objective analyses. Similarly, those low base rate and non-obvious predictions which are confirmed may have greater salience than those which are not. Those predictions in offender profiles that proved inaccurate or even misleading may be more likely to be downplayed or forgotten. Indeed, this is a well-known technique used by performers such as magicians, known as 'cold reading' although it seems this may also be used in a non-deliberate manner. Use of this method though has been extensively and rightly criticised as being both unscientific and potentially harmful (Gladwell, 2007). This can be compounded by what have been called 'Barnum' effects, which involve direct efforts to trick an audience. This is achieved by giving vague, ambiguous and often universally applicable descriptions, which will frequently be accepted as being accurate descriptions of something specific (Forer, 1949). This is a technique used by fortune telling and mind-reading acts, and the use of such methods, even if not done consciously, has been raised as a potential criticism of some early efforts at psychological profiling (Gladwell, 2007).

The next major development in profiling also came from North America and was driven by concerns about the quality and consistency of existing practice. This involved the US Federal Bureau of Investigation (FBI) which established a Behavioural Science Unit (BSU) in 1972 to address these concerns. This unit researched the question of whether more effective profiling could be developed and more broadly set out to explore ways in which the behavioural sciences could make greater contributions to investigation and detection. In doing this, the BSU aimed at developing more scientifically grounded forensic methods, analogous to those which had proved so productive in the physical sciences. This began with work on psychological profiles of likely perpetrators in unsolved cases which had proved intractable. Many of which were in fact 'cold cases' with no current lines of investigation, so there was little to be lost by trying psychological profiling. A central actor in this early work was Howard Teten, a former Californian police officer who importantly also had a background and training in forensic science. Teten had begun working for the FBI in the 1960s and along with a small group of colleagues, developed an approach to profiling that they called Criminal Investigation Analysis (CIA). This involved a process of gathering and testing data about crime scenes and offender behaviours. The early methods pioneered by the BSU were progressively developed and evaluated and this work went on to be widely popularised in fiction (Teten, 1989). This was not least because profiling here typically involved very rare, high-profile, difficult to solve crimes, such as serial sexual homicide cases. Offences of this kind had often proved to be particularly difficult when using traditional detection methods, with victims often appearing to be chosen randomly.

The CIA approach was initially developed through the study of offenders identified in apparently similar cases, as a means of developing better insights. Data here were gathered by means of structured interviews and analysis of collateral data. This was then used to develop better systematic descriptions of likely perpetrators of ostensibly similar crimes, with the aim of developing profiles of practical use to investigative teams, such as generating new lines of inquiry and insights into potential suspects (Ressler, Douglas, Groth et al., 1980). This work was described as involving four stages: data assimilation, crime classification, crime reconstruction and profile generation (Ressler, Burgess, Douglas et al., 1986). The final stage, profile generation, used a standardised reporting format which summarised socio-demographic and psychosocial characteristics. Given that this research involved developing profiles based on samples of known offenders, it rested on an assumption that known and unknown offenders would show significant consistency. If correct, this would mean that profiles based on known offenders would have practical utility in similar types of crime. Whilst the early work in this area focussed on notorious and high-profile cases in North America, the methodology was subsequently extended to a growing range of criminal behaviour.

The development of profiling outside North America occurred slightly later and often independently. As a result, this work has evolved in a rather different manner. A common theme here has been the stress on improving accuracy, based on the use of scientific method to develop practice and the associated evidence base (Canter, 1989; Kocsis, 1999; Crighton, 2021). This can be seen to involve two distinct methodologies which went on, somewhat misleadingly, to be described as 'statistical' and 'clinical' approaches. Both terms are shorthand over-simplifications but stress the difference between profiles based on individual 'clinical' judgements and those based on group data. Here, 'clinical' profiles can be seen to draw on the work of Brussel and other similar profilers, typically involving the generation of descriptive profiles of likely characteristics of perpetrators of crimes. In contrast, 'statistical' approaches have emphasised formal analysis of group-based data, typically drawing on multi-variate forms of statistical analysis. In turn, these generate descriptions of the likelihood of offender characteristics linked to various forms of crime.

The 'clinical' approach to profiling largely dominated early work in this area and at least initially was often welcomed by investigators. Systematic efforts at evaluation of these profiles though proved to be disappointing, and this was associated with a growing dissatisfaction in those who used such profiles. Independent research highlighted concerns around the reliability, validity and utility of these profiles. One review of this area, undertaken in the United Kingdon (UK), highlighted some major failings in this methodology. These included very wide variations in the form and content of these 'clinical' profiles. The utility of this kind of psychological profile within investigations was also a focus of serious concern, with the suggestion that they were contributing little and had clear potential for adverse effects (Copson, 1995). These findings were highlighted by concerns that were explored in the UK Courts where the practical use of profiles came under legal scrutiny in the high-profile case of *R* v. *Stagg* [1994]. This case acted as a turning point for research and practice in the field, making the growing concerns public. In this case, it was noted that the distinction between profiling and investigation had become increasingly blurred, leading to serious errors. Subsequently, this case and the emerging independent research acted as major drivers for change and improvement profiling, with this taking the form of efforts to put the work on a firmer scientific footing (Alison, Bennett, Mokros et al., 2002; Fox and Farrington, 2018; Fujita, Watanabe, Yokota et al., 2013).

Current practice in psychological profiling

Currently, dominant approaches to profiling rest on two fundamental ideas: behavioural consistency and homology. Behavioural consistency refers to the assumption that behaviours exhibited in one event will tend to show consistencies across other events. Homology refers to the assumption that similar behaviours, observed at the scene of an event, will tend to be associated with similar characteristics in individual actors. Based on these two key assumptions, it is argued that it will be possible to make valid inferences from information gathered from the scene of events, such as terrorist incidents or violent crimes, to generate profiles of the actor or actors involved. Profiles of this kind in turn have practical use in informing prevention, investigation and detection of crimes (Gudjonsson and Copson, 1997; Alison, Bennett, Mokros et al., 2002; Kocsis, 2006; Fujita, Watanabe, Yokota et al., 2013). At a theoretical level, there is a consensus that it is possible to use available data in this manner, to derive valid profiles of likely perpetrators (Kocsis, 2006). Using this general framework, a variety of methods have been used to do this and a range of different terminology has been developed to describe this. Arguably though, three main approaches have come to dominate the field: Criminal Investigation Analysis (CIA), Crime Action Profiling (CAP) and Investigative Psychology (IP) (Crighton, 2021).

Criminal Investigation Analysis (CIA)

The term 'CIA' captures a range of methods that were developed primarily by the FBI in North America (Teten, 1989; Ressler, Douglas, Groth et al., 1980; Ressler, Burgess, Douglas et al., 1986). This approach is based on the development and practical application of what is described as empirically grounded information, resting largely on use of self-report data from convicted offenders and systematic analysis of crime scenes. The CIA approach stresses the value of analysing crime scenes and uses terminology such as 'staging' and 'signature' to describe observed consistencies across these. Some early and influential distinctions emerged because of this approach to analysis, perhaps the best known and most enduring of which has been a distinction between 'organised' and 'disorganised' perpetrators. This distinction was seen as reflecting clear differences in areas such as the extent of pre-planning and the level of emotional and behavioural control shown. The CIA methodology was subsequently developed to consider a wide range of offences, with the method becoming codified into a manual, the *Crime Classification Manual* (Douglas, Burgess, Burgess et al., 2019). This provided a series of templates for profiles that could be used by investigative teams.

Crime Action Profiling (CAP)

CAP was developed independently but shares some characteristics with the CIA approach (Kocsis, 1999, 2006) in that it was initially developed with a focus on specific difficult to solve crimes. The approach significantly differed in the breadth of factors included within profiles, such as the inclusion of logistical factors surrounding profiling and data collection. CAP also drew more on formal, largely statistical methods, for processing information to form profiles, using the method of multidimensional scaling (MDS) (Jaworska and Chupetlovska-Anastasova, 2009). This formal analysis is used extensively as a means of generating profiles and specific predictions of likelihood (Kocsis, 2003, 2006).

Investigative Psychology (IP)

This approach was developed at the UK (Alison and Kebbell, 2006; Canter, 2010), and similarly to CAP, it relies on the use of formal statistical techniques to analyse information. This has included extensive use of MDS, as the basis for developing psychological profiles, although the approach has also stressed the contribution of psychology to wider investigative processes. As with other profiling, it began as a means of trying to address more intractable forms of criminal behaviour but has been developed across a wider range of events.

Developments in profiling

Profiling moved from its early pioneering phase of development to the point where it now forms a mainstream aspect of forensic psychology. The credibility and utility of work in this area has also increased as a function of progressive improvements in methodology, which have addressed many of the serious and justified criticisms of earlier work. As touched on above, these had included suggestions that some early efforts in this area were often unscientific, being based unwittingly on psychological effects well known to magicians and entertainers.

A key tenet of applying scientific method to profiling has been systematic efforts to evaluate the accuracy of profiles. Historically, this often-yielded mixed results, driving fundamental change in practice. Studies from the 1990s had looked at areas such as the accuracy of individual profilers, how they compared to control groups of non-profilers and how accurate investigators perceived them to be. The results here were often disappointing (Fox, Farrington, Kapardis et al., 2020). One study of this kind looked at data from a series of murder and rape cases used as the basis for comparison. Here, all the cases had been successfully solved, allowing for comparison of profiles to the real characteristics of offenders. Participants in the study were asked to construct profiles and to do this through completing a series of multiple-choice questions. The results suggested that experienced profilers tended to be significantly better at predicting the characteristics of the cases of rape but that they did not differ from the control group when looking at the murder cases (Pinizzotto and Finkel, 1990). In a similar vein, another study looked at rape and arson cases, and here, the experienced profilers did perform better than the control group, but there were two notable limitations. Firstly, the study involved a small number of profilers, so any conclusions need to be treated with considerable caution. Additionally, there was reported to be a high degree of statistical variance among this group (Kocsis, 2003). This finding largely mirrors some of the work into other areas of expert decision making, which suggests that whilst some 'experts' perform very well others perform very poorly (Crighton, 2023).

Such studies are open to criticisms, such as the use of small-sample sizes, in terms of both the number of cases analysed and the numbers of profilers involved. Evidence in this area often rests on evaluations of only a handful of profilers, who are willing to have their work subject to such independent scrutiny. Because of this, such studies have typically had very low levels of statistical power. This means that small, moderate and sometime even large effects may be undetectable. Conclusions are therefore necessarily tentative as a result, with low levels of statistical power meaning that positive and negative effects will be missed. The experimental paradigms used in this area have also been criticised for often presenting materials in highly artificial ways. Case information is typically presented in very limited formats involving only written information, with the responses of participants also being highly constrained. Experimental paradigms of this kind are therefore very different from what profilers would typically be faced with and the ways in which they would normally work. Given these differences, there is a need for considerable caution in extrapolating to real-world practice. That said, the very wide variation in performance that has been reported suggests good reasons to be concerned and a need for high levels of care in this area.

Ideas of behavioural consistency in profiling have received support from the developing research base, as well as from the wider evidence base into the development of criminal behaviour. Both areas of research suggest the emergence of consistencies in behaviour early in life, with these generally persisting over time (Basto-Pereira and Farrington, 2020; Farrington, Coid, Harnett et al., 2006; Skinner, Farrington and Shepherd, 2020). Findings of this kind provide support for the idea that patterns of stable behaviour follow a clear developmental sequence and that, in turn, this will tend to be reflected in later behaviour. Emerging evidence has also provided some support for behavioural consistency across crime scenes (Proulx, Aubut, Perron et al., 1994; Jackson and Bekerian, 1997; Proulx, St-Yves, Guay et al., 1999; Alison and Kebbell, 2006).

The assumption of homology, that similar crime scene behaviours will be associated with similar offender characteristics, has generally enjoyed weaker support, with some studies failing to show the presence of any significant homology. One study attempted to test this hypothesis by integrating what was felt to be predictive crime scene data, using the statistical technique of logistic regression. The result here did not show substantive improvement over base rates for most of the predictors analysed (Davies, Wittebrood and Jackson, 1998). Another study looked at this area using a sample of 50 convicted rapists. Here, it was reported that the group studied appeared relatively homogeneous, regardless of differences in the observed offence characteristics (House, 1997). A subsequent study looked at a larger sample of 100 males, all convicted of the rape of strangers. This group was analysed in terms of 28 dichotomous variables. Here again, there was an absence of clear evidence to link crime scene behaviours and the characteristics of the offenders (Mokros and Alison, 2002). Such findings have drawn into question the validity of the assumption of homology and the strength of this, should it be present. Drawing on this, some have suggested a resemblance between the early work on profiling and naïve personality theories (Alison and Kebbell, 2006). Naïve personality theories tended, just like some early profiling, to be nomothetic. That is, they were aiming at general 'laws' to yield group-based predictions. Early profiling work can be criticised on similar grounds to these naïve theories, most importantly perhaps for failing to adequately consider the power of situational effects leading to attributional errors (Mischel, Shoda and Ayduk, 2007).

Work into the contribution of profiling to broader investigative processes has been slower to develop, and the early studies in this area often had serious methodological weaknesses. Early work typically involved weak self-report methods, such as surveys of satisfaction. These would typically ask a sample of investigative officers to retrospectively say how useful they had found profiles to be (Pinizzotto and Finkel, 1990). Whilst such research often yielded moderately positive results, some of the problems with this are perhaps obvious and such results in fact say little about the real contributions of profiling investigative processes. In general, investigators tended to be positive, but these retrospective comments are not a meaningful evaluation. There is a bias here towards positive recall and responses, likely to be amplified in turn by a focus on successfully resolved cases, whether profiling played a part in the resolution or not. Studies of this kind also tended to involve small samples, again generating problems with very low statistical power. In combination with other uncontrolled potential biases, this led to extensive and justified criticism of such evaluations (Copson, 1995).

Later work sought to move on from this, adopting more methodologically rigorous approaches (Alison, Smith and Morgan, 2003). This included the use of questionnaire-based methods which concerned events in real cases. Here, for example, participants were randomly given one of two alternative profiles (A or B). These provided distinct outlines of perpetrator characteristics, with profile A being a genuine profile and B representing a control profile. This control profile being matched for content but including a set of fabricated characteristics, designed to be clearly distinct from the genuine profile. Results from this kind of study have been enlightening, showing the clear limitations of earlier work. In this experimental paradigm, those given profiles tended to rate both as being 'generally accurate.' Participants rarely if ever felt that a profile was 'generally' or 'very inaccurate.' This supports a hypothesis that, when faced with such a task, people are in fact trying to make sense of it. They seem to do this by trying to achieve a fit between the profile and the characteristics they have been given. Evidence in this area has been added to, leading to the suggestion that many early profiles, would typically include information that would not be open to confirmation or refutation. This would apply even after a perpetrator had been detected and convicted. Included here would be the use of vague or inconsistent statements, open to very broad interpretation. Further criticism here was that profiler reports at that time would often provide no basis for the advice contained within the profile (Alison and Kebbell, 2006; Alison, Smith and Morgan, 2003; West and Alison, 2006).

There was initially some resistance to independent evaluation of practice and preliminary findings, and ideas were at times applied in the absence of convincing evidence. Questions of racial and other biases often received little attention. Methods developed in North America were applied to very different contexts, with serious risk of misleading investigators (Siggins, 2002; Harcourt, 2003, 2004; Palermo and Kocsis, 2005).

The accuracy of profiling

Four recent systematic reviews have looked at the accuracy of psychological profiling across various forms of crime (Dowden, Bennell and Bloomfield, 2007; Snook, Eastwood, Gendreau et al., 2007; Bennell, Mugford, Ellingwood et al., 2013; Fox and Farrington, 2018). Some trends in profiling are evident from these reviews, which have also provided good evidence on quality, accuracy and utility. The earliest of these reviews reported a substantial growth of work in the area, reflected by an increased quantity and quality of research (Dowden, Bennell and

Bloomfield, 2007). This growth though followed initially low levels of generally poor-quality work. By the early 2000s, an increased proportion of work had been peer reviewed with some improvements in the methodological quality of work also reported.

A later narrative review study limited its consideration to work published in peer review journals, with 130 relevant publications on profiling being included (Snook, Eastwood, Gendreau et al., 2007). It is striking that only four of these were judged to meet the standard for inclusion in a meta-analysis, looking at accuracy of identification. Such a small sample size means that any conclusions from this review need to be treated with considerable caution, with the analysis suggesting an accuracy rate of 62% when using profiles. This compared to an accuracy rate of 38% without using profiles.

Bennell, Mugford, Ellingwood et al. (2013) also undertook a review of published work in the area but limited this to work which involved case linkage analysis (CLA). CLA is an approach to profiling which assesses the ability to statistically link crimes to an individual, based on the analysis of crime scene data. This review suggested there had been significant improvement in the evidence base, compared with the earlier reviews. Here, 17 articles were judged to be of suitable quality for inclusion in the analysis and the results suggested clear variations in the accuracy associated with CLA. This was assessed by using the area under the curve (AUC) statistic as a measure of accuracy, with around half of the results considered falling into the 0.70–0.89 range, suggesting a clear improvement over random chance (0.50). Encouragingly, two studies were found to have high levels of accuracy, with AUC values of around 0.90. In contrast, three studies were reported to show low levels of accuracy falling in the 0.50–0.69 range, with one study showing a below the chance level of performance (<0.5). The use of CLA was most common in pro-filing of burglary and sexual assault offences, but the accuracy here was poorer than for homicide offences. Indeed, the method also performed relatively poorly when applied to offences of robbery and car thefts (Bennell, Mugford, Ellingwood et al., 2013; Chapman, Smith and Bond, 2012).

The most recent and most detailed meta-analysis was undertaken by Fox and Farrington (2018). This provided the most extensive review of the evidence base to date and drew on research undertaken between 1979 and 2016. A total of 426 relevant publications were identified, but strikingly only 18 studies were felt to meet the standard for inclusion in the meta-analysis. The reviewers assessed the quality of work by using the Cambridge Quality Checklist (Murray, Farrington and Eisner, 2009) and the Cochrane Effective Practice and Organization of Care (2017) framework. The reviewers noted a continuation of the earlier growth seen in the published research in profiling. Improvement in the quality of research though was reported to have been slower, and this had been associated with a growing dominance of a small number of research centres. Much of the early work in the field showed a concentration on homicide and sexual homicide. More recently, there had been an expansion to other areas including arson and higher-frequency offences including robbery, burglary, car theft and online crimes. As with the earlier reviews, the analysis suggested wide variation in levels of accuracy across studies

(Fox and Farrington, 2018). One study of 237 homicide cases in the United States reported an exceptionally high level of accuracy, with an AUC of 0.96 and standard error (SE) of 0.02 (Melnyk, Bennell, Gauthier et al., 2011). This study was a clear outlier though, with the accuracy of other studies being significantly lower than this. The accuracy of studies concerned with sexual violence tended to be lower than for homicide, with a UK-based study of 365 cases, reporting an accuracy level using the AUC statistic of 0.87 (SE 0.02) (Slater, Woodhams and Hamilton-Giachritsis, 2015). A larger study with greater statistical power, involving 720 cases, was conducted in Japan and this reported comparable but slightly lower accuracy than the UK study, with an AUC of 0.83 (SE 0.03) (Yokota, Watanabe, Wachi et al., 2017). Whilst these levels of accuracy are poorer than for the profiling of homicides, the results still suggest good levels of performance that are well above chance.

Analysis of the results for other types of offence was generally less encouraging. Accuracy of identification here was reported to have been better when measures of geographic proximity were used and studies have typically used inter-crime distance (ICD) as a measure of this (Woodhams, Davies, Galambos et al., 2021). Profiling of robberies showed a notable drop in accuracy, with an AUC of 0.75 (SE 0.09) when using ICD to profile offenders (Burrell, Bull and Bond, 2012). Profiling of more common crimes, such as car thefts, showed markedly lower accuracy, although this finding was based on a small sample size. Here, a study conducted in the UK found levels of accuracy in line with random chance, with an AUC of 0.56 (SE 0.04) reported (Fox and Farrington, 2018). The results of this most recent review did not suggest any evidence of publication bias impacting on the results. Overall, the authors concluded that the accuracy of profiles appeared to be slightly higher for offences against the person than for property crimes, with a composite measure of all crime scene behaviours yielding the highest level of accuracy (Fox and Farrington, 2018).

Applying profiling to politically motivated violence

The approaches to psychological profiling of politically motivated forms of violence have generally been quite similar to those used for other forms of violence, and a similar distinction can be drawn between 'clinical' and 'statistical' approaches. As a result, many of the same criticisms can be made here, although given the stakes that may be involved, these can be more acute. Use of 'clinical' approaches here can be seen to have emerged with the work during World War II of the US OSS in creating profiles of key political leaders, who had caused so much devastation across the world. This method has continued to be applied, although the theoretical basis for it has become wider compared to it early reliance on Freudian psychodynamic concepts (Post, 2003). This form of profiling, as touched on above, has the major advantage that profilers can directly observe, to varying degrees, the behaviour of the target of the profile. There is often of wealth of video and audio materials on world leaders, often showing change and developments over time. This material does have limitations, typically involving public events where behaviour is likely to be more constrained and limited. Nonetheless, this provides psychological profilers a much wider range of data than would be typical in other areas of profiling.

This form of profiling shares several weaknesses that appear inherent to these 'clinical' approaches. These would include the difficulty in determining the reliability of these profiles. Essentially, it is unclear how far profilers would agree in their assessments. This can though be addressed to some extent by completion of team-based profiles, where the aim is to develop more detailed agreed profiles. Another significant problem here is determining the validity of such profiles. There is a lack of obvious benchmarks which the accuracy of profiles can be tested against. The method is also open to the kinds of effects that have been an issue throughout the history of profiling, such as the presence of 'cold reading' and 'Barnum' effects (Meehl, 1956). These might result in an undue emphasis being placed on weakly founded psychological profiles. Linked to this, the utility of these kinds of profiles is also unclear and meaningful evaluation of this is challenging. The risk here is, of course, the same as that seen in the profiling of criminal offenders. In that case, senior investigating officers were generally positive about profiles, even where these had proved to be of little value in investigations (Copson, 1995; Copson, Badcock, Boon et al., 1997). These challenges are though clearly not insuperable, and there is clear potential to assess the validity and utility of this form of profiling given the skills to do so (Çuhadar, Kaarbo, Kesgin et al., 2020).

Psychological profiling has also been applied in ways that are more closely analogous to that seen in offender profiling. Here, the method has been used with the aims of prediction and identification. The aims here have been to identify patterns that are more likely to be associated with those who engage in politically motivated forms of violence, which can then be used to predict those who are likely to act and identify them. This application of profiling is open to the criticism that it involves seeking to apply unwarranted typologies to the area of politically violent acts. This critique is based on the view that the 'types' identified in profiles lack both validity and utility. It has been noted that politically motivated actors show the presence of high levels of individual and group variation and also that, historically, they appear demographically and psychologically similar to the general population (Crenshaw, 2012; McGuirk, 2018; Sarma, Carthy and Cox, 2022). Development of profiles in this context can therefore be criticised as reflecting similar naïve personality theory approaches that caused criticism in other areas, failing to adequately address the power of environmental effects.

The application of 'clinical' profiling can also be criticised for its heavy reliance on the prior experience and training of profilers and the potential for this to introduce a variety of known and unknown biases (Ainsworth, 2001). When applied to the area of politically motivated violence, this may be particularly acute. Here, even highly experienced profilers will necessarily be working from small numbers of cases, which may also be highly atypical (Kocsis, 2006).

'Statistical' approaches that aim to predict and identify here also face a number of criticisms and challenges. The most obvious concern here focusses on issues of sampling and sample sizes. A major concern has been the suitability of formal analytic methods when applied to comparatively rare events. A lack of adequate statistical power to detect trends has therefore been a recurrent concern. There is though some good news here, with formal means that are designed to address the challenge of working with small samples of data (Ramsay, 1980). Although these do not provide a complete solution to concerns around working with small samples, these do suggest that this is not an insuperable problem.

The accuracy of the data has also been a problem, since this often draws on written records, often criminal justice records of various kinds but also sources such as health and social services records. This kind of information suffers from various well-known problems (Fox, Farrington, Kapardis et al., 2020; Home Office, 2025). Significant weaknesses here would include large amounts of information often being missing, of poor quality or unreliable and inaccurate. Information of this kind has generally been collected for other purposes and so is not gathered for the purpose of formal analysis. Taking this kind of data and subjecting it to formal analysis can be criticised for building on inadequate foundations and creating a false impression of precision. Such effects can be exacerbated by the efforts to address this by 'cleaning up' the data using various statistical techniques, making the foundations even more opaque. In addition, the challenge here goes beyond these issues of data quality. Those engaged in politically motivated violence are often equipped and motivated to actively provide disinformation (Jaspersen and Montibeller, 2020; Basu, 2021) adding an additional layer of complexity to the development of empirically based profiles. Again though, given the skills and motivation to do so, these are concerns that can be addressed. It is entirely possible to gather and analyse good quality information for these groups. There are no fundamental reasons why this cannot be used to develop 'statistical' profiles and test the accuracy and utility of these.

As noted earlier, profiling in this area has been handicapped by problems with definition of terms. This has sometimes been associated with a focus on legal categories rather than behaviour, which has muddied the waters. Ostensibly, similar events have been treated as distinct and quite different behaviours have been treated as similar, based on legal categories, needlessly complicating analysis. Questions over whether states can engage in terrorism has been a particular complication here, with an apparent bias of focussing on non-state actors and groups. A variety of terms have been used which at least partially create this problem, with terms such as state atrocities, hybrid warfare and asymmetrical warfare often capturing state actions indistinguishable from those of non-state actors. The UK's experience of Northern Ireland Related Terrorism provides an illustrative example of this, with state actors and agencies being accused of engaging in behaviours indistinguishable from non-state actors. Similarly, the actions of the Russian state, in seeking to destabilise neighbouring states provides another example where the acts of state and non-state actors often appear indistinguishable (Jackson, 2008; Galeotti, 2016; Muradov, 2022). Adding to this are clear overlaps between those engaging in politically motivated forms of violence and general criminality. Here, for example, individuals or groups may be engaged in acts of terrorism have also been observed to engage in organised crime, violent crime and sexual violence (Jupp and Garrod,

2022). Whatever the strengths of these distinctions in other areas of research and practice, they do give rise to problems in the development of psychological profiles in this area.

Data mining

Since the 1970s, there has been an exponential growth in the availability and use of information technology and digital communications (Hilbert and López, 2011). More recently, social media has massively expanded. In combination, these trends have resulted in enormous growth in the quantity of data produced, which can also be accessed, gathered and analysed. In relation to profiling, this has been something of a double-edged sword. On the one hand, it presents a potentially rich source of information about those who are at risk of engaging in politically motivated violence, as well as those who make the transition from beliefs to actions. On the other hand though, the sheer quantity of this data presents its own not inconsiderable challenges, making it hard to pick out useful information from background 'noise.' Massive and international flows of data also make it easier to hide from scrutiny (Zhang and Morris, 2023).

Efforts to address the challenges involved can be described under the general term of 'data mining.' This broad term has been used to describe various methods for picking out patterns from large quantities of information. These techniques have often been developed for commercial purposes, such as identifying potential customers, or the targeting of information or advertising at individuals. Notably, for these kinds of application, high levels of precision are not necessary and even modest trends can be valuable in terms of advertising or shifting political discourse. This kind of 'mining' for patterns may also be useful for profiling and again this has been led by the commercial sector. This can though be extended, for good or ill, to psychological profiling of politically motivated violence. Such use raises serious ethical and political concerns, in addition to those which are already present in commercial applications.

There is no universal agreement on how exactly to describe 'data mining,' and there are nuances around the term in different contexts. For present purposes though, this is simply summarised as a process involving five broad stages. The first of these is the selection of potential data sources, and this is followed by a stage of 'pre-processing' of data. This concerns taking information and putting this into the form of useable data. The third stage can be seen to involve transformation of these data into forms that can be searched by computer, which enables the next stage of data analysis. The final stage here is interpreting the outputs of this process. Overall, the process of 'data mining' can be summarised as either matching searchable data to previously known patterns or profiles, or 'fishing' for unknown patterns or profiles (Han, Kamber and Pei, 2012). In turn, these can be divided into those which are 'subject'-based and those which are 'goal'-based (Zarsky, 2011). 'Fishing' for unknown patterns here is sometimes described as 'dragnet' methods and may use various algorithms, combined with the considerable power of high-speed computing: with this increasingly using machine learning to refine and improve these algorithms (Mahesh, 2020). Crucially though, the value of this is dependent on how good these algorithms are. Using poor algorithms here will simply yield meaningless or actively misleading results (Saini and Bansal, 2024). Even when judiciously used, there are other intrinsic limitations. The method is dependent on high-level skills to determine how to extract, process and interpret data (Bilalli, Abelló, Aluja-Banet et al., 2018). This is crucial since the method in searching for unknown patterns may produce outputs that are meaningless or unintelligible. The method also generates the practical, legal and ethical problems around what to do with data that is deemed irrelevant to the purpose it was gathered for. This is necessarily generated in vast quantities, creating temptations to retain this or use it for other purposes. There is a fundamental tension here, in democratic societies at least, between storing this for security purposes and the rights of citizens. In authoritarian societies, it may be used as means of imposing ever greater social control, oppression and opaque manipulation of the populace. This creates the paradox of a technology initially used to protect against political motivated violence being used as a means of inflicting it.

Notably, work in this area is generally not in the public domain, so its use and potential abuses have not been open to scrutiny. Some examples have though been subject to detailed legal or political scrutiny and this provides some insight. Two important examples have been reviewed here, one coming from Germany and the other from the United States (McGuirk, 2018, 2021). In Germany, the use of 'data mining' was scrutinised by the Federal Constitutional Court. Here, an approach called 'Rasterfahndung' had been used as a counter-terrorism method. This can be translated as 'dragnet investigation' in English and had first been introduced in the 1970s. Then, it had been used to try and identify members of the Red Army Faction, a left-wing terrorist group. Data were trawled, based on a police observation that members of this group tended to pay electricity bills using cash. Here, power companies had given the names of customers paying by cash, which were compared against registry office data, looking for false identities. Where this was not the case individuals were eliminated and the Police went on to search the remaining properties. This dragnet approach led to the arrest of one person. The same method was used again in the early 2000s in an effort to detect Islamist terrorism and the legality of this was challenged. As a result, the method was subject to legal scrutiny, largely concerned with issues of privacy and constitutional rights, much of which was made public (Müller and Richter, 2008).

The example from the United States followed on from the implementation of the Homeland Security Act (HSA) 2002, which had enabled wide scale data mining. This was seen to have resulted in the collection of a very wide range of information, which included large amounts of financial data. This resulted in political scrutiny coming from the US Congress, much of which was also made public. Here, Congress found that trawling had been conducted using both subject and pattern-based approaches and that vast amounts of data had been involved. This had been focussed on improving security processes in air travel but clearly had wider potential application, with the results going on to inform a computer-assisted passenger pre-screening system (CAPPS). This was later revised into a CAPPS II system and in turn by systems called 'Secure Flight,' 'Automated Targeting System' (ATS) and 'Terrorism Information Awareness' (TIA) covering both air passengers and air freight (Lake, 2004).

These examples suggest rather mixed results, with use proving especially problematic when 'looking' for unknown patterns. The reviews in both in Germany and the US also suggested a lack good evidence for the methods used, which seemed to have limited ability to deal with events in real time. The utility in some settings therefore appeared to be poor. There also seemed to be serious challenges in the pre-processing stage, made acute by the large quantities of unstructured data. This is a problem that has been made worse by the growth and diversification of digital information available, with much of the available data lacking clear structure (Saini and Bansal, 2024).

The Federal Constitutional Court went on to express serious concerns over significant infringement of human rights and the disproportionality of the approach, meaning essentially that the infringements of rights were not offset by the usefulness of the method in protecting the public. The concerns here seem to focus on use of 'dragnet' methods, rather than searching against known patterns. The US Congress seems to have reached very similar conclusions but raised additional concerns around systematic racial biases. As a result, funding was largely withdrawn for much of this kind of work in the US, although similar but modified methods have subsequently re-emerged.

Using profiling to predict and identify from at scene behaviours

Considerable efforts have been made to identify those who are engaged in politically motivated violence or who may be more likely to engage, based on profiles of observable behaviour. Typically, this has been seen as an addition or adjunct to the use of other primarily physical methods to ensure accurate identification. These would include use of fingerprints, iris scanning and increasingly computerised facial recognition and gait analysis. Profiling here has been largely focused on the assessment of observable psycho-physiological reactions. These have been used to develop profiles for those thought likely to present a greater likelihood of engaging in attacks. These kinds of profile have generally been used to direct additional scrutiny and questioning, rather than achieving precise identification or prediction. As such, the method is geared towards avoiding false negatives (misses) and generating false positives. The indicators used to form profiles here can be captured under the broad label of 'body language.' Within this, a great deal of the focus here has been on reactions thought to be associated with anxiety due to stress, although this has increasingly been extended to the area of language analysis (Archer, Lansley and Garner, 2020).

Various criticisms have been made of this form of profiling. Most importantly perhaps, reliance on behavioural and verbal indicators of this kind rests on several assumptions. These often include the idea that those engaged in attacks will experience marked stress and anxiety, hypothesised to be consistently observable under specific circumstances. Both ideas have limited empirical support. The challenge here is increased by the nature of the environments typically involved and the openness of behavioural and linguistic indicators to a range of counter measures. This is likely to be a particular concern in the case of state-supported actors or groups. Even where this is not the case, this form of profiling is likely to experience powerful effects due to powerful interactional effects between individuals and environments (Mischel, 1979; Hardie, 2020).

There is limited public information available on the effectiveness of this form of profiling. Others have expressed concern that for the identification of some categories, such as suicide bombers, seeking to identify anxiety here may be inaccurate or actively misleading (Lester, Yang and Lindsay, 2004). Importantly, it is established that different types of emotional states impact on suicidal ideation and behaviours (Burr, Rahm-Knigge and Conner, 2018). To some extent, these concerns can be addressed, although it is generally unclear how well, and consistently, this has been done.

Profiling of this kind is widely used and has been particularly evident in areas such as aviation, where such profiles are used in airports and in some jurisdictions onboard aircraft. An example of this comes from Israel, where this form of profiling was developed following a series of terrorist hijackings of aircraft, beginning in the 1960s (Whitaker, 2010). At the time, this was a novel threat and the response involved multi-layered defences, called a 'four circles' approach. This described a layered approach to security with the first or outer 'circle' referring to the wider airport zone. Here, security checks and scans can be carried out based only on a suspicion, in turn informed by profiles. The second circle refers to the airport terminal, with continual screening of the environment, undertaken by trained staff. Again the work of these staff will be informed by profiles of likely perpetrators, as well as their own experience. These are used to identify individuals for 'enhanced questioning.' The third circle captures the use of 'data mining' techniques on passenger information. The fourth circle refers to the use of what has been referred to as 'special' questioning techniques, details of which are undisclosed, presumably to maintain their value and reduce the risk of counter-measures.

Another example of this application of profiling comes from the US, with the development of the Behavioural Detection and Analysis (BDA) program, which involves Screening Passengers by Observation Techniques (SPOT) (Department of Homeland Security, 2011). Again, this is a part of a layered approach to security, with SPOT being focussed on profiling based on psycho-physiological indicators. These may be used as an adjunct method for filtering people into more enhanced screening and checks, including the use of 'data mining' techniques. The use of SPOT has been described as involving specially trained staff, who will have completed a four-day course. Based on the publicly available information, this appears to be largely based on profiles of facial expressions, in turn based on experimental lab-based work on emotional expression (Ekman and Friesen, 2003). This reliance has been the focus of criticism, with the application of such experimental studies to applied settings raising potential concerns (McGuirk, 2021). In addition, it is also far from clear that four days training would be adequate to identify and profile the subtleties of body language.

Using sensitive characteristics in profiling

Sensitive characteristics typically include individual characteristics such as race, ethnicity, age, gender and country of origin. Views on using these to develop profiles in this area have often been polarised. At one extreme, some have adopted a purely utilitarian view, arguing that use is justified by the seriousness of potential outcomes. This view reaches its logical conclusion with the use of mass surveillance and opaque manipulation techniques (Xu, 2021). At the other extreme, it can be argued that such characteristics should never be used for profiling. Most though have stressed the importance of maintaining human rights, seeing the use of some characteristics to be generally wrong in principle and requiring exceptional justification (Tesón, 2005; Luban, 2014).

Particular concerns have emerged around the use of race, ethnicity and religion to create profiles. This has been criticised as a means of disadvantaging or harassing some groups. Responses to this have been varied. For example, the European Court of Human Rights (EctHR) has taken the view that sensitive characteristics may be used for this purpose subject to limitations. These included the need for use to be justified in pursuit of a legitimate aim and being proportionate to that, as well as appearing 'reasonable.' Additionally, the need for this to be open to review was stressed (De Londras and Tregidga, 2021). Concerns have persisted though around psychological profiling involving a large amount of racial profiling or providing an apparently scientific basis for discrimination and disproportionate actions (Ravich, 2007; Meyer, 2010).

Profiles of involvement in politically motivated violence

Profiling has shown promise here distinguishing between individuals based on motivation and type of actor. For example, looking at the distinctive features of lone actors in comparison to those engaged in small terrorist cells or larger terrorist groups and movements. The dominant method here has involved use of various forms of multidimensional scaling (MDS). These have previously been widely used in other areas of profiling, although use in the context of politically motivated violence is comparatively recent (Wilson, Canter, Smith et al., 1996; Wilson and Smith, 2000).

Early research yielded promising results here, suggesting significantly different profiles in terms of demographics, geographic locations, preparatory acts, sex and motivations (Smith, Damphousse and Paxton, 2006). Later, work looked at those engaged in Extreme Right-Wing Terrorism (ERWT) and showed elevated levels of identified mental illness (Chermak and Gruenewald, 2015). Other research has focussed on profiling lone actors, systematically analysing their behaviour and looking for differences in areas such as ideology or networks. This work has suggested that, while there is no uniform profile for lone actors, some distinct characteristics were more evident prior to attacks. These included other people more often becoming aware of these perpetrators expressing grievances, extreme political views and for some, an explicit intention to act violently. Lone-actor terrorists often appeared to be socially isolated. Despite this though, some relevant behaviours were often observed by others in the lead up attacks. These typically involved visible acts around planning and logistics, with evidence of lone actors acting impulsively being rare (Gill and Corner, 2013; Gill, Horgan and Deckert, 2014).

Investigative Psychology and typologies of behaviour

Multiple attempts have been made to develop typologies of the various forms of politically motivated violence (Shultz, 1978; Marsden and Schmid, 2011; López Werner, 2024). For example, a study conducted in the US analysed 171 of those convicted Al-Qaeda-related offenses (AQROs) or who had undertaken suicide attacks between 1997 and 2011 (Simcox and Dyer, 2013). Based on analysis of background factors including demographic, offence-related and network connections, the presence of five distinct profiles was suggested: active participants, aspirants, facilitators, trained aspirants and ideologues. Similar research looking primarily at Europe, North Africa, the Middle East and Pakistan (Nesser, 2006, 2018) suggested four distinct profiles: entrepreneurs, protégés, misfits and drifters. Comparison of these suggests one of the main difficulties with typologies, where different profiles emerge being largely dependent on the method of analysis used and views of those constructing the typology. As such, these have been primarily descriptive, often being based on work in specific areas. Whether findings of this kind will generalise remains unclear. They can also be criticised for being heavily reliant on the background and experience of those constructing the typology, suggesting outputs that may be idiosyncratic and lacking in wider validity (McGuirk, 2018). This does not rule out the possibility of developing widely applicable descriptions, but current work in this area has not achieved this and should be seen as an initial step in developing understanding, based on observation, description and categorisation. Returns from this are though diminishing and multiplying descriptive typologies of this kind is a largely unproductive exercise.

One of the ways this work has been taken forward has been the use of formal analysis to develop profiles with known properties. These have largely drawn on various forms of multi-dimensional scaling (MDS) and related methods of analysis to generate profiles, with this method used to effectively profiling multiple areas (Wilson, Canter, Smith et al., 1996; Wilson, 2000; Wilson and Smith, 2000). Recent examples have included the development of profiles of those engaged in ERWT and terrorists motivated by other ideologies. ERWT has been a relatively neglected area of research, but there has been a recent growth of interest (Spaaij, 2010; Moskalenko and McCauley, 2020). Historically, the focus had typically been elsewhere, and following World War II, this was primarily on those motivated by left-wing ideology. Focus then moved to terrorism linked to the conflict over Palestine, and following the 9/11 attacks, trans-national groups motivated by religious ideology. The relative neglect of ERWT is surprising. Between 1990 and 2010, this was reported to be the most common form in terms of number of incidents (Gruenewald, Chermak and Freilich, 2013). Suggestions that this is a function of ERWT being a recent phenomenon are misplaced and there is a lengthy history of this kind of activity. The growth in information technology and digital communications though has clearly facilitated this and altered its presentation (Ravndal, 2018; Graham, 2021).

Changes in the presentation of violence here includes the growth of 'leaderless' and lone-actor attacks. This can be seen to reflect systematic changes in strategy and tactics. At a strategic level, this has allowed attacks to take place in the absence of apparent organisational structures or formal leadership. These have been largely replaced with the broadcasting of ideas and methods using information technology, which are widely disseminated in the hope of being taken up by sympathetic individuals. This has been observed to serve some important functions. It means that groups advocating political violence no longer require a formal presence or memberships, protecting them from legal liability. Using such methods is also a low-cost activity both financially and organisationally. At a tactical level, it also serves several functions. These include reducing the vulnerability of planned attacks to detection and prevention, reducing vulnerability to many traditional counter-terrorism methods (Kaplan, 1997).

Research into ERWT has identified profiles for both actors and methods. A study by Hewitt (2003) looked at this area of terrorism in the US, based on open-source data which included Federal Bureau of Investigation (FBI) annual reports. This involved a descriptive analysis of individual and group-based ideologically motivated actors. Work such as this has suggested a greater preponderance of lone-actor attacks and growing use of these 'leaderless' methods (Michael, 2012). Actors here appeared to have often come to adopt strongly held political views with little or no engagement with others, or where they do interact this often appeared to be primarily as a means to express their own idiosyncratic beliefs. They had typically developed political and ideological views by accessing increasingly extreme materials online, rather than participating in groups or organisations. Going on to act appeared to be the result of such growing individual motivation and the perception that this was supported by others, from online views that expressed views and attitudes that they felt were concordant. Here, there was generally little or no direction or formal control from others, beyond acting as an 'echo chamber' for ideas (Williams, 2024). Where a degree of organisation was observed in ERWT, this tended to be based on small cell tactics, rather than reliance on larger organisational structures.

Recent evidence looking at these lone actors (or the so-called 'lone wolf') more generally has reinforced the idea that the internet has a central role, providing a means of easier engagement and development of views (Alfano, Carter and Cheong, 2018). Lone actors though often appeared to become more focussed on their individual views, experiences and grievance than those who engaged with groups. Group membership here seems to generate norms that appear largely absent for lone actors. These individualised views can often be seen in the publication highly personal manifestos and ideologies that do not fit neatly with views of political groupings (Siggery, Hunt and Tzani, 2023). These often appear to anticipate increased and high levels of public acceptance because of publication. Lone actors may also spend large amounts of time accessing extremist material online, leading to a process that has been described as 'self-radicalisation' (Bates, 2012). This finding may be linked to elevated levels of social isolation and psychological disturbance.

Lone actors also appear more likely to pick single targets for attack but to inflict multiple casualties when doing so. In this respect showing a pattern commonly seen in other areas of violence such as school shootings (Gerard, Whitfield, Porter et al., 2016; Flannery, Dabkowski, McMaster et al., 2025). Commonly, these kinds of attack have involved shootings, particularly in the US, or the use of improvised explosive devices or attacks using motor vehicles. These have typically been directed towards soft targets, such as buildings associated with local or state administration or public events, rather than military or law enforcement targets. Attacks were also found to typically involve strangers, with the main aim apparently being to cause the maximum number of casualties. Lone-actor terrorists also seemed to be more likely to die during such attacks, with higher rates of being killed during the act by law enforcement staff.

A study by Gruenewald, Chermak and Freilich, (2013) looked at a sample of lone actor terrorism acts which occurred between 1990 and 2010, drawing on the US Extremist Crime Database (ECDB) (Freilich, Chermak, Belli et al., 2014). Data for 139 incidents were analysed, where at least one actor involved was identified as involved in ERWT. Far right was operationally defined here as involving antiglobal sentiments, suspicion of centralised authority and government, reverence for aspects of liberty (particularly firearms and taxation), commitment to conspiracy theories, seeing the threat as imminent and engagement in paramilitary activities and preparations. Within this study, mainstream Christian right-wing views were excluded. Lone actors were defined as those with no group membership at all stages and no evidence of external control or command. Given the small sample size involved, there is a need for caution around the findings from this study. However, it suggested some significant differences in the profiles of these lone actors. They appeared more likely to have a history of serious mental health problems, with 40% having a history of mental illness compared to 8% for group-based actors. They were also more likely to be living alone or living without family or intimate partners and were significantly more likely to use firearms, with 85% doing so compared to 40%. Targeting of more than one victim and being killed by law enforcement officers was also more common, 11% versus 3%. Lone actors also tended to be significantly older, with an average age of 35 compared to 27. They were significantly more likely to have served in a branch of the military, with 25% having such experience compared to 8%. Surprisingly perhaps, they also showed lower levels of parental divorce and curiously were also more likely to be based in the North East of the US and less likely to be in the West. The researchers went on to conduct a multivariate analysis of this data, deriving five predictor variables that effectively identified lone actors. These were: (1) prior military experience; (2) mental illness prior to the attack; (3) age; (4) alienation from their partner through divorce, separation or death; and (5) the attack having taken place in the post-9/11 period (Gruenewald, Chermak and Freilich, 2013).

Based on this study, the authors went on to reject the view, expressed previously, that efforts to profile this group are unlikely to be useful in counter terrorism terms (Barnes, 2012). This view had rested on several arguments, which included the view that single-actor attacks were very rare and often poorly planned and executed. It was also suggested that they would lack reliable indicators prior to the event, which fitted with other research findings that there was little in the way of psychological characteristics that usefully distinguished terrorists from the general populace. Such views have been associated with a stress on counter terrorism methods other than profiling, as being more effective approaches. This included a stress on areas such as community engagement, 'counter-radicalisation' work, improvements to physical security and the use of established detection and investigation methods. The point concerning the relatively low frequency of events is a universal problem for counter terrorism work, as indeed it often is for other areas of forensic practice. Lone actors though are not as unusual as had been suggested, with it being reported that of identified plots in the US, around four in ten had involved lone-actor attacks (Strom and Hickman, 2010; Strom, Hollywood and Pope, 2016). Indeed, this *modus operandi* appears to have grown in importance, with ideas that this is invariably inferior to group based or small cell-based attacks, requiring reconsideration. The clear tactical disadvantages associated with this form of terrorism being offset by its resistance to some traditional counter terrorism methods. Most obviously, concealment of plans is easier here. There are far fewer chances of information leaking through informants or penetration by state agencies. Finally, the continued growth of electronic communications and information technology has enabled much easier access to tactical and technical information and relatively secure communications. Materials that would in the past have been difficult and risky to obtain have become relatively easy to access. In part, because of this, lone actor attacks have often come to appear in terms of tactics and materials largely indistinguishable from small cell and directed attacks.

Despite the growing challenges though, recent counter-terrorism responses do seem to have had significant successes in addressing lone attacks. Differences have been apparent in the profiles of this type of attack, although further research is clearly needed in this area. There is a need to look for the best ways to profile lone actors, small cell and group-based actors. The strategies used to respond to attacks may also benefit from work, with three key elements suggested here. The first of these is the need for better working across multiple agencies, with too much work in this area still afflicted by isolated and often narrow siloed working. There is also a pressing and growing need to address the impact of the digital communications and information technology. Technology has clear roles in terms of motivation and networking. Finally, there is a need to improve the quality and accuracy of threat assessment work. As will be discussed later, efforts to address risk and uncertainty in this area have often been poorly grounded in the wider evidence base and poorly developed.

At a practice level, these suggest ways in which more effective prevention strategies might be developed. For example, lone actors appear significantly more likely to have contact with some agencies of the state, such as the military and mental health services. Efforts to draw on and integrate information from these agencies provides a way to increase the effectiveness of counter terrorism efforts. Development of what have been termed 'fusion centres' in the US is an example of systematic efforts to achieve this, integrating information for multiple agencies. Similarly, the development of Contest and Prevent policies in the UK has increasingly, if somewhat belatedly, focused more on this kind of approach to counterterrorism. The association between lone-actor terrorism and prior military service also suggests the value of links to the armed forces in general and military intelligence in particular. Links to services dealing with the most severe and enduring forms of mental health problems also appear especially important in this area. Ease of access to like-minded individuals, alongside the ease with which contradictory views may be avoided also seems to be an important driver and open that appears open to a range of responses aimed to counter these effects. Not least of the concerns here is the action of various opaque algorithms that may have negative effects on already distressed individuals. Use of psychological profiling seems to offer promise here for better addressing lone actor and other forms of terrorist attacks. There is also scope for work to better distinguish those likely to engage in politically motivated violent attacks from those violent offenders without political motives or interests.

Profiling behaviour in politically motivated hostage incidents

Profiling of hostage taking and the threats of hostage taking incidents, as an aspect of politically motivated violence, has also become a focus for research and practice development (Enders and Sandler, 1999). A key assumption here has been that these hostage incidents and threats will show identifiable patterns, as seen in other areas of profiling. An important active debate here has also concerned the application of rational decision-making models to this area (Clarke and Felson, 1993). These have been contrasted with other models that have stressed the role of psychological disorder (Post, 2007). The former approach has become increasingly dominant in research into terrorist hostage taking, with this coming to be seen as a strategy and tactic based largely on processes of rational decision making. Two main factors have acted to complicate this and influence the predictability of such events. The first of these concerns the tendency for hostage taking, as an aspect of politically motivated violence, to primarily be conducted by groups or small cells. This introduces an added layer of complexity when compared to much of the work on hostage incidents without any political motivations, with these involving group processes and sometimes inter-group processes between actors and those in a control or command relationship with them (Brandt and Sandler, 2009). In addition and in common with many other aspects of politically motivated violence, the planning of acts will typically be covert in nature, with many including active efforts to misdirect and deceive (Ammar, 2023).

Even so, research in this area has suggested a degree of predictability and the capacity to successfully model and profile the interactions involved (Martin, 1985; Wilson, 2000). The psychological concept of 'scripts' has been used here as a useful explanatory construct. In essence, this refers to psychological patterns which tend to shape activity in various situations (Abelson, 1981). These can be seen to form behavioural 'schemas,' or frameworks which help to organise and interpret information and guide how individuals interact with the environment. This construct fits well with ideas around behavioural consistency that underpin work on psychological profiling (Donald and Canter, 1992; Wilson, 2000; Canter and Allison, 2018).

In the case of novel situations, individuals will often approach these with no pre-existing scripts of this kind. Equally though, they do not approach these as a blank slate: being able to draw on the organisation of previous learning. As a result, it has been suggested that behaviour will frequently revert to prior experience, adopting accepted and well-learned social roles and rules. In turn, it has been suggested these will draw heavily on the way individuals interpret the social context (Donald and Canter, 1992). This idea has been applied to the study of terrorist hostage taking incidents, as a means of profiling patterns of behaviour and the qualities of incidents. The aim of this work has been to increase the predictability of these volatile high-risk events (Wilson and Smith, 2000). Politically motivated hostage incidents will often be novel events for perpetrators. For those who have previously engaged in hostage taking, access to their previous behaviours will be available to profilers. But for others, where there is no access to prior behaviours, the use of scripts has been put forward as a useful method for analysis.

Hostage incidents of this kind are also, very clearly, not random in nature. Generally, they will involve significant planning, with this often being careful and detailed in nature. As a result, it has been suggested that study of the planning and actions during incidents has considerable practical use (Brandt and Sandler, 2009). For example, a retrospective study undertaken in the UK undertook a content analysis of 160 cases, based on publicly available accounts (Wilson, 2000). Analysis here looked at the behaviours observed and the demands that were made by perpetrators during incidents. The reliability of these assessments was evaluated between independent raters, and this was reported to fall within the range of 0.88–0.9. This would suggest generally high levels of agreement between different assessors. Reflecting the historic period studied, the incidents were divided into Palestinian linked groups, other group actors and unaffiliated actors. Analysis looked at the ways in which control was established, how resources were controlled, the planning that seemed to be involved and apparent motivations of the perpetrators (Wilson, 2000). Formally, analysis of this was conducted using a statistical method called measurement system analysis (MSA). MSA is similar to many of the other formal methods of analysis used in profiling and is suited to analysis based on multiple dichotomous variables (Wilson, 2000; Fox and Farrington, 2018). A relatively high coefficient of contiguity of 0.95 has been reported for this analysis when applied to serial criminal behaviours such as rape (Wilson, Canter and Jack, 1997). Contiguity here refers to a claimed measure of 'closeness' or 'nearness' (Roussas, 1972). Here, a level of 0.95 would essentially be seen to suggest a high degree of such 'closeness' between the profile and the serial criminal behaviour.

For the analysis of behavioural styles seen during terrorist hostage incidents, this was found to be slightly lower at 0.91, with evidence of clear differences between the profiles for each of the groups studied (Wilson, 2000). In relation to the analysis of resources, this coefficient was reported to be 0.99, but the results for the analysis of demands were less clear with a result of 0.88. It is perhaps unsurprising that the demands made proved harder to accurately model than the behaviour and resources involved. Commonly though, the demands concerned the release of specific prisoners, the release of a general group of prisoners or demands for onward travel. These clearly give some insight into the grievances and the nature of the groups studied. Interpreting this is limited though by the fact that the demands made during incidents may not be consistent throughout and some of these may not reliably taken at face value.

Overall, the study concluded that there were clear patterns of behaviour seen during this kind of hostage incident and that, as with a range of criminal behaviours that had been studied, these could be usefully profiled (Wilson, 2000). Many of the methods employed in psychological profiling therefore appear relevant to this form of hostage taking, with potential for creating useful models for practice and research. Based on the data set that was analysed, these were reported to be stable within a 1- to 3-year time frame but beyond this evidence of significant change was reported. This appeared to be a function of politically motivated actors adapting and changing their approaches. This is perhaps unsurprising and can be seen as a reflection of the dynamic and changeable nature of these forms of violence. This does though provide an opportunity to develop more systematic understanding of change and continuities in this area, as part of the need for ongoing revision and adaption of profiles, to match these processes of change.

Evaluation

It has been suggested that the application of profiling to politically motivated violence generates distinct and often insuperable problems (McGuirk, 2018). The lack of any consistent 'psychopathology' in terrorist actors has been identified as a particular challenge, when compared to the profiling of most forms of crime. For some forms of this kind of violence, the issue of crime scene destruction is also relevant. Acts such as suicide bombings often involve severe damage, and as a result, it has been suggested that there may be little behavioural evidence left to analyse. Since much of the profiling of criminal behaviours has relied on detailed analyses of crime scenes, it is suggested this may critically limit the scope to gather useful information. The strongest form of this line of argument suggests that the common use of profiling, as a means to detect unknown offenders, is not relevant here. Even where this view is rejected, more prosaic concerns around the quality of data available in such incidents has been noted. Typically, this needs to be drawn from existing records and damaged scenes. As with many areas of forensic practice, this often involves missing, limited, poor quality or inaccurate information (Richardson, Schultz and Crawford, 2019). Using often flawed or inaccurate data as a basis for formal analysis risks masking these weaknesses.

Some of the criticisms raised of profiling here appear stronger than others. Concerns that profiling is based on estimates of likelihood rather than certainty appear misplaced. The observation is clearly true but the conclusion that accurate estimates of likelihood are not of value seems erroneous. Setting a benchmark of perfect accuracy would eliminate the use of forensic science. Some other concerns that have been aired seem to a significant extent based on historic notions of profiling and appear less compelling in relation to contemporary research and practice. This typically involves analysis of a broad range of available information and goes beyond crime scene analysis. Concerns around data quality and sampling though are certainly justified. These are also challenges that are hard to resolve, although efforts have been made here with the development of research databases allowing for access to larger numbers of cases. This has though been handicapped by the lack of access to classified data by independent researchers (Sageman, 2004, 2014; Monahan, 2016)

Information in the academic literature on such applications of profiling is limited, and this makes evaluation and efforts to look at the impacts on practice difficult. States have been reluctant to share data on how effective the methods are believed to be and independent evidence on efficacy is often lacking. There have been efforts here to develop more open forms of data that can be used for research, with the creation of databases in related areas such as the ECDB or the Global Terrorism Database (GTD) (LaFree and Dugan, 2007). These provide access to pooled data, greatly aiding efforts at evaluation work in this area. They do though have clear limitations and large amounts of data have remained inaccessible to those with the necessary skills to make best use of it.

Summary and conclusions

Psychological profiling in this context involves the use of scientific methods to aid in detection or management, through the prediction and description of likely characteristics. This is based on gathering of relevant information and generation of profiles. Use of such approaches in security and intelligence settings can be traced back to the work of the United States Office of Strategic Services (OSS) in the United States during World War II.

Profiling the various forms of politically motivated violence throws up unique challenges and challenges that are common to other areas of profiling. It involves rare events, which may include a very wide range of targets. Those engaged in these forms of violence may also be well resourced and motivated to provide active disinformation. Profiling has though been aided by exponential growth in the capacity to gather and process data. This has been somewhat double edged, with sheer volumes of data swamping existing systems of analysis. Various forms of 'data mining' have emerged from this, designed to match to known patterns or profiles in this data, or more controversially to trawl for unknown patterns or profiles assumed to exist. These approaches to profiling are likely to grow further, with developments in machine learning and artificial intelligence enabling the processing of more varied forms of data.

Profiling of individual psychological reactions has also become a part of layered security measures in settings targeted for attacks, such as ports and airports. In simple terms, these can be described as relying on 'body language,' typically focussed on indicators of stress and anxiety. Such applications of profiling have been criticised as being based on weak evidence and poorly founded assumptions. Despite being widely used, independent evaluation of their efficacy or utility of these methods is lacking.

Profiling of those engaged in, or likely to engage in, politically motivated violence in other areas has been limited. Development here has been a comparatively recent phenomenon and this seems to be linked to past research findings, which suggested a lack of distinguishing demographic or psychological characteristics. Recent work has questioned whether this still holds true, with a growth of the research into profiling and its wider application to terrorism and related areas. Drawing largely on statistical methods of analysis, this suggests differences in terms of the profiles of actors, methods used and behaviours during incidents. This work suggests that these methods have significant potential to improve practice and to be developed further.

The specialist area of terrorist hostage incidents has also been a focus for research and practice development. Work here has suggested a significant degree of predictability in behaviours and as a result the ability to develop useful profiles of incidents and perpetrators. This has suggested the presence of structures underlying these types of incidents that seem to be based on the rational decision making of perpetrators and those linked by command or control relationships. Methods of psychological profiling therefore appear relevant to this form of hostage taking, with the potential to develop effective models for practice and further research.

Evaluating the accuracy and utility of profiling in relation to politically motivated violence presents serious challenges. Much of the available data has been and continues to be inaccessible to those with the skills to best use it, whilst organisations holding data often lack the skills to undertake necessary research. Efforts have been made to addressed, through the development of open databases: such as the ECDB and GTD. These have sought to make more data available to researchers. This has been associated with significant advances in the quality of research and utility of work in this area. It cannot though address the large amounts of classified data which remains unavailable for high quality analysis.

References

Abelson, R. P. (1981). Psychological status of the script concept. *American Psychologist*, *36*(7), 715–729.

Ainsworth, P. (2001). *Offender Profiling and Crime Analysis.* London: Willan.

Alfano, M., Carter, J. A., and Cheong, M. (2018). Technological seduction and self-radicalization. *Journal of the American Philosophical Association*, *4*(3), 298–322.

Alison, L., Bennett, C., Mokros, A., and Ormrod, D. (2002). The personality paradox in offender profiling. A theoretical review of the processes involved in deriving background characteristics from crime scene actions. *Psychology, Public Policy and Law*, *8*, 115–135.

Alison, L. and Kebbell, M. (2006). Offender profiling: limits and potential. In M. Kebbell and G. Davies (Eds.), *Practical Psychology for Forensic Investigations and Prosecutions*. Chichester: John Wiley.

Alison, L. J., Smith, M. D., and Morgan, K. (2003). Interpreting the accuracy of offender profiles. *Psychology, Crime and Law, 9*(2), 185–195.

Ammar, J. (2023). Disinformation: the Jihadists' new religion. In R. Arcos, I. Chiru and C. Ivan (Eds.), *Routledge Handbook of Disinformation and National Security*. London: Routledge.

Archer, D., Lansley, C., and Garner, A. (2020). Keeping airports safe: the value of small talk. Available online https://e-space.mmu.ac.uk/625153/3/Chapter%2012%20-%20Arc her%20et%20al%20revised.pdf. Retrieved February 5, 2025.

Barnes, B. D. (2012). Confronting the one-man wolf pack: adapting law enforcement and prosecution responses to the threat of lone wolf terrorism. *Boston University Law Review, 92*, 1613–1662.

Basto-Pereira, M. and Farrington, D. P. (2020). Life-long conviction pathways and self-reported offending: towards a deeper comprehension of criminal career development. *British Journal of Criminology, 60*, 285–302.

Basu, N. (2021). Learning lessons from countering terrorism: the UK experience 2017–2020. *Cambridge Journal of Evidence-Based Policing, 5*, 134–145.

Bates, R. A. (2012). Dancing with wolves: today's lone wolf terrorists. *The Journal of Public and Professional Sociology, 4*(1), 1–14.

Bennell, C., Mugford, R., Ellingwood, H., and Woodhams, J. (2013). *Linking Crimes Using Behavioural Clues: Current Levels of Linking Accuracy and Strategies for Moving Forward*. Wiley Online Library. https://doi.org/10.1002/jip.1395

Bilalli, B., Abelló, A., Aluja-Banet, T., and Wrembel, R. (2018). Intelligent assistance for data pre-processing. *Computer Standards & Interfaces, 57*, 101–109.

Brandt, P. T. and Sandler, T. (2009). Hostage taking: understanding terrorism event dynamics. *Journal of Policy Modeling, 31*(5), 758–778.

Brussel, J. (1968). *Case Book of a Crime Psychiatrist*. New York: Bernard Geis.

Burgess, A. W., Baker, T., Greening, D., Hartman, C. R., Burgess, A. G., Douglas, J. E., and Halloran, R. (1997). Stalking behaviours within domestic violence. *Journal of Family Violence, 12*(4), 389–403.

Burr, E. M., Rahm-Knigge, R. L., and Conner, B. T. (2018). The differentiating role of state and trait hopelessness in suicidal ideation and suicide attempt. *Archives of Suicide Research, 22*(3), 510–517.

Burrell, A., Bull, R., and Bond, J. (2012). Linking personal robbery offences using offender behaviour. *Journal of Investigative Psychology and Offender Profiling, 9*, 201–222.

Canter, D. V. (1989). Offender profiles. *The Psychologist, 2*(1), 12–16.

Canter, D. V. (2010). Offender profiling. In J. M. Brown and Campbell, E. A. (Eds.), *The Cambridge Handbook of Forensic Psychology*. Cambridge: Cambridge University Press.

Canter, D. and Alison, L. (2018). *Profiling in Policy and Practice*. London: Routledge.

Chapman, R., Smith, L. L., and Bond, J. W. (2012). An investigation into the differentiating characteristics between car key burglars and regular burglars. *Journal of Forensic Sciences, 57*(4), 939–945.

Chermak, S. and Gruenewald, J. A. (2015). Laying a foundation for the criminological examination of right-wing, left-wing, and Al Qaeda-inspired extremism in the United States. *Terrorism and Political Violence, 27*(1), 133–159.

Christie, A. (1936). *The ABC Murders*. London: Collins Crime Club.

Clarke, R. V. and Felson, M. (Eds.) (1993). *Routine Activity and Rational Choice: Volume 5*. New York: Routledge.

Cochrane Effective Practice and Organization of Care Review Group. (2017). Data collection checklist. Retrieved from www.methods.cochrane.org/sites/methods.cochrane.org.bias/files/public/uploads/EPOC%20Data%20Collection%20Checklist.pdf

Conan Doyle, A. (2001/1897). *A study in scarlet*. Contributor Iain Sinclair (Ed.), London: Penguin Classics. First published 1897.

Copson, G. (1995). *Coals to Newcastle? Part 1: A Study of Offender Profiling*. London: Home Office.

Copson, G., Badcock, R., Boon, J., and Britton, P. (1997). Articulating a systematic approach to clinical crime profiling. *Criminal Behaviour and Mental Health*, *7*, 13–17.

Crenshaw, M. (1981). The causes of terrorism. *Comparative Politics*, *13*(4), 379–399.

Crenshaw, M. (2012). The causes of terrorism. In J. Horgan and Braddock, K. (Eds.), *Terrorism Studies: A Reader*. London: Routledge.

Crighton, D. A. (2021). Offender profiling. In D. A. Crighton and Towl, G. J. (Eds.), *Forensic Psychology* (3rd ed.). Chichester: Wiley.

Crighton, D. (2023). *Risk Assessment in Forensic Practice*. London: Routledge.

Çuhadar, Ç. E., Kaarbo, J., Kesgin, B., and Özkeçeci-Taner, B. (2020). Turkish leaders and their foreign policy decision-making style: a comparative and multi-method perspective. *Turkish Studies*, *22*(1), 1–27.

Davies, A., Wittebrood, K., and Jackson, J. L. (1998). *Predicting the Criminal Record of a Stranger Rapist*. Special Interest Series Paper 12. London: Home Office Policing and Reducing Crime Unit.

De Londras, F. and Tregidga, J. (2021). Rights, proportionality and process in EU counter-terrorism law-making. *International Journal of Constitutional Law*, *19*, 665–693.

Department of Homeland Security. (2011). *Screening of Passengers by Observation Techniques (SPOT) Program*. Washington: Department of Homeland Security.

Donald, I. and Canter, D. (1992). Intentionality and fatality during the King's Cross underground fire. *European Journal of Social Psychology*, *22*(3), 203–218.

Douglas, J., Burgess, A. W., Burgess, A. G., and Ressler, R. K. (2019). *Crime Classification Manual: A Standard System for Investigating and Classifying Violent Crime* (2nd ed.). San Francisco: Jossey-Bass.

Dowden, C., Bennell, C., and Bloomfield, S. (2007). Advances in offender profiling: a systematic review of the profiling literature published over the past three decades. *Journal of Police and Criminal Psychology*, *22*(1), 44–56.

Ekman, P. and Friesen, W. V. (2003). *Unmasking the Face: A Guide to Recognizing Emotions from Facial Clues*. Los Altos: Malor Books.

Enders, W. and Sandler, T. (1999). Transnational terrorism in the post–cold war era. *International Studies Quarterly*, *43*(1), 145–167.

Farrington, D. P., Coid, J. W., Harnett, L. M., Jolliffe, D., Soteriou, N., Turner, R. E., and West, D. J. (2006). *Criminal careers up to age 50 and life success up to age 48: new findings from the Cambridge Study in Delinquent Development* (2nd ed.). Home Office Research Study 299. London: Home Office.

Flannery, D. J., Dabkowski, E., McMaster, R., Ogonek, M., and Deo, V. (2025). Gun violence and its influence on school safety and security. In N. D. Thomson (Ed.), *Handbook of Gun Violence*. London: Academic Press.

Forer, B. (1949). The fallacy of personal validation: a classroom demonstration of gullibility. *Journal of Abnormal and Social Psychology*, *44*, 118–123.

Fox, B. and Farrington, D. P. (2012). Creating burglary profiles using latent class analysis: new approach to offender profiling *Criminal Justice and Behavior, 39*(12), 1582–1611.

Fox, B. and Farrington, D. P. (2018). What have we learned from offender profiling? A systematic review and meta-analysis of 40 years of research. *Psychological Bulletin, 144*(12), 1247–1274.

Fox, B., Farrington, D. P., Kapardis, A., and Hambly, O. C. (2020). *Evidence-Based Offender Profiling.* London: Routledge.

Freilich, J. D., Chermak, S. M., Belli, R., Gruenewald, J., and Parkin, W. S. (2014). Introducing the United States Extremist Crime Database (ECDB). *Terrorism and Political Violence, 26*, 372–384.

Fujita, G., Watanabe, K., Yokota, K., Kuraishi, H., Suzuki, M., Wachi, T., and Kuraishi, H. (2013). Multivariate models for behavioral offender profiling of Japanese homicide. *Criminal Justice and Behavior, 40*(2), 214–227.

Galeotti, M. (2016). Hybrid, ambiguous, and non-linear? How new is Russia's 'new way of war'? *Small Wars & Insurgencies, 27*(2), 282–301.

Gerard, F. J., Whitfield, K. C., Porter, L. E., and Browne, K. D. (2016). Offender and offence characteristics of school shooting incidents. *Journal of Investigative Psychology and Offender Profiling, 13*(1), 22–38.

Gill, P. and Corner, E. (2013). Disaggregating terrorist offenders: implications for research and practice. *Criminology & Public Policy, 12*, 93–101.

Gill, P., Horgan, J., and Deckert, P. (2014). Bombing alone: tracing the motivations and antecedent behaviors of lone-actor terrorists. *Journal of Forensic Sciences, 59*(2), 425–435.

Gladwell, M. (2007). Dangerous Minds criminal profiling made easy. The New Yorker, *November 12.* www.newyorker.com/magazine/2007/11/12/dangerous-minds

Graham, A. (2021). Explaining white supremacy and domestic terrorism. In M. Haner and Sloan, M. M. (Eds.), *Theories of Terrorism Contemporary Perspectives.* New York: Routledge.

Gruenewald, J., Chermak, S., and Freilich, J. D. (2013). Distinguishing "loner" attacks from other domestic extremist violence: a comparison of far-right homicide incident and offender characteristics. *Criminology & Public Policy, 12*(1), 65–91.

Gudjonsson, G. H. and Copson, G. (1997). The role of the expert in criminal investigation. In J. L. Jackson and Bekerian, D. A. (Eds.), *Offender Profiling: Theory, Research and Practice.* Chichester: Wiley.

Han, J., Kamber, M., and Pei, J. (2012). *Data Mining: Concepts and Techniques.* Waltham: Morgan Kaufmann Publishers.

Harcourt, B. E. (2003). The shaping of chance: actuarial models and criminal profiling at the turn of the twenty-first century. *University of Chicago Law Review , 70*, 105–134.

Harcourt, B. E. (2004). Rethinking racial profiling: a critique of the economics, civil liberties, and constitutional literature, and of criminal profiling more generally. *University of Chicago Law Review , 71*, 1275–1387.

Hardie, B. (2020). *Studying Situational Interaction: Explaining Behaviour by Analysing Person-Environment Convergence.* London: Springer Nature.

Hewitt, C. (2003). *Understanding Terrorism in America* (1st ed.). London: Routledge.

Hilbert, M. and López, P. (2011). The world's technological capacity to store, communicate, and compute information. *Science, 332*(6025), 60–65.

Home Office. (2025). Independent report. Prevent Learning Review: Axel Muganwa Rudakubana (accessible) Published 5 February 2025. London: Home Office. Available online www.gov.uk/government/publications/prevent-learning-review-southport-attack/prevent-learning-review-axel-muganwa-rudakubana-accessible#detailed-timeline-with-learning-outcomes. Accessed February 5, 2025.

House, J. C. (1997). Towards a practical application of offender profiling: the RNC's criminal suspect prioritization system. In J. L. Jackson and Bekerian, D. A. (Eds.), *Offender Profiling: Theory, Research and Practice*. Chichester: Wiley.

Jackson, L. and Bekerian, D. A. (Eds.) (1997). *Offender Profiling Theory Research and Practice*. Chichester: John Wiley.

Jackson, R. (2008). The ghosts of state terror: knowledge, politics and terrorism studies. *Critical Studies on Terrorism, 1*(3), 377–392.

Jaspersen, J. G. and Montibeller, G. (2020). On the learning patterns and adaptive behavior of terrorist organizations. *European Journal of Operational Research, 282*(1), 221–234.

Jaworska, N. and Chupetlovska-Anastasova, A. (2009). A review of multidimensional scaling (MDS) and its utility in various psychological domains. *Tutorials in Quantitative Methods for Psychology, 5*(1), 1–10.

Jupp, J. and Garrod, M. (2022). Legacies of the troubles: the links between organized crime and terrorism in Northern Ireland. *Studies in Conflict & Terrorism, 45*(5–6), 389–428.

Kaplan, J. (1997). Leaderless resistance. *Terrorism and Political Violence, 9*(3), 80–95.

Kocsis, R. N. (1999). Criminal profiling of crime scene behaviors in Australian sexual murders. *Australian Police Journal, 53*, 113–116.

Kocsis, R. N. (2003). Criminal psychological profiling: an outcome and process study. *Law and Human Behaviour, 14*, 215–233.

Kocsis, R. N. (2006). *Criminal Profiling International Theory, Research, and Practice*. Totowa: Humana Press.

LaFree, G. and Dugan, L. (2007). Introducing the global terrorism database. *Terrorism and Political Violence, 19*(2), 181–204.

Lake, J. E. (2004). *CRS Report for Congress. Border and Transportation Security: Overview of Congressional Issues. RL32705, O. C.* Washington, DC: Library of Congress.

Lester, D., Yang, B., and Lindsay, M. (2004). Suicide bombers: are psychological profiles possible? *Studies in Conflict & Terrorism, 27*(4), 283–295.

Lively, J. (1981). The Europe of the enlightenment. *History of European Ideas, 1*(2), 91–102.

López Werner, E. A. (2024). Typology of terrorist profiling using centrality metrics: hinge figures, influential operatives and trusted assets. *Terrorism and Political Violence*, 1–16. https://doi.org/10.1080/09546553.2024.2342866

Luban, D. (2014). *Torture, Power, and Law*. Cambridge: Cambridge University Press.

Mahesh, B. (2020). Machine learning algorithms- a review. *International Journal of Science and Research, 9*(1), 381–386.

Marsden, S. V., and Schmid, A. P. (2011). Typologies of terrorism and political violence. In A. Schmid (Ed.),. *The Routledge Handbook of Terrorism Research*. London: Routledge.

Martin, L. J. (1985). The media's role in international terrorism. *Terrorism, 8*(2), 127–146.

McGuirk, N. (2021). *Terrorist pProfiling and lLaw eEnforcement: Detection, pPrevention, dDeterrence*. London: Routledge.

McGuirk, N. K. (2018). An evaluation of the theory and the practice of terrorist profiling in the identification of terrorist characteristics. Unpublished PhD dissertation University of Birmingham, UK.

Meehl, P. E. (1956). Wanted – aA Ggood Ccookbook. *American Psychologist,, 11* (6), 263–272.

Melnyk, T., Bennell, C., Gauthier, D. J., and Gauthier, D. (2011). Another look at across-crime similarity coefficients for use in behavioural linkage analysis: Aan attempt to replicate Woodhams, Grant, and Price (2007). *Psychology, Crime and Law,, 17*, 359–380.

Meyer, D. L. (2010). The SPOT program: hHello racial profiling, goodbye fourth amendment. *University of Maryland Law Journal Race, Religion, Gender and Class, 10*, 289–339.

Michael, G. (2012). Leaderless rResistance: tThe nNew fFace of Tterrorism. *Defence Studies, 12*(2), 257–282.

Ministry of Justice. (2024). *Accredited oOfficial sStatistics Criminal Justice Statistics qQuarterly: December 2023*. London: OGL.

Mischel, W. (1979). On the interface of cognition and personality: bBeyond the person–situation debate. *American Psychologist, 34*(9), 740–754.

Mischel, W., Shoda, Y., and Ayduk, O. (2007). *Introduction to Personality: Toward an Integrative Science of the Person* (8th ed.). New York: Wiley.

Mokros, A., and Alison, L. (2002). Is profiling possible? Testing the predicted homology of crime scene actions and background characteristics in a sample of rapists. *Legal and Criminological Psychology,, 7*, 25–43.

Monahan, J. (2016). The individual risk assessment of terrorism: rRecent developments. In G. LaFree and J. D. Freilich (Eds.),. *The hHandbook of the cCriminology of tTerrorism*. New York: John Wiley.

Monahan, J., and Skeem, J. L. (2016). Risk assessment in criminal sentencing. *Annual Review of Clinical Psychology, 12*(1), 489–513.

Moskalenko, S., and McCauley, C. (2020). *Radicalization to tTerrorism: What eEveryone nNeeds to kKnow*. New York: Oxford University Press.

Müller, F., and& Richter, T. (2008). Report on the Bundesverfassungsgericht's (Federal Constitutional Court) Jurisprudence in 2005/2006. *German Law Journal, 9*(2), 161–193.

Muradov, I. (2022). The Russian hybrid warfare: the cases of Ukraine and Georgia. *Defence Studies, 22*(2), 168–191.

Murray, J., Farrington, D. P., and Eisner, M. (2009). Drawing conclusion about causes from systematic reviews of risk factors: tThe Cambridge qQuality Cchecklists. *Journal of Experimental Criminology,, 5*, 1–23.

Nesser, P. (2006). Structures of jihadist terrorist cells in the UK and Europe. In Proceedings of the *Joint* FFI/King's *College Conference* on "the *Changing Faces* of *Jihadism," April 2006*. London: Kings College.

Nesser, P. (2018). *Islamist Terrorism in Europe*. Oxford: Oxford University Press.

Palermo, G. B. and Kocsis, R. N. (2005). *Offender Profiling: An Introduction to the Sociopsychological Analysis of Violent Crime*. Springfield: Charles C Thomas Publisher.

Petherick, W. (2005). *Serial Crime: Theoretical and Practical Issues in Behavioral Profiling*. Burlington: Academic Press.

Pinizzotto, A. J. and Finkel, N. J. (1990). Criminal personality profiling an outcome and process study. *Law and Human Behavior, 14*(3), 215–233.

Post, J. M. (Ed.) (2003). *The Psychological Assessment of Political Leaders: With Profiles of Saddam Hussein and Bill Clinton*. Detroit: University of Michigan Press.

Post, J. M. (2007). *The Mind of the Terrorist: The Psychology of Terrorism from the IRA to al-Qaeda*. New York: Palgrave Macmillan.

Proulx, J., Aubut, J., Perron, L., and McKibben, A. (1994). Troubles de la personalité et viol: Implications théoriques et cliniques [Personality disorders and violence: Theoretical and clinical implications]. *Criminologie, 27*, 33–53.

Proulx, J., St-Yves, M., Guay, J. P., and Ouimet, M. (1999). Les aggresseurs sexuels de femmes: Scénarios délictuels et troubles de la personalitié [Sexual aggressors of women: Offence scenarios and personality disorders]. In J. Proulx, Cusson, M., and Ouimet, M. (Eds.), *Les Violences Criminelles*. Quebec: Les Presses de L'Université Laval.

Ramsay, J. O. (1980). Some small sample results for maximum likelihood estimation in multidimensional scaling. *Psychometrika, 45*(1), 139–144.

Ravndal, J. A. (2018). Explaining right-wing terrorism and violence in Western Europe: grievances, opportunities and polarisation. *European Journal of Political Research, 57*(4), 845–866.

Ravich, T. M. (2007). Is airline passenger profiling necessary? *University of Miami Law Review, 62*, 1–53.

Ressler, R. K., Burgess, A. W., Douglas, J. E., Hartman, C. R., and D'Agostino, R. B. (1986). Sexual killers and their victims: identifying patterns through crime scene analysis. *Journal of Interpersonal Violence, 1*, 288–308.

Ressler, R. K., Douglas, J. E., Groth, N. A., and Burgess, A. W. (1980). Offender profiles: a multidisciplinary approach. *FBI Law Enforcement Bulletin, 49*, 16–20.

Richardson, R., Schultz, J. M., and Crawford, K. (2019). Dirty data, bad predictions: how civil rights violations impact police data, predictive policing systems, and justice. *New York University Law Review, 94*, 193–233.

Roussas, G. G. (1972). *Contiguity of Probability Measures: Some Applications in Statistics.* Cambridge: Cambridge University Press.

Sageman, M. (2004). *Understanding Terror Networks.* Philadelphia: University of Pennsylvania Press.

Sageman, M. (2014). The stagnation in terrorism research. *Terrorism and Political Violence, 26*(4), 565–580.

Saini, J. K. and Bansal, D. (2024). Computational techniques to counter terrorism: a systematic survey. *Multimedia Tools and Applications, 83*(1), 1189–1214.

Sarma, K. M., Carthy, S. L., and Cox, K. M. (2022). Mental disorder, psychological problems and terrorist behaviour: a systematic review and meta-analysis. *Campbell Systematic Reviews, 18*(3), e1268.

Shultz, R. (1978). Conceptualizing political terrorism: a typology. *Journal of International Affairs, 32*(1), 7–15.

Siggery, A., Hunt, D., and Tzani, C. (2023). Language profile of lone actor terrorist manifestos: a mixed methods analysis. *Behavioral Sciences of Terrorism and Political Aggression, 15*(3), 390–408.

Siggins, P. (2002). *Racial Profiling in the Age of Terrorism.* Santa Clara: Santa Clara University. www.scu.edu/ethics/focus-areas/more-focus-areas/resources/racial-profiling-in-an-age-of-terrorism/

Simcox, R. and Dyer, E. (2013). *Al-Qaeda in the United States.* London: The Henry Jackson Society.

Skinner, G. C. M., Farrington, D. P., and Shepherd, J. P. (2020). Offender trajectories, health and hospital admissions: relationships and risk factors in the longitudinal Cambridge study in delinquent development. *Journal of the Royal Society of Medicine, 113*, 110–118.

Slater, C., Woodhams, J., and Hamilton-Giachritsis, C. (2015). Testing the assumptions of crime linkage with stranger sex offenses: a more ecologically-valid study. *Journal of Police and Criminal Psychology, 30*, 261–273.

Smith, B. L., Damphousse, K. R., and Paxton, R. (2006). *Pre-Incident Indicators of Terrorist Incidents: The Identification of Behavioral, Geographic and Temporal Patterns of Preparatory Conduct*. Fayetteville: University of Arkansas.

Snook, B., Eastwood, J., Gendreau, P., Goggin, C., and Cullen, R. M. (2007). Taking stock of criminal profiling: a narrative review and meta-analysis. *Criminal Justice and Behavior*, *34*(4), 437–453.

Spaaij, R. (2010). The enigma of lone wolf terrorism: an assessment. *Studies in Conflict & Terrorism*, *33*(9), 854–870.

Strom, K. J. and Hickman, M. J. (2010). Unanalyzed evidence in law-enforcement agencies: a national examination of forensic processing in police departments. *Criminology & Public Policy*, *9*(2), 381–404.

Strom, K. J., Hollywood, J. S., and Pope, M. W. (2016). Terrorist plots the United States: what we have really faced, and how we might best defend against it. In G. LaFree and J. D. Freilich (Eds.), *The Handbook of the Criminology of Terrorism*. Chichester: John Wiley and Sons.

Tesón, F. R. (2005). Liberal security. In R. A. Wilson (Ed.), *Human Rights in the "War on Terror."* Cambridge: Cambridge University Press.

Teten, H. D. (1989). Offender profiling. In W. G. Bailey (Ed.), *The Encyclopaedia of Police Science*. New York: Garland.

West, A. and Alison, L. (2006). Conclusions: personal reflections on the last decade. In L. Alison (Ed.), *The Forensic Psychologists Casebook: Psychological Profiling and Criminal Investigation*. Cullompton: Willan.

Whitaker, R. (2010). Behavioural profiling in Israeli aviation security as a tool for social control. In E. Zureik, Lyon, D., and Abu-Laban, Y. (Eds.), *Surveillance and Control in Israel/Palestine*. London: Routledge.

Williams, T. J. V. (2024). Hiding in plain sight: An exploration into online radicalisation and social media safeguarding. Unpublished PhD thesis, University of Huddersfield.

Wilson, M. A. (2000). Toward a model of terrorist behavior in hostage-taking incidents. *Journal of Conflict Resolution*, *44*(4), 403–424.

Wilson, M. A., Canter, D., and Jack, K. (1997). *The Psychology of Rape Investigation: A Study in Police Decision Making, Final Report*. Swindon: ESRC.

Wilson, M., Canter, D., Smith, A., and Drillings, M. (1996). *Modelling Terrorist Behavior: Developing Investigative Decision Making Through the Analysis of Empirical Databases. ARI Research Note 96-37*. Virginia: United States Army Research Institute for the Behavioral and Social Sciences.

Wilson, M. and Smith, A. (2000). Rules and roles in terrorist hostage taking. In D. Canter and Alison, L. (Eds.), *The Social Psychology of Crime*. London: Routledge.

Woodhams, J., Davies, K., Galambos, S., and Webb, M. (2021). A descriptive analysis of the temporal and geographical proximities seen within UK series of sex offenses. *Journal of Police and Criminal Psychology*, *36*(4), 706–715.

Xu, X. (2021). To repress or to co-opt? Authoritarian control in the age of digital surveillance. *American Journal of Political Science*, *65*(2), 309–325.

Yokota, K., Watanabe, K., Wachi, T., Otsuka, Y., Hirama, K., and Fujita, G. (2017). Crime linkage of sex offences in Japan by multiple correspondence analysis. *Journal of Investigative Psychology and Offender Profiling*, *14*, 109–119.

Zarsky, T. Z. (2011). Governmental data mining and its alternatives. *Penn State Law Review*, *116*, 285–330.

Zhang, C. and Morris, C. (2023). Borders, bordering and sovereignty in digital space. *Territory, Politics, Governance*, *11*(6), 1051–1058.

6 Risk, ambiguity, uncertainty and intractability

Questions of how to deal with risk, ambiguity, uncertainty and intractability in politically motivated violence are important areas, all of which are the subject of live debate in forensic practice. These rest on a number of fundamental concepts and assumptions, and a basic understanding of these is necessary to understanding of this area. Understanding though often appears severely limited across forensic practice, where the issues involved in ambiguity, intractability and uncertainty have been largely neglected or simply conflated with risk. This seems linked to a great deal of poor and misguided practice, resting on weak or even implausible assumptions and ideas. Better understanding of the key concepts and essential distinctions here is important to critically reviewing practice in this area, as well as giving a firmer foundation for looking at ways in which practice may be improved and developed.

Key concepts

The term 'risk' is used in varied ways across different subject areas and the term itself remains somewhat controversial, with no universally agreed definition. Alternative and at times conflicting uses of the term risk have been suggested, with some of these being more plausible than others. One of the most important and influential attempts to define risk was set out in an extended essay just over a century ago (Knight, 1921) although this has had limited effects on current forensic practice. Frank Knight was an economist at the University of Chicago, and in his essay, he set out to address the linked areas of risk and profit, as they were understood at that time. The review though went well beyond this narrow economic focus, with a consideration of the scientific and philosophical foundations of the area. This analysis was clearly based on the assumption that risk needed to be firmly grounded in scientific exploration and hence the application of scientific method. Much of Knight's thinking here was strongly influenced by the ideas of French philosopher and mathematician René Descartes (Descartes, 1644/2006). This included acceptance of the fundamental importance of inferences, in turn based primarily on prior experience of similar situations. Both our perceptions and inferences though will inevitably be imperfect. These imperfections will in turn

DOI: 10.4324/9781003429579-6

be compounded by our having limited knowledge about the likely results of our actions, as well as our inability to carry out any planned actions exactly as intended (Knight, 1921).

Drawing on these assumptions, Knight took on the challenges involved in dealing effectively with the world. This is highly complex and the challenges faced are considerable, requiring the ability to cope with a practically infinite number of 'objects' in the world. This needs to be done within limited and constrained mental capacity. This challenge was though made more manageable, Knight argued, because of the consistency of properties for many of these 'objects.' These would often remain quite constant across different contexts and under different conditions. Even where these 'objects' did change, he argued this would typically be in predictable ways. Knight went on to hypothesise that quantitative aspects of the properties of 'objects,' along with our ability to deal with these, was fundamental to coping with the complexity involved. In essence, many of the 'objects' perceived in the world would differ in degree but not in kind, suggesting that significant properties would often be common to large groups of 'objects.' This makes the challenge of dealing with the world more manageable within the limited cognitive resources available.

At a fundamental level, Knight assumed that because of human cognitive limitations, many areas of the world may not in fact be knowable to us. He was though quite optimistic in his view of this assumption, suggesting that its practical effect would be limited. This optimism rested in turn on an assumption that the extent of what may be 'knowable' to us would be likely to greatly exceed our actual powers of observation. Based largely on this analysis, Knight suggested that in many areas of life, there would always be a need to rely on correlational and probabilistic judgements. These and the judgements based on them would allow for an 'intelligent ordering' of things, with this being based on contingencies that would not otherwise be observable. He argued that this was likely to be an ongoing issue within the social sciences, in contrast to the physical sciences which had often developed based on directly observable contingencies. Within the areas of interest to the social sciences, analysis often concerned complex systems, where there was a limited ability to control the variables involved.

In dealing with this challenge, Knight suggested that concepts of probability were central to an adequate understanding of risk, distinguishing between three different forms of this. The first of these involved what is often called *a priori* probability, which refers to events and distributions of events that can be logically determined in advance. It is this form of probability which tends to dominate introductory textbooks on statistics, which typically involve examples of estimating the probability of events such as rolling dice or the outcomes of spinning a roulette wheel. In examples of this kind, the events are typically independent, although this is not necessary. This means that one event does not affect another, so one spin on a roulette wheel would not influence the outcome for a subsequent spin. Each spin of the wheel, assuming it is a fair wheel, will have an equal probability of landing on any number. Probability of the outcomes can then can be logically or axiomatically determined. Taking a simpler example, the chance of throwing a six, using a fair six-sided die, can be logically defined as being one in six. The distribution of likely outcomes can also be similarly defined. Ambiguity describes cases where the probabilities involved are calculable but are not known. It would therefore include cases involving dice but where these are biased or loaded in an undisclosed manner, or slot machines with undisclosed bias.

Knight distinguished this *a priori* kind of probability from relative frequency conceptions of probability. Relative frequency probability involves the likelihood of events that cannot be logically or axiomatically determined in advance, in the way outlined above. This form of probability has a much wider range of application than *a priori* probability and as a result has been widely used in trying to deal with a range of applied problems. It has also formed a basis for scientific study and experimentation in a number of fields. This form of probability is concerned with the relative frequency of events that is seen in samples that are felt to be relevant. An illustrative example of this would be estimating the likelihood that individual in a population is a particular height. Such information cannot be logically derived as an *a priori* probability and similarly the population distribution here is not one that can be logically derived. Probability in this example can though be based on estimates, in turn drawn from a sample of observations from a relevant population. By using a large enough sample, it is then possible to calculate a distribution of heights and to estimate the proportion of the population who are a given height.

Where *a priori* probabilities can be calculated this kind of estimation, based on relative frequencies is unnecessary. This kind of knowledge though turns out to be the exception, largely limited to kind of examples drawn on by early developers of statistics and seen in introductory texts on statistics. Using this distinction, Knight went on to argue that the difference between these two approaches to probability was based primarily on how accurately the classification instances could be grouped together. For relative frequency estimates of probability, the aim would then be to develop more precise sub-groups, with greater levels of homogeneity. In relation to the question of the risk of given outcomes, this method could be used to yield more precise estimates, allowing closer approximation of the 'true' probability of these. These 'true' levels though would be one of the areas that would remain unknowable to us, being open only to potentially ever closer and more accurate approximations.

Perhaps the most influential aspect of Knight's work though was the critical distinction he made between 'risk' and 'uncertainty,' a distinction that was independently made by John Maynard Keynes in his work on probability (Keynes, 1921). This distinction saw risk as a measurable quality of the probability of something happening: either in terms of an *a priori* probability or a relative frequency estimate of the probability. So, in rolling a fair die, the probability of rolling a six would be 1/6 and in the example of height, the probability of being 70 inches tall might be 1/50. Crucially, this definition of risk depends on being able to define the 'state space,' which essentially refers to the ability to set out all the possible states of the system (Chopin and Papaspiliopoulos, 2020). Simple examples of this include physical systems, such as those involving simple pendulums, electrical circuits or signal detection. By contrast, Knight suggested that uncertainty concerned those situations where this is not possible and as such this concerned the unmeasurable random part of likelihood (Knight, 1921; Keynes, 1921). Knight therefore argued that uncertainty involved situations where there was no way to determine axiomatically or otherwise estimate probability empirically.

Following on from this conclusion, the flux involved in many situations is associated with a significant degree of uncertainty and Knight suggested, that this reflected a genuine indeterminacy, change and discontinuity. As a result, he suggested that for some situations a resolution to this lay in grouping and the application of probabilistic reasoning: converting such problems, wherever possible, into relative frequency probability distributions. An archetypal economic example of this is the use of insurance as a means of dealing with risk. This involves grouping data in commercially useful ways, alongside the use legal provisions to limit cover. However, Knight clearly recognised that this was not always a feasible approach and as a result suggested that, for many situations, conditions of uncertainty would inevitably apply. This kind of problem would, he argued, continue to require reliance on intuitive human judgements. Knight viewed this as a weak form of classification but the best that could be achieved under such conditions.

Intractability has also been used in different ways. Here, the term is used to refer to those problems where the all the possible future states and consequences of all actions can be known, all the probabilities are known but an optimal course of action cannot be determined, either by computers or by people (Gigerenzer, 2024). This includes a surprising number of real-world examples and chess is often used as an example of this. However, there are many other real-world examples. Put very simply, this follows from exponential growth in the number of calculations needed.

Risk assessment

Risk assessment can be defined as a process of using 'risk factors' to estimate the likelihood of an outcome occurring in a population (Kraemer, Kazdin, Offord et al., 1997; Kraemer, Stice, Kazdin et al., 2001). These risk factors though have often been poorly defined in forensic practice, with the term often used to refer to anything that may increase the likelihood of a vaguely defined outcome or event. The idea of 'protective factors' has also been suggested, with these often being similarly defined, encompassing anything that decreases likelihood. This distinction can be criticised as being largely redundant, with many 'protective' factors being the converse of 'risk' factors. So, for example, a risk factor may be the presence of 'unstable' family relationships and a protective factor may be the presence of 'stable' family relationships. It has also become common across forensic practice to refer to 'static' and 'dynamic' factors. This terminology has a long history of use, where static factors have been seen as unchanging or unchangeable, in contrast to dynamic factors which are seen as changing or changeable.

The definition suggested by Kraemer and colleagues provides a sound starting point. It is though not adequate and much of current forensic practice does not fit well with this, generating significant problems. The suggested distinction between 'static' and 'dynamic' factors is also especially problematic. This distinction was considered in detail by Knight (1921) and rejected. Knight recognised this as an already established distinction in the area of risk but was critical of the simple dichotomy, seeing it as both misleading and unhelpful. He argued that there was no dichotomy but generally a continuum of progressive change, noting that it was often not possible to draw sharp and significant distinctions between progressive change and fluctuations within groups (Knight, 1921). This may be illustrated with reference to some areas of forensic practice, where this terminology of 'static' and 'dynamic' has been used. For example, the idea that 'static factors' can be defined as those which cannot be changed or influenced and are based on historical events or characteristics. Examples given of this have included gender, age, offending history and previous convictions (National Offender Management Service, 2016). At least some of these examples though appear open to varying degrees of influence and change, as suggested by Knight.

The approach taken here is to work from better developed terminology, which in turn drew on work largely from public health research and practice (Kraemer, Kazdin, Offord et al., 1997; Kraemer, Stice, Kazdin et al., 2001). This involves a clear distinction between risk correlates and risk factors. A risk correlate here is defined as something that is systematically related to a given outcome of interest but that has not been shown to precede it. So these would include concomitants that accompany something, as well as outcomes that follow something. Concomitants can in turn be further distinguished as fixed or variable markers. Fixed risk markers being unchangeable characteristics, whilst variable risk markers refer to things that do change, and may change continuously. Risk factors are distinguished from these correlates as being something that can be shown to be systematically related to an outcome or event of interest but that can also be shown to precede it.

Risk factors can be further distinguished into those which are variable and those which are causal. Variable risk factor is used here to refer to things that may be altered and a concrete example of this would be an individual's level of educational attainment. This can of course be changed, through a process of education, which may in turn be associated with a reduced likelihood of a subsequent event. The term causal risk factor though is restricted to variable risk factors where manipulation can be demonstrated to change the outcome (Coid, Kallis, Doyle et al., 2015). The most frequently suggested example of such a causal risk factor in forensic practice is perhaps that of substance use.

Risk management, resilience and robustness

Risk management has also been used in differing ways. In the wider field of risk, this term has generally been used to refer to the broad process of dealing with questions of risk. This would include risk analysis, assessment, treatment, overall decisions around the acceptability of risks and evaluation of the processes of dealing with risk. As such, this captures a full range of activities that may be involved in trying to deal with a defined risk. Use of this term in forensic practice has commonly been quite different from this, typically being limited to the area of risk treatment, or efforts to reduce the likelihood and mitigate the effects of occurrence. This parochial terminology has some negative effects, most seriously perhaps in unhelpfully stressing the primary objective of risk management as risk reduction. This is an unwarranted simplification of the term, which neglects the importance of developing understanding and striking appropriate balances between differing and competing interests. Drawing on forensic practice for illustrative examples here, such a focus would suggest undesirable and unbalanced approaches, such as never giving parole to serious offenders, or always mandating constant observation with any patient expressing suicidal ideas. In relation to terrorism, the immediate aftermath of the 9/11 attacks on the US is illustrative. On that day the risks of further attacks were initially managed by, amongst others actions, grounding all commercial flights. This was a highly effective 'risk treatment' in the immediate aftermath of attacks but not a desirable one in the longer term, hence the decision to resume flights as part of a wider risk management strategy. The easiest way to reduce risks is often simply not to undertake activities which involve uncertainty. Yet often, this will not be possible, or if it is possible, may be clearly undesirable. Life from birth onwards carries significant and varied risks and risk management is better understood as the processes involved in striking appropriate balances across these.

The terms risk resilience and risk robustness have rarely been seen in forensic practice but are common in the wider field of risk. In relation to the area of terrorism and related areas of politically motivated violence, both have considerable relevance and wide application. Again these terms have been used in various ways. Here the term risk robustness is used to refer to the ability to cope with anticipated deviations from normal functioning. So, for example, how well a system of ensuring the security of a setting such as an airport can deal with an outbreak of flu and associated staff absences. Risk resilience, by contrast, is used to refer to the ability to withstand unexpected events or surprises. An example here might be the ability of a system or setting to withstand some form of unanticipated attack (Moffitt, Stranlund and Field, 2005). Notably, several recent trends appear to act in ways that may significantly reduce resilience and robustness (van Der Vegt, Essens, Wahlström et al., 2015). For example, efforts to improve 'efficiency' of prisons or hospitals by ensuring very high levels of bed occupancy and low levels of staffing will significantly reduce risk robustness and resilience. This is because built in 'redundancy' that might be used to deal with demands created by anticipated and unanticipated deviations from normal conditions has been progressively removed.

Current practice in risk assessment

Two approaches to 'risk assessment' have come to dominate forensic practice. The first of these has involved the use of actuarial or algorithmic methods to estimate the likelihood of specified outcomes. The other main approach has involved the use of structured professional judgement (SPJ) or checklist-based approaches. These have frequently been called risk assessment instruments (RAIs) and often claim to be more than checklists of risk factors.

Actuarial methods are based on the use of statistical reasoning, which is used to consider data on relevant population samples. These are used to try and estimate the probability of future events (Dawid, Musio and Murtas, 2017). Use of this method can be seen to be based on formal, logical or axiom-based approaches, seeking to achieve optimised outcomes. This kind of methodology has a significant history within forensic practice and has long been proposed by some as a replacement for human decision making. Those who have argued for this see the use of these formal methods as a way to avoid inherent biases that people show in making judgements. An early example of this involved decision making about supervised release from prison custody by parole boards, with the advocacy of actuarial predictors as a replacement for human decision making (Lundberg, 1926; Sarbin, 1944).

Actuarial approaches to political violence

Actuarial approaches to the risk assessment of political violence have involved using the same formal means of combining and analysing data seen in other areas of forensic practice. Use in this context though has been subject to specific as well as more general criticisms. Some of the criticisms made of actuarial approaches are quite weak, often being based on false premises. These would include those which stress the limitations in data that can be used to assess risk. Here, it is sometimes argued that the method limits this to simple numerical data, with other forms of data excluded. This is at best only partially true. There is some truth in this criticism but only to the extent that data needs to be in a form, or put into a form, that allows for numerical analysis. This does not though, as sometimes suggested, mean that qualitative data cannot be accommodated. Advocates of these kinds of formal logical methods have in fact observed that a broad-based view of the kinds of data that can be used may be taken, often drawing on a wide range of theoretical perspectives. What distinguishes actuarial methods is not the data used but the way that data is processed and analysed once gathered (Meehl, 1954, 1956).

Actuarial methods have also been criticised for their poor ability to deal with low frequency events, tending to perform best where the likelihood of an event is around 50%. When dealing with low-frequency events, these methods tend to perform poorly, typically by producing large numbers of false positives. They have also been criticised for performing poorly with high impact events that have low base rates. These may dramatically affect the accuracy of otherwise good predictors and these kinds of event invariably cause difficulties for actuarial approaches (Meehl, 1954, 1956; Towl and Crighton, 1996, Crighton and Towl, 2008). An illustrative example of this is the 'broken-leg' problem. Essentially, this concerns the fact that even highly accurate algorithms for predicting given outcomes may fail completely, when faced with a rare but high impact event. In this example, a highly accurate model to predict cinema attendance may subsequently fail at an individual level, where the person suffers a serious injury such as a broken leg. This concern is of salience in efforts to apply actuarial methods to terrorism, since this often involves rare high impact events, which are also subject to high levels of aleatory uncertainty (or unknown unknowns).

Advocates of actuarial methods in this area have tended to recognise these limitations, acknowledging that efforts to try to predict individual acts of terrorism are unlikely to be useful (Woo, 2002; 2021). In place of this actuarial methods here have typically defined risk as the product of a hazard and vulnerability, in turn actuarially modelling these hazards. However, this kind of approach typically involves a high degree of judgement around the assumptions made and also a high degree of flexibility in application. As a result, this version of the actuarial method can be criticised as diverging markedly from the traditional reductionist scientific approaches described by Knight (1921). In these, analysis typically progresses using 'bottom-up' approaches, where the understanding of simple systems precedes the understanding of more complex ones (Aven and Renn, 2009; Aven, 2015). The application of actuarial methods to analysing hazards and risk in terrorism has typically used 'top-down' approaches that assume understanding of higher-level systems before simpler ones. One example of this would be the use of network models, which stress the analysis of complex of associations (Gunaratna, 2002). This has been expanded to suggest an analogy of explanatory value between terrorism and the kinds of swarm intelligence seen in areas of animal and insect behaviour (Woo, 2002). This approach is open to the criticism that it stands normal scientific method on its head, going beyond credible evidence. It is perhaps not surprising that such efforts have so far proven inadequate to the task of addressing the risk of various forms of politically motivated violence.

The challenge of dealing with the risk of politically motivated violence is made greater, since it generally involves asymmetries. This includes asymmetry in areas such as planning and leadership. Insurgent and terrorist groups typically lack comparable resources and structures to states and accordingly opt not to use traditional means. Most conclude that it is not sensible to directly attack an opponent they cannot hope to defeat by such confrontation. Asymmetry can be both a weakness and strength, but it is certainly not understood well enough to predict its effects with any accuracy. Some insights are possible and the main weaknesses of terrorists and insurgents in particular are relatively obvious. Compared to states, they are usually not able to draw on as wide a range of assets, such as economic, human and military resources. They do though have less obvious strengths, many of which can be seen as a function of scale. These would include being able to respond quickly and flexibly to threats, not having to work through large often bureaucratic structures and lacking legal constraints, following from commitment to the rule of law. These aspects and many more interact, in poorly understood ways, to exploit vulnerabilities in more powerful but less agile targets. Current trends in terrorist organisations have also suggested ongoing change in this area, with reported moves towards the use of less formal structures, amplifying asymmetry. An example of this would be the emergence of Hamas, with far less formal structure than the Palestine Liberation Organisation (PLO) which it displaced. Similarly, Al-Qaeda (AQ) appears to have involved a hybrid of hierarchical and networked forms that made it harder to infiltrate and counter (Ronfeldt and Arquilla, 2001).

Some advocates of actuarial methods have stressed the value of using logical rational models, such as Game Theory (Ho, Rajagopalan, Skvortsov et al., 2022).

This has been suggested as a means of looking at specific areas, such as the way in which terrorists or insurgents may prioritise targets. Game theory is suggested here as a good basis for developing probability distributions for potential targets or hazards. These in turn, it is argued, can be based on mathematical expressions for the functional dependence between targets likelihood and their utility. In line with this, it is suggested that the probability of success can also be statistically modelled in a similar manner, along with the effects of this on the expected marginal utility of attacks. This kind of modelling though is open to criticisms. Foremost of these is that it inevitably depends on a series of assumptions and assignment of subjective probabilities. The final estimates of risk put forward may appear to be very precise. The accuracy and usefulness of these estimates though will only be as good as the foundational assumptions and information on which they are based.

Another approach to the use of actuarial methods in this context has concerned the function of 'securitising' risk, or at least some parts of it (Woo, 2002, 2021). Securitisation refers here to the use of these methods to model the financial risks involved. In many respects, this is quite like the use of relative frequency probability to develop insurance products. The aim then becomes one of modelling the financial risks associated with say a terrorist attack, then using this to seek to manage the associated costs. This is though some way from the normal understanding of efforts to assess the risk of politically motivated violence. In many respects, it can be seen as mirroring other highly sophisticated efforts to use logic-based models to assess financial risks, which perhaps reached a peak on the early 2000s. Those efforts to manage financial risk went on to be extensively criticised, having been heavily implicated in financial collapses, most notably in 2008, where many of the assumptions on which they were based appeared at best poorly founded (Taleb, 2015).

Checklist-based assessments

Checklist-based assessments are non-actuarial approaches to estimating how likely a given outcome is. They differ from actuarial approaches in that they do not involve the formal combination and analysis of data, although data analysed in this manner may be incorporated. They are similar in that they generally claim to be assessing the risk of defined events, such as the occurrence or recurrence of violence. This is normally estimated in the form of qualitative verbal descriptions: such as 'low,' 'moderate' or 'high.' These checklist-based assessments assume that the consideration of multiple areas will result in more accurate judgements. Assessments of this kind also make contested claims to be able to improve significantly on the accuracy of unaided judgements, often described as 'clinical' assessments or more pejoratively as 'unstructured clinical' assessments.

Initial development of this checklist methodology has been elaborated on over time, with the creation of more extensive lists of 'factors,' more detailed descriptions of these and the inclusion of additional analysis. Revisions have tended to stress more analysis of background information and expansion and elaboration of outcomes. This has typically included notions of constructing clinical 'formulations' to account for behaviours as well as events or outcomes. In some cases, the method has been extended to include the development of imaginary alternative scenarios, for example, with the construction of scenarios involving escalatory or less serious outcomes. Developments of this kind have often been, rather oddly, described in terms of 'generational' change. This seems a somewhat grandiose use of language in this context not reflecting the reality of changes which appear relatively insubstantial. The changes involved might more plausibly be seen as refinements and embellishments to a common methodology, rather than reflecting any substantive changes. The only exception to this being, perhaps, what have been described as 'fifth-generation' checklists. In most respects, these appear similar to earlier forms but seek to automate the process of assessment, removing people from the decision-making process and replacing them with logical rationality-based automated processes, reliant on machine learning and artificial intelligence to try to predict events in real time (Garrett and Monahan, 2020). This might more reasonably be seen as a paradigm change from previous checklist-based assessments.

The use of checklist-based methods has grown dramatically across forensic practice, with this largely displacing other alternatives. Advocates of this form of assessment stress its accuracy for making predictions and its flexibility in dealing with individual needs and characteristics. As such, the method is argued to deal effectively with problems seen in actuarial methods, such as dealing effectively with high-impact, low-frequency events: by allowing for these to be added to the areas addressed. Whatever the merits or otherwise of these arguments, exponential growth of this method can be seen to have been driven in part by growing professional and commercial interests. Many checklist-based assessments have been developed and actively marketed, targeting similar areas. In recent years, the method has also been progressively expanded to include a growing range of behaviours and populations, with this now including forms of politically motivated violence, 'extremism' and 'radicalisation.' This has involved the marketing of these products, which have been derived from models that are based on offending that is not ideologically based.

A recent review identified multiple checklist-based assessments claiming to assess the risk of these areas. Of these, the reviewers judged that seven were suitable for inclusion, based on meeting basic quality criteria for this kind of assessment (van der Heide, van der Zwan and van Leyenhorst, 2019). The quality criteria used included the checklist being developed to specifically address the area of 'extremist' violence and that it contained indicators to determine the level of risk for this or alternatively for the extent of 'radicalisation' of the individuals assessed. Additionally, only those checklists developed after 2010 were included, although the basis for this apparently arbitrary criterion is unclear. Using these criteria, eight assessments were excluded from consideration. The seven included assessments were the Violent Extremism Risk Assessment 2nd revision (VERA 2R), Extremism Risk Guidance 22+ (ERG 22+), Significance Quest Assessment Test (SQAT), Islamic Radicalisation model 46 (IR46), Radicalisation Risk Assessment in Prisons (RRAP) and Radar and the Vulnerability Assessment Framework (VAF).

Notably, some of these assessments show a significant degree of overlap. The ERG 22+ which is used in England and Wales is very closely related Vulnerability Assessment Framework (VAF). They are essentially the same checklist of areas for assessment but with a focus in the VAF on community use. Both assessments also appear to have marked similarities to the earlier VERA 2 assessment (van der Heide, van der Zwan and van Leyenhorst, 2019). This has been adopted in Scotland in its revised form, the VERA 2R, in preference to the ERG 22+ and VAF (Pressman and Flockton, 2014). Interestingly, all these assessments appear to have eschewed reference to politically motivated violence, adopting instead notions of 'extremism' or 'vulnerability' focussed on beliefs or 'psychopathology.'

The use of assessments of this kind has been variously described. For example, the developers of the ERG 22+ see it as having a 'critical role' in informing decisions around management, monitoring, supervision and interventions needed in this area. This is further extended to include assessment of how these processes have affected risk, where individuals should be located within the criminal justice system, whether they should be released, reintegrated or recalled to custody (Lloyd and Dean, 2015). This wide span of use is based on evaluation of 22 areas, divided into three 'dimensions': described as 'Engagement,' 'Intent' and 'Capability' (Elliott, Randhawa-Horne and Hambly, 2023). Each of the areas included are scored using what are termed 'assessor metrics.' For the engagement and intent 'dimensions,' these are scored 0, 1 or 2, with overall categories assessed as 'low,' 'medium' or 'high.' For the 'capability' dimension, the items and overall category are assessed as 'minimal,' 'some' or 'significant.' Generally, the approach can be seen as similar to most of the other checklist-based assessments commonly used in correctional and forensic mental health settings (Yang, Wong and Coid, 2010).

There are clear problems with transferring this approach to the assessment of terrorism, 'extremist' violence or 'vulnerability' to engaging in such activities. These range from some quite trivial concerns, through to more fundamental difficulties. Regrettably, much of the focus has been on addressing the relatively trivial. For example, it is possible to improve how reliably such checklists can be completed by different assessors, normally called inter-rater reliability. Faced with a task of scoring someone across a pre-defined checklist of areas, the levels of agreement between assessors will typically be moderate or even poor. This will largely depend on how clearly defined these areas and the criteria for assessing them are. In scientific terms though, this is a trivial problem. Areas of assessment can be defined more precisely by operationalising the terms. Assessors can then be trained and drilled in how they evaluate these, so that the scoring tends towards greater group consensus. Such improvements in inter-rater agreement have indeed been a focus of work in this area. This can though be criticised as missing the more fundamental problems with transferring this method from correctional and mental health settings. Most importantly here is the question of what these assessments are measuring, if anything. Each of the checklists covers a range of areas, but there is in fact little convincing evidence to support the assumption that these are valid risk factors for various forms of politically motivated violence.

Cargo cult science

Current approaches in forensic practice, to areas of politically motivated violence, appear to have been very largely transplanted from other areas, such as the
assessment of the risk of criminal reconvictions. How effective current practice
has been in these areas is contested (Crighton, 2023). Applying this to the risk of
'radicalisation,' 'vulnerability' or terrorism or other forms of politically motivated
violence raises multiple questions. So too does the claimed breadth of application
of the method, claiming to take in very different contexts and functions, ranging
from assessed risk in the community to the evaluation of efficacy of risk treatment.

The popularity and growth of checklist-based assessment has been associated
with a growth in significant professional and commercial interests. The theoretical
and empirical foundation for the method is though weak. Performance of the method
in practice tends to be modest at best. This growth of checklist-based assessments
has also been strongly criticised as undermining more useful and productive work
(Wald and Woolverton, 1990). Despite the concerns though, the approach has
continued to be very actively marketed, sometimes drawing on claims of being
the 'gold standard' method of assessing risk. Claims of this kind appear problematic, even in more routine areas of forensic practice, such as assessments involving
sexually motivated criminal violence. Here, checklists have been applied to broadly
defined risks, such as 'sexual violence' with a range of claimed 'risk factors' being
addressed. Risk analysis has typically been quite superficial, involving some history taking, problem 'formulation' and, in some assessments, creation of hypothetical future scenarios.

Checklist assessments which claim to assess the risk of terrorism or alternatively notions such as 'extremism,' 'vulnerability' or 'radicalisation' are fundamentally the same. They use terms that are broad, often poorly defined and that
neglect a great deal of complexity. There is a tendency to use vague definitions of
concepts such as 'terrorism,' 'extremism,' 'vulnerability' or 'radicalisation.' These
assessments involve assessment of individuals based on standard lists of claimed
'risk factors,' with the analysis of these, statistical or otherwise, being generally
elementary in nature. Perhaps the most striking problem here though is the fundamental lack of knowledge about risk correlates, outcomes and the fixed or variable
factors that might be involved in various forms of politically motivated violence
(Sageman, 2014; Monahan, 2016). Very little is in fact known about what constitute risk factors, how these might be distinguished from correlates and how these
might be shown to be systematically related to outcomes. There is no credible evidence to date of individual causal risk factors for any form of political violence,
with little apparent effort to address this serious failing by means of good quality,
credible research in this area (Sageman, 2014; Monahan, 2016).

Creation of checklist assessments in this area can be seen, at best, as being
premature. It can also be criticised as transferring a flawed method, already open
to serious criticism, to an area where there is little understanding. In doing this,
the completion of these assessments creates the false impression of scientific
understanding, whilst generating unnecessary costs and detracting from potentially

more useful activity. Activity that would include credible research to improve basic understanding. At a practice level, resources would also be better targeted at better training of practitioners and efforts to better calibrate their judgements and communications around risk and uncertainty. In many other fields, this is routine and effective, yet it appears largely absent in forensic practice (International Organisation for Standardization, 2018; Dressel and Farid, 2018). Taking the UK example, there is evidently scope to look at how effective those involved in the varied parts of the Contest policy are at assessing referrals and to proactively feed this back. Providing feedback draws on peoples natural capacities, here the ability to learn from experience, something which can be shown to be effective in improving the accuracy of assessments of risk (Dressel and Farid, 2018).

There is little independent evidence on the performance of checklist-based assessments in relation to terrorism, 'extremism,' 'vulnerability' or 'radicalisation' and the ability of these to assess areas such as risk, or the efficacy of risk treatments, remains largely opaque. There have though been some efforts to independently evaluate these checklist methods of assessment, in relation to other areas of forensic practice, such as the prediction of general reoffending or violent offending. Here, this method of assessment has been consistently shown to have a relatively low ceiling of performance, typically above random chance but clustering around modest levels of predictive accuracy (Yang, Wong and Coid, 2010). Such limitations are well known to practitioners and researchers, yet have not checked the growth in popularity and dominance of this method. Nor have they slowed its spread to new, less well understood and high stakes areas, such as terrorism.

A key study in this area perhaps suggests a reason for this. In this study, researchers looked at a wide range of checklist-based risk assessment instruments, finding that they appeared to be largely interchangeable. This was demonstrated by the remarkable easy with which they could be created. Similarly, effective checklist assessments were produced quickly and easily by taking randomly drawn items from other checklists and forming these into a new instrument. These were memorably described as 'coffee can' instruments, since items were drawn from a coffee can. These randomly generated checklist assessments were seen to perform similarly to the originals (Kroner, Mills and Reddon, 2005). The explanation for this finding appeared to be that all of the checklist assessments were, in fact, drawing on a small pool of well-known and moderately good correlates of criminality. As a result, all were able to achieve the modest but consistent levels of performance seen (Kroner, Mills and Reddon, 2005). Given this ease of construction, along with the growing marketisation of practice, the rapid spread of the method perhaps becomes more intelligible. The serious limitations of this approach have been repeatedly identified to little effect. The neglect of these concerns is though hard to defend. When applied to forms of politically motivated violence though, such concerns are amplified. Assumptions that this checklist method will continue to perform at a similar level to those used in other areas of forensic practice appear highly questionable and indeed given the potential outcomes involved, deeply concerning.

This persistence and growth in the use of a method, that appears to work on a quite different basis from the one often claimed, has led to suggestions that this method of assessment is in fact an example of 'cargo cult' science (Crighton, 2023). The term cargo cult science was used by the physicist Richard Feynman, to describe an activity which on the surface looks like science. It describes activity that copies the methods used by scientists whilst not meeting any of its fundamental requirements (Feynman, 1974). Checklist-based risk assessments generally invite this criticism, appearing to be a scientific method and often being marketed based on this premise. They do not though add to understanding, rather seeming to draw on a small pool of correlates. As such, a lot of the material in this form of assessment appears to be superfluous, padding out assessments to take the form of scientific methods. The concerns of using cargo cult science are if anything even more pronounced with the extension of the method to assessment of politically motivated forms of violence. Here, there is no evidence that this pool of general correlates will carry over at all. Here, general indicators of criminality that may work in other contexts may be largely irrelevant or indeed be actively misleading (Crenshaw, 1981; Monahan, 2016).

Going back to basics

Arguably, attempts to assess risk in terrorism have two primary functions. One of these is concerned with legal decision making, including areas such as prosecution, sentencing and also the determination of whether someone is suitable to have various forms of restriction eased or ended (Kruglanski, Crenshaw, Post et al., 2008; Monahan, 2012, 2016). The second primary function has been identified as detection of 'insider threats.' That is threats from those who have access to some areas of the state, for example, as employees or sub-contractors, who may use this to cause harm. This would include efforts to identify agents or assets of hostile states or actors, or those who may otherwise pose a risk (Department of Defense, 2010; Bunn and Sagan, 2014; Schouten and Saathoff, 2014).

Both areas present with serious problems and a number of reasons have been suggested for this (Monahan, 2012, 2016; Sageman, 2014). As touched on above, the most serious of these is the shortage of credible knowledge in this area. Little is known about risk indicators and factors. As noted above, this has not stopped the creation of apparently 'scientific' checklist-based assessments or actuarial models to assess 'risk.' This has suggested far greater understanding than actually exists in areas such as 'radicalisation,' 'extremism' and politically motivated violence. Indeed, for some assessments, this has extended to suggestions that these are good enough to determine response to risk treatments. Such a reading of the evidence though would be unfounded. These areas are not well understood and it has been argued that there is in fact a pressing need for high-quality research, to develop understanding (Sageman, 2014; Monahan, 2016).

Generally, scant evidence has been put forward to support many suggested 'risk factors' other than ones that are demographically obvious, such as perpetrators tending to be young and male. Observations of this kind add little to the field, with the notion that young men tend to be more likely to engage in violent acts hardly constituting a significant insight. As a result of this paucity of evidence, both actuarial and checklist assessments in this area have rested on weak assumptions. Suggestions that the resulting products are accurate enough to assess the impact of varied forms of risk treatment, lack supporting evidence and so lack credibility. A secondary but perhaps linked problem here is that these assessments often appear to assume that it is possible to talk about concepts such as terrorism, 'radicalisation' or 'extremism,' as unitary entities. Again this seems to be a poorly grounded assumption. It is possible and indeed seems more plausible that terrorism, 'extremism' and 'radicalisation' may develop in quite different ways and adopt different forms. This may in fact involve processes that differ in important ways, suggesting in turn a need for different approaches to risk treatment and risk management.

Promising suggestions for further research and exploration have been made here, including areas such as ideology, affiliations, 'grievances' and moral emotions (Monahan, 2016). The suspicion that ideology will be important here is a consistent theme across varied forms of politically motivated violence. Many of those who engage in terrorism, insurgency and other politically motivated violence often appear driven by specific and strongly held views. There is though a vast gulf between holding strong ideological beliefs and then going on to engage in violence based on these. Explaining these transitions presents a major challenge. Promising areas of research and methods have though been put forward, such as focussing on the role of social affiliation (Sageman, 2008; McCauley and Moskalenko, 2011). The role of information technology and digital communications in general and use of the Internet in particular have also been identified as an important area for further research. This may particularly concern the dissemination of information and techniques that would otherwise be hard to access.

Useful theoretical accounts for this transitioning from firmly held beliefs to violent action has been suggested, such as the 'coalition-commitment' hypothesis. This provides a helpful frame to understand and account for the role of religious beliefs in transitions from beliefs to violent action. This hypothesis also has the advantage of providing a broad explanatory framework, not restricted to any specific religion. It assumes that part of the function of most religions is to foster altruism or 'parochial altruism' within groups (Ginges, Atran, Sachdeva et al., 2011). Collective religious activities are then seen as having a significant role in fostering popular and social support for political views, in support of the wider group. This analysis can though be extended to secular forms, where similar arguments around developing a group sense of altruism may apply in parallel ways.

This has clear links to the larger research base into social categorisation, which suggests that group membership alone can be sufficient to generate intergroup discrimination, hostility and violence. This has been explained in terms of the social comparison processes, operating between groups, with the need for a positive ingroup identity driving this. As a result of these comparisons, mutual differentiation between groups may support varying levels of conflict. Differentiation between groups based on religious beliefs may be seen as an extreme example of this, but in fact such differences can be 'minimal' and still drive behaviour (Turner, 1975).

If this kind of thinking is correct, then areas such as kinship, friendship and romantic affiliations are likely to be central to the transition from ideological commitment to political violence. Efforts to deal with this may need to focus much more on interpersonal relationships than individual characteristics (Taylor, Roach and Pease, 2015; Monahan, 2016). Following this line of thinking, some general areas have been suggested as promising avenues for further research in particular family relationships, romantic partnerships, friendships and 'virtual communities.' Within these specific characteristics have also been suggested to be crucial, such as the degree of perceived interpersonal closeness. This rests on the assumption that closer relationships are likely to have more pronounced effects than more distant ones. As well as closeness, whether these relationships involve others who condone or support the use of violence as a means of reaching political goals may be an important driver.

The role of feelings of 'grievance' has also been identified as an important focus for research. The suggestion that this contributes to the development of extreme views and progression of this to violent acts seems both plausible and persuasive. Feelings involving personal losses seem important here, with deaths of loved ones seeming to have particular relevance. This has led to suggestions that this may act in an especially powerful way through its interaction with and impact on individual feelings around mortality (Pyszczynski, Abdollahi, Solomon et al., 2006). It is odd that 'grievances' linked to these kinds of loss, which often appear strongly justified, have been largely neglected as an area of research in forensic practice. This is more surprising still, given robust findings from a range of meta-analytic studies into how deaths of this kind affect people. These effects often appear without conscious realisation but show moderate to large effect sizes across studies (Burke, Martens and Faucher, 2010). Drawing on this work, it has been hypothesised that stronger feelings of inter-dependence with others may serve to reduce feelings of anxiety, possibly by increasing the individual's perceptions of their own wider significance. Ideas of living on, through the wider group, have been put forward as potentially important here (Orehek, Sasota, Kruglanski et al., 2014; Monahan, 2016).

It has also been proposed that efforts to adequately understand and assess some forms of politically motivated violence will need to more seriously address moral questions. In general, it has been suggested this needs to consider the violation of a groups norms in general and the 'sacred values' of groups in particular. Where these are involved, then efforts to apply of economic models and incentives do not only appear to be an effective means to develop understanding. An example of how economic models fail here can be drawn from the Israeli–Palestinian conflict. Here, previous unsuccessful resolutions have been suggested on the basis of exchanging 'land for peace' (Monahan, 2016). Such attempts appear based on the idea that material incentives of this kind would increase the motivation towards peace, presumably based on the economic utility of such an exchange. Yet, these proved counter-productive in this conflict and were in fact associated with increased levels of violence, with people acting counter to this analysis. By contrast, the presence of symbolic compromises or incentives, such as recognising the rights of others, has been associated with reductions in violence (Ginges, Atran, Sachdeva et al., 2011; Monahan, 2016).

The question of 'identities' has also been put forward as an important area for research and practice development (Monahan, 2012, 2016). Here, the important role of strong feelings of group identification has been suggested as a promising area to look for risk factors. The psychological pathway involved here may, in many respects, be like that reported for religious groups and other closely bonded groups. As such, it might involve the development of 'family-like' relationships, as part of the process of group formation and bonding. It may also involve processes of making 'sacrifices' and 'extreme sacrifices' which increase the level of commitment to the group (Turner, 1975; Tajfel and Turner, 1979; Monahan, 2016). This appears quite different from what is seen in acts of politically motivated violence carried out by lone actors, which also seem to diverge from research which has suggested that those engaged in terrorists groups and cells did not differ from the wider population in terms of demographic or psychological characteristics (Crenshaw, 1981). Lone actors do appear to show systematic differences in terms of their identities (Gruenewald, Chermak and Freilich, 2013; LaFree, 2013; McCauley and Moskalenko, 2014).

This is further complicated by the observation of marked demographic differences between lone actors motivated by different causes. Those professing support for Islamist groups, for example, tended to show higher rates of being students, of seeking legitimisation from authority figures, of engaging in virtual activity and of evidence of links to some form of command-and-control. Those associated with extreme right-wing terrorism were more likely to be unemployed, to have lower levels of university experience and to engage in dry runs of terror attacks. Single issue terrorists also showed some distinct characteristics, tending to show higher levels of being in a relationship, higher levels of criminal convictions and warnings and to have higher levels of mental illness (Gill, Horgan and Deckert, 2014).

Validating risk factors

Going from prospective to well-validated risk factors for terrorism, insurgency or other forms of politically motivated violence involves substantial methodological challenges. It has been repeatedly observed that it is not possible to prospectively validate these, in the way that can be done for other forms of violence (Monahan and Skeem, 2014; Monahan, 2016; Braddock, 2019). As a result, case control designs are probably the best that can be done (Cronbach and Meehl, 1955). This involves identifying factors that both precede and correlate with acts or views, then comparing these for terrorist, 'extremist' or 'radicalised' groups against matched control groups. There has been a lamentable lack of progress here and the reasons for this remain largely hidden. Some potential drivers of this may suggest themselves though. Most obviously perhaps, this is an area where independent researchers, with the necessary skills to undertake this kind of research, have generally been excluded. This has been a consistent pattern despite those with access to such data lacking skills necessary to undertake good quality research in this area (Sageman, 2014; Monahan, 2016). Much of this blockage appears to have been driven by concerns around secrecy and confidentially, limiting both access and the pool of expertise being drawn on. Efforts have been made to address this with the creation of larger shared databases, such as the United States Extremist Crime Database (ECDB) (Freilich, Chermak, Belli et al., 2014) and the Global Terrorism Database (GTD) (LaFree and Dugan, 2007). These have though been limited to data in the public domain, leaving a great deal of classified data untapped (Sageman, 2014). Correcting this neglect does not seem to be an insuperable challenge. Indeed, similar concerns have been successfully addressed in other areas, where a balance between security and expertise needs to be delivered. This appears to be a relatively easy problem to resolve, given a willingness to do so.

Improving practice

Dominant approaches to risk have been traced back to the 1940s and 1950s where they developed, following the end of the second world war, as part of the Cold War that followed. This period saw growing political conflict between one bloc led by the United States and another led by the Soviet Union, which resulted in an arms race. This era also saw a dramatic growth of optimisation models, which were based on logical or axiomatic rationality (Gigerenzer, 2024). This included efforts to model the conflict in this way, using methods such as game theory (Emery, 2021). Some key events seem to have fuelled this analysis and were linked to the fears of imminent and major conflict between these two blocs. These included the Berlin crisis 1958–1962 (Schick, 2016), the Cuban Missile Crisis 1962 (Allison and Zelikow, 1971), the crushing of the Prague Spring in 1968 (Bischof, Karner and Ruggenthaler, 2009) and the Vietnam War 1956–1975 (Wiest, 2003). This was an era dominated by the threat of global nuclear war and military planning doctrines concerned with 'mutually assured destruction.' Given this, both parties to this conflict would have had strong motivations to better understanding how the other would behave. This is reflected in extensive state and military support given to academic researchers to look at ways of eliminating, reducing or managing threats.

This supported the development of work into optimal approaches to risk, which would be based on objective predictors and logical or axiomatic analysis that would yield an 'optimal' solution. This idea was taken to its logical conclusion by some in the maths division of the RAND Corporation for example, who looked to develop 'pure' and universally applicable rational methods, which might be used to resolve any political problems (Emery, 2021). It is unclear how far these researchers actually believed this but the ideal here would have been that these would be implemented automatically by digital computers, without human intervention (Erickson, Klein, Daston et al., 2013; Emery, 2021). In many respects, this idea never went away, but in current debates, it has changed in presentation. The view has persisted and spread beyond wargaming that by using 'logical rationality' approaches, the problems associated with the sloppy thinking and emotions afflicting human decision making can be avoided. This kind of thinking has led to the application of sophisticated formal methods, which failed to work as anticipated when applied, creating serious failures in policy and practice (Milstein, 1974; Ilbas, 2012). The most graphic example of this was perhaps the application of these models to the war in Vietnam. Many of those in the US administrations involved were drawn from an educational elite, with those in power being increasingly drawn from a narrow range of academic and indeed socio-economic backgrounds. Many had very high-level training in economics and management and this came to be reflected in the way the war in Vietnam was run, based on managerialist methods. This included a stress on the use of 'metrics' to evaluate progress, probably the most notorious of these being the use of 'body count' as a 'performance indicator.' Use of these methods rested on the assumption that war could be understood and fought in terms of loss and utility, which drew in turn from formal econometric models. When moved from academia and applied to the risks and uncertainties associated with war, the results can be seen as nothing short of disastrous. These models did not work in the expected way when applied to real world problems. This can be seen to stem from the use of what have been termed 'small-world' models. These are in essence models where all the possible states of the system are known (Fischbacher-Smith, 2015; Gigerenzer, 2024). This is attainable when creating theoretical models, when the parameters of the model can be limited and specified. 'Small-world' models though are not effective when applied to 'large-world' cases, such as wars, which involve uncertainty and intractability (Daddis, 2012; Fischbacher-Smith and Smith, 2015; Gigerenzer, 2024).

It has been observed that many of those who developed such 'small-world' models were very aware of these limitations (Gigerenzer, 2008, 2010; Katsikopoulos, Simşek, Buckmann et al., 2020). Others who adopted their models often appeared less aware, or less concerned. A key turning point here has been identified as the work of the economist Milton Friedman, who completed what has memorably been described as an 'extraordinary coup' (Gigerenzer, 2024). This involved the 'small-world' maximisation of subjective expected utility theory coming to be seen as a universal theory, able to account for rational decision making and being universally applicable. In reality, this has evident limitations and weaknesses, which were clearly understood by those who developed it. Friedman though saw these as just 'anomalies.' This view seems to have become dominant, with criticisms of this theory largely forgotten (Gigerenzer, 2024). Those with the best understanding of the theory had caveated it, noting its narrow application and unsuitability for dealing with conditions involving uncertainty and intractability. This would mean the approach was only normative in the case of 'small worlds' where future states and consequences were known (Savage, 1954; von Neuman and Morgenstein, 1944, 1947, 1953). The model also appears intended to describe the way people behave, rather than providing a normative description of how they 'should' behave since the later would have been of little relevance to efforts to prevent conflict (Gigerenzer, 2024).

Another curious twist has been observed here, which involved the assertion that psychological realism was not important. This stated that the only important thing was that people behaved 'as-if' to maximise their subjective expected utility, not that they behaved in ways that actually do so (Friedman, 1953). Again the remarkable character of this claim has been observed along with its practical effect, that most neo-classical economists have showed little interest in the actual processes involved in decision making (Gigerenzer, 2024).

Perhaps the most striking recent example of failure here would be the financial crisis of 2008. Here, the US Federal Reserve 'small-world' models failed, as did similar models used across much of European banking and finance. This in turn led to the testimony of the then Chairman of the US Federal Reserve, expressing his shock and disbelief that those involved had not acted in the way predicted by these models (Taleb, 2015). A later review of this area looked at how well behaviour in the larger world was in fact predicted by the utility functions developed from these 'small-world' models (Friedman, Issac, James et al., 2014). This found that the power to make predictions out of sample fell into the 'poor to non-existent' range, with no evidence that they were convincing superiority to naïve theories. These kinds of models have been shown to excel at data fitting rather than prediction. They seem to prosper by rarely being tested in ways that put them at risk of refutation (Gigerenzer, 2024).

Are people irrational?

There is a substantial body of highly cited psychological research to suggest people are fundamentally irrational, which in turn supported the imposition of methods claiming to correct for this. This view is though a recent development that stems from the 1970s. Before this, cognitive and developmental psychology had supported a view of people as being generally good if slightly conservative intuitive statisticians (Peterson and Beach, 1967). Research in developmental psychology had shown that most children showed a clear sequence of acquiring statistical reasoning (Inhelder and Piaget, 1958; Piaget, 1962). This was not addressed in the research tradition that began in the 1970s and referred to here as 'cognitive illusions' research. This differed from earlier work in cognitive and developmental psychology in important ways. It used logical rationality as the benchmark for evaluating human decision making, with divergence from these models seen as demonstrating error. This was also accompanied by an important change in methodology, with testing using physical devices and objects being replaced by written hypothetical problems (Gigerenzer, 2008).

From the 1970s, this approach became increasingly dominant in cognitive psychology, with the claims around these divergences becoming increasingly broad and confident (Gigerenzer and Murray, 2015). This in turn supported a view that people were so poor at making decisions and that the use of opaque manipulation was justified as this would result in 'better' decisions. Here, the 'better' decisions were those suggested by logical rationality models (Gigerenzer, 2024). This came to be widely described as 'nudging' and was increasingly influential across psychology, politics and public administration (Thaler and Sustein, 2008).

A critical observation here has been the utility of such thinking to some parts of the state and its negative impacts on others. It is a perspective which clearly locates problems of poor decision making within individuals, with this in turn being a result of fundamental irrationality. This supported efforts to modify individual decision making. However, this rather neglects the role of the environment and social or economic conditions. Taking this approach means that dysfunctional markets and the conduct of businesses does not need to be addressed (Gigerenzer, 2024). The enthusiasm of governments and administrators for this view is perhaps understandable, supported as it was by the production of a stream of apparently supportive research findings from academic settings. Taking the UK state as illustrative, a Behavioural Insights Team (BIT) was established in 2010 (Behavioural Insights Team, 2010). This team was based within the Cabinet Office of the UK government and initially listed nine examples of such 'nudging.' These concerned smoking, organ donation, teenage pregnancy, alcohol, diet and weight, diabetes, food hygiene, physical activity and social care. These are undoubtedly serious political and policy challenges for the UK government. However, taking the example of diet and weight as illustrative, this stressed individual behaviour linked to the claimed effects from priming and salience. The suggestion here was that people could be primed to buy healthier food by, for example, the use of messaging on shopping trolleys (Behavioural Insights Team, 2010). Other states showed similar enthusiasm for focussing on individual judgements, 'nudging' individual behaviour in ways that protect from irrational decision making. In the US, a 'Regulation Czar' was set up by the US administration (Ferguson, 2010).

These opaque efforts to modify behaviour have been described as a 'new paternalism.' This has been designed to protect people from their own psychological irrationality, rather than protecting them from the imperfections of markets and the plain criminality seen in some major organisations (Le Grand, 2022). It has also been noted that this adopts a view of human psychology with clear echoes of the ideas of B.F. Skinner in his book *Beyond Freedom and Dignity* (Skinner, 1971), suggesting that 99% of behaviour is automatic and easily manipulable by priming (Gigerenzer, 2024). Such claims in fact lack foundation, with many failures to replicate the various forms of priming effects that were claimed to exist. Assessment of the efforts to 'nudge' behaviour in the manner suggested has also yielded unimpressive results. Meta-analysis of 212 studies in this area suggested 'small-to-medium' effective size but also a moderate publication bias, meaning that studies which had no effect or negative effects have tended not to be published (Mertens, Herberz, Hahnel et al., 2022). Correcting for this bias in the meta-analysis, the small-to-medium effect was reported to disappear, with no benefit in any domain found (Maier, Bartos, Stanley et al., 2022).

Claims of effectiveness in this area may also have been tainted by the contentious area of academic fraud and manipulation. Traditionally, the dominant view of this has been that it is a rare phenomenon, involving only a small number of cases of abuse. The widespread assumption has been that these can be effectively addressed by traditional academic processes, such as 'blind' peer review. Concerns have increasingly emerged, extending across many fields of research an practice, suggesting such assumptions are inaccurate, naïve, complacent and harmful (Goldstein, 2010; Wilson, 2020; Simonsohn, Simmons and Nelson, 2021).

How people make good decisions

Using heuristics is a generally effective and economical way to make good decisions, analogous to visual perception which is usually accurate and functional allowing people to interact with a complex world (Gregory, 1997). Both though can sometimes result in the occurrence of illusions, either visual or cognitive. The research tradition in these two areas though has been very different. The approach to cognitive illusions has come to be focused, almost exclusively, on the observation of failings and then labelling these as vaguely defined concepts: primarily 'availability,' 'anchoring' and 'representativeness.' The vagueness around these constructs has persisted along with the commitment to optimisation models as the benchmark for evaluation. Heuristic decision making has been assumed to be inferior to the results generated by these models (Gigerenzer and Gaissmaier, 2011). The crucial dependence between heuristics and environment has also been neglected (Simon and Newell, 1958; Gigerenzer, 2008).

Politically motivated violence can be seen as involving both uncertainty and intractability requiring a more serious consideration of heuristic decision making than has previously been seen. These heuristics also need to be better understood, both in terms of the inferences involved and the preferences that result. Analysis of this kind is not new and an early and highly influential example would be Simon's work on 'satisficing.' Here, the careful analysis of what people do in seeking to solve problems was seen as essential to measuring the accuracy of heuristics (Simon, 1977). This approach has resulted in important findings, including 'less is more' effects. Here, the use of apparently simple heuristics produces more accurate prediction than the use of complex models, as well as having advantages of economy of effort and transparency (Gigerenzer, Todd and The ABC Research Group, 1999). In contrast to much of the work on priming effects and cognitive illusions, these findings have also proved to be replicable.

An initial response to these findings suggested that whilst heuristics might perform better than complex linear models, they would be outperformed by more complex non-linear optimisation models. These would include various methods, for example neural networks and neural net training algorithms (Jones, 2004). These involve the use of increasingly complex and opaque formal methods of analysis. Experimental evaluation though has failed to support claims that these methods would perform better than apparently simple heuristics which have performed better than the most complex of these models, such as random forests (Biau and Scornet, 2016) and support vector machines (Hearst, Dumais, Osuna et al., 1998). Again heuristics performed here with much greater efficiency and economy of conscious effort and appear able to do this by relying on natural inbuilt skills. Much of this inbuilt processing is in fact highly complex but this does not require conscious effort (Körding and Wolpert, 2004; Brighton and Gigerenzer, 2015).

Ecological rationality and better decision making

The term ecological rationality refers broadly to how people deal with complex problems and the dependence of this on context (Todd and Gigerenzer, 2007; Gigerenzer, 2008; Hertwig, Leuker, Pachur et al., 2022). This draws attention to the fundamental importance of the interaction between cognition and environment (Simon and Newell, 1958). This has been explained using the analogy of a pair of scissors, where it is impossible to understand how they work without reference to both blades and the interaction between them. Ecological rationality applies this analogy to cognition, stressing that this involves two parts that are not intelligible in isolation from each other. Human cognition only works within an environment, so that trying to study it separately from this can be seen as absurd (Simon, 1977; Gigerenzer, 2008). Proponents of ecological rationality stress the continuity here with the historic traditions of cognitive psychology, reaching back to its foundation by psychologists such as James, Dewey and Brunswick (Rizzo, 2023; Gigerenzer, 2024).

This suggests that the kind of 'small-world' models discussed above, cannot usefully be transplanted to 'large-world' contexts, such as business or political decision making. It might be worth noting here just how recently concepts of mathematical probability, on which these 'small-world' models are based, emerged. Despite centuries of development in mathematics and philosophy, this occurred primarily from the 17th century onwards (Daston, 1995). This suggests a form of thinking that does not come naturally or easily to us and indeed for most of human history people have needed to deal with natural frequencies, not conditional probabilities. These natural frequencies need to be addressed within environments, rather than being hypothetical problems. So, the use of hypothetical written problems about probabilities involves entirely artificial creations, very different from the problems that people can effectively deal with. Despite this fact, this is the paradigm that has come to dominate the research into cognitive illusions (Gigerenzer and Hoffrage, 1995). So it is perhaps not surprising that people have clear difficulties in dealing with these novel and artificial exercises.

People do though show a good ability to deal with problems involving uncertainty and intractability, which are similar to the kinds of problems that present themselves in 'large-world' problems. Research here suggests that people can do this by applying multiple strategies, often switching between these. This adds emphasis to the need to understand the processes involved here, with research suggesting a clear developmental sequence, with competence changing progressively through overlapping stages (Siegler, 1999). Where problems are appropriately structured, children at the appropriate developmental stage are competent in solving problems involving probability and logic. This includes solving the Bayesian conditional probability tasks often used to demonstrate the presence of cognitive illusions. Problems of this kind when given in the form of natural frequencies, rather than as hypothetical conditional probabilities, do not appear problematic for most adults and children. Even where they do make errors, these are generally a result of using strategies rather than guessing. The strategies used here are typically non-Bayesian: such as using a representative thinking approach. This involves considering how frequently two events co-occur, ignoring base rates and also ignoring false-positive rates. Interestingly this naïve strategy corresponds to the null hypothesis statistical testing (NHST) method, which has so unhelpfully dominated many areas of psychological research (Meehl, 1967, 1978).

In practice, the most important finding coming out of this research is the centrality of how information is presented. Presenting information in formats that fit how people naturally deal with problems, greatly improves performance. This is a robust finding that has been replicated across a groups and problem areas. Performance here also seems dependent on a developmental sequence in problem solving, suggesting four stages: described as guessing, counting, pre-Bayesian and Bayesian stages (Siegler, 1999). At an early age, most people appear to develop the ability to reason in a Bayesian manner, but they do this on the basis of context dependent natural frequencies.

Several implications flow from these findings and these appear very different from those suggested by cognitive illusions research. Ecological rationality stresses the importance of environments designed to get the best out of natural decision making, rather than stressing removal of people from the process. Efforts to replace natural approaches to decision making, with methods based on formal logic, are seen as at best being misguided. In important areas of application, which would include varied forms of politically motivated violence, active harm may result. One of the major strengths of natural heuristics here is that they show better levels of robustness, continuing to work effectively when formal methods fail. This has been demonstrated in a seminal study that compared the effectiveness of formal optimising and heuristic approaches. This involved efforts to predict educational outcomes, based on a selection of data for a sample of high schools in Chicago. The objective here was to predict schools the highest dropout rates (Dawes and Corrigan, 1974). Drawing on the existing evidence base, it was assumed that some cues would be of relevance. These included attendance rates, the socio-economic makeup of the school catchment, ethnic makeup of the school, class sizes, performance on standardised test scores, and so on. Cues of this kind were used as the basis for a formal optimising method of prediction, in this case involving multiple regression analysis. The results from this formal analysis were then tested against three natural heuristics: tallying, take the best and minimalist. A tallying heuristic simply involves the counting of cues in favour of a given outcome or prediction but does not weight any of the cues. A take the best heuristic involves making decisions on one cue at a time, with the order based on the cues judged to be the best predictors. This is what experts typically do when undertaking assessments. A minimalist heuristic is similar to take the best but here there is no judgement around which cue or cues are the best and these are chosen in random order.

In this study, the multiple regression analysis and the tallying heuristic used all the available cues. In contrast, the take the best heuristic used on average 2.4

cues and the minimalist heuristic 2.2. The multiple regression analysis achieved the optimal results, in terms of fitting to the historic data. Importantly though, this did not translate into the best prediction of outcomes. In this respect, both the tallying and take the best heuristics performed better and did so based on simple counting or ordering of the cues. This was explained as the result of the regression analysis extracting too much information from the data set, in pursuit of an optimal result. This led to 'overfitting' of the data, essentially meaning that more of the random variation was incorrectly seen as being predictive. This resulted in the better fitting but poorer prediction. The tallying and take the best heuristics did better and were more robust because they simply ignored much of this background 'noise' or random variation, with a greater focus on genuinely predictive information.

Heuristic decision making though is clearly not infallible, and it seems clear that it may perform poorly, or be tricked, in particular environments. Examples are useful in explaining the reasons why this happens and one of these involves what have been called 'dread' risks. The most common example of this is probably the risk of air crashes, although terrorist attacks provide another less common example. People experience elevated levels of fear in relation to these kinds of events, despite reassurances around the low probability of occurrence. This has resulted in these kinds of risk being given considerable emphasis, often in stark contrasts other areas of risk that may result in much higher levels of death and serious injury. For example, a striking contrast here is between healthcare settings and air travel. The levels of unnecessary deaths and serious injuries to patients has been and indeed remains very much higher than for commercial air travellers. Despite this, questions of improving patient safety have, at least until very recently, received far less attention and action than air travel. Various explanations have been proposed for this but none appear able to fully explain this effect, which is of clear relevance to various areas of politically motivated violence. An example of this was drawn from the period shortly after the 9/11 attacks on the US. This looked at deaths linked to travel during this period. Many people were observed to have switched from commercial flying to travelling by road. Driving is though a significantly more dangerous activity than commercial flying, in terms of both fatalities and serious injuries. This shift therefore resulted in many more deaths and injuries being experienced in the US than would otherwise have happened. This was estimated to be around 1,600 deaths resulting from this change in behaviour, which in fact exceeded the number of deaths from the 9/11 attacks (Gigerenzer, 2008; Gaissmaier and Gigerenzer, 2012). Terrorist attacks often appear to aim at generating just these kinds of dread risk effects, by amplifying fear in a wider audience and causing ongoing harms.

Keeping things simple

Forensic practice in recent years has tended to stress the use of increasingly complex methods in decision-making concerned with areas of risk, ambiguity and uncertainty. Evidence of this is seen in the growing use of actuarial and checklist-based approaches in the assessments involving these areas. Actuarial methods have drawn on increasingly complex methods and models, whilst checklist-based methods have also taken on increasingly elaborate forms. This move seems in part predicated on an assumption that these changes will lead to better accuracy in prediction. In as far as a theoretical basis for this change is made explicit, this seems to draw on optimisation approaches and models, largely developed in economics and management. It is a clearly anti-psychological approach that appears to see little value in looking at how people solve these kinds of problems. Yet, this rests on the unsupported assumption that greater complexity will yield 'better' results. Evidence here suggests that using complex methods does not in fact lead to more accurate predictions in the way assumed and also that these methods may also be lacking in robustness and resilience (Fischbacher-Smith, 2015, 2016; Crighton, 2023). Simpler heuristics methods often appear better in these respects, with additional advantages of speed and economy (Gigerenzer and Gaissmaier, 2011). Heuristics are able to achieve this feat by drawing on abilities that are highly evolved or highly trained, which in turn draw on often complex but largely automatic processing that does not require conscious effort (Körding and Wolpert, 2004).

Classification

Classification refers here to determining a rule to assign objects to one of a given set of classes. This can serve the function of diagnosis, prediction or indeed a mix of both. Classification can be addressed by use of formal methods and this can be shown to work well in stable and controlled worlds, such as laboratory-based studies. In these 'small worlds,' the logic-based rules used can be progressively modified and refined to produce improved optimal results. Faced with the kind of problems involved in the 'large-worlds' seen in business, industry and politics though, this is not the case. Here, efforts to fine tune models may in fact lead to large prediction errors.

Simple rules or heuristics often perform well here and enjoy the major advantages of being easy to use, easy to understand and have the important character of being transparent in operation. Using these rests on fundamental cognitive abilities, such as counting and ordering, requiring little effort. As noted above, tallying heuristics involve counting the reasons to classify into a group and summing these. Take the best heuristics involve working through ordered cues, as seen in areas such as healthcare triage. For example, use of 'fast-and-frugal tree' (FFT) methods are common here and will typically involve a series of binary questions, leading either to classification or a further binary question. Staying with healthcare triage, an example of this involves using the reminder of: breathing, bleeding, breaks and burns. Used in emergency situations, this forms an FFT where the first binary decision is whether the casualty is breathing. If not, then they are classified as falling into the highest risk category and needing immediate intervention (or risk treatment) in the form of immediate efforts at resuscitation. If they are breathing, then the assessor can move on to the next binary question, concerned with evidence of active blood loss. If present then they can be classified as falling into the second highest risk category, with risk treatment indicated in the form of immediate efforts to arrest blood loss. If there is no active blood loss, then the assessor can move on to the next binary question or questions: in this example involving two further binary questions. Importantly using this heuristic serves to focus efforts on those most in need to risk treatment, maximising the reduction in mortality and morbidity that can be achieved. It also enjoys the major advantage of being accurate, robust and fast. It places few cognitive demands on those using the method and has transparent decision rules, so it is clear to all how and why decisions are being made, whilst also allowing for deviations where these are felt to be justified.

An important aspect of classification in these kinds of real 'large-world' problems is that these will, using the definition suggested earlier, generally concern uncertainty rather than risk. This applies to politically motivated violence, where the state space is not known and there is no means to determine cue weights or optimal classification rules. As with other areas of forensic practice, the future may differ from the past in unpredictable ways, so that that predictions based on past events are not only inaccurate but may be seriously misleading (Russell, 2001; Taleb, 2015). Uncertainty here simply cannot be addressed using probability theory in the way that risk can (Knight, 1921; Keynes, 1937; Gigerenzer, 2008, 2010).

Under such conditions of uncertainty, use of heuristics can be used to improve decision making. This is based on accepting that classification here needs to recognise the unstable nature of the 'large-world' problems. Under these conditions, effective classification needs to be based on what successful experts do, rather than relying on optimised rule-based methods that are based on 'small-world' models. This involves a shift in research to look at what these experts do, in a search for rules that can be more widely applied. In doing this, transparency has also been noted as a fundamental value for both practitioners and society more widely (Gigerenzer, 2008, 2010). Transparency is a key value here since it allows the testing and adjustment of decision rules, with the aim of progressive improvement. Recent trends in practice though have often been the opposite of this, with the use of increasingly opaque methods coming to increasingly dominate. This has extended to the use of what are called 'black box' methods which rely on artificial intelligence and deep learning. These methods raise concerns around lack of transparency but also results that are hidden from human comprehension. This is a serious, growing concern, with adverse impacts on democratic and civil rights (Katsikopoulos, Simşek, Buckmann et al., 2020; Cotter, 2023).

Using heuristics to cope with politically motivated violence

The example here is taken from a review of how problems involving uncertainty might be better dealt with in real world situations (Katsikopoulos, Simşek, Buckmann et al., 2020). This looked at the critical role of staffing checkpoints in areas where active conflict and terrorist attacks were ongoing. Those staffing checkpoints faced a categorisation problem, whether those approaching the checkpoint were civilians going about their daily business or were suicide attackers using civilian vehicles. Categorising traffic in this manner, into hostile or not hostile groups, involved making critical life and death decisions, both for those staffing the checkpoints and travellers. Classifying vehicles as hostile would result in the use of escalating force, up to and including lethal force. Work at checkpoints like this is also generally undertaken by junior and often relatively inexperienced personnel, who may be working in isolated conditions without easy access to senior colleagues.

There are a few potential responses to this kind of problem. One of these would be to apply logic-based approaches, based on the 'small-world' theoretical models as discussed above. Here, the assumption would be that the model used would transfer to this larger real-world situation or 'wild' setting or at least transfer 'well enough.' This would involve seeking an optimised solution based on historic data, then drawing on formal analysis, which might be something as simple as multiple regression analysis or as complex as using random forest or neural net techniques. Such a model would then require assessment of the cues deemed to be predictive, based on the fitting of data to a sample of previous cases. The results could then be used to direct various responses. The problems with this kind of approach have been discussed in some detail above.

Another possible approach here would involve use of some form of checklist, specifying a range of areas to be considered, followed by options for responding. This method has commonly been adopted by military leaderships, with the issuing of checklist directives for the legal use of military force. The results of this have though been variable. The approach seems to be effective where conditions allow ample time to think and to seek approval from more senior colleagues before using and escalating levels of force. Such conditions though are often not met and certainly did not appear typical of checkpoints in a conflict zone, where the assessment of threats would necessitate rapid decision making. Detailed checklists of actions seem to have limited use in reducing categorising errors in these circumstances and this may reflect more fundamental problems with the approach. Notably, these provide no classification rules. The method also appears largely silent on what might prompt different responses, such as when to use force, when and how to increase the level of force and when to stop using force altogether (Katsikopoulos, Simşek, Buckmann et al., 2020).

The researchers here went on to analyse what was happening when faced with this kind of problem. This was based on an analysis of official 'Battle Damage Assessment Reports' (BDAR) of encounters between soldiers at checkpoints and incoming vehicles. This involved a sample of 1,060 reports. The main finding here was that the military personnel involved seemed to be relying on a single cue: whether the oncoming vehicle is complying (i.e., slowing down or stopping) (Keller and Konstantinos, 2016). Of the 1,060 reports, seven had involved suicide bomb attacks. For all 1,053 other reports, this single cue of non-compliance was present. In 1,020 of these cases, force had been used as soon as the vehicle driver failed to comply but was not increased if they subsequently complied. The researchers summarised this single cue decision making as a 'compliance heuristic,' which essentially said increase the level of force if the oncoming vehicle is not complying with instructions (Katsikopoulos, Simşek, Buckmann et al., 2020).

In 857 cases, this had led to an escalation in force which resulted in 35 civilian casualties, and in the other 196, a further escalation to use extreme force had resulted with 169 civilian casualties.

In seeking a better approach the researchers looked at an alternative method of categorisation. This drew on a literature and document review for cues that could be predictive, as well as practical, in real-world conditions. Vehicles having more than one occupant was identified as an important cue for a lower level of threat (Bagwell, 2008). In addition, the way that skilled personnel solved this kind of problem was analysed. This suggested use of three cues: whether the vehicle had multiple occupants, whether the driver complied with instructions and whether there were any further valid threat cues. Further threat cues included such things as having specific intelligence reports about suspicious vehicles in the area, for example reports concerning a particular make and colour of vehicle. This was used to develop a practical heuristic which would be easy to recall, quick to use and that would yield accurate results. This 'Checkpoint Tree' used a take the best heuristic, assessing cues in order of importance, rather than a tallying heuristic where cues would have been given equal weight. This was adopted to support faster decision making, which typically would have occurred after the first or second cue. Drawing on the way skilled personnel assessed threats, the researchers assumed that the vehicle having multiple occupants was likely to be a particularly good indicator of low threat.

Empirically assessing the accuracy of this heuristic proved challenging but was possible because of a leak of classified documents. This included the BADR's of 'critical encounters' that took place between 2004 and 2009 (Katsikopoulos, Simşek, Buckmann et al., 2020). The seven suicide attacks during this period had all involved a single attacker, driving a vehicle. None had been successfully prevented. In the remaining incidents, involving vehicles that did not have hostile intent but that were incorrectly classified as threats, 58 civilians were reported to have been killed and 146 injured.

In looking at the seven cases of successful suicide attacks, the researchers concluded that there was insufficient information to fully test the Checkpoint Tree, beyond the first cue. It was not possible in these cases to assess whether drivers complied with instructions, or whether additional intelligence information was available and used. They did though note that the Checkpoint Tree heuristic could not have performed worse, since all the attacks had succeeded. Based on the remaining 1,053 cases, they concluded that the reports did include enough information to test the Checkpoint Tree. In these cases, this correctly classified 975 cases as involving civilians and incorrectly classified 78 as involving suicide attackers. The number of civilian casualties that may have arisen from these 78 false alarms was estimated, based on the assumption that the Checkpoint Tree was memorised and applied. Here, mis-classifying someone as a suicide attacker would not necessarily imply the person would be killed or injured. The researchers though recognised the difficulty in estimating the number of casualties that would have resulted from use the Checkpoint Tree. However, they noted that it would be a safe assumption that the upper limit would be 78, where all these false alarms resulted in an escalation to the use of lethal force. There was though evidence to suggest that checkpoint personnel did show an escalation of force, depending on circumstances, so this upper limit seems unduly pessimistic. Even so, this compared well to the results for using checklist guidance and in fact relying on a single-cue heuristic, where there had been 204 casualties. Two key points can be taken from this study. The first of these is that there is no perfect way to deal with these situations, with both the approaches studied leading to misclassification. The second is that by using a better heuristic, in the form as the Checkpoint Tree, the way in which these uncertain situations were dealt with could be greatly improved: in this case with a reduction in civilian casualties of at least 60 per cent (Katsikopoulos, Simşek, Buckmann et al., 2020).

In such attacks, it is clearly the case that various methods and tactics can be used, with changes that are reactive and adaptive. This adds to the uncertainty involved here, so in the example given above, it would be possible to stage attacks with more than one passenger in the vehicle. This would obviate the value of the first cue in the Checkpoint Tree, and when dealing with politically motivated violence, this is a reasonable concern, which would reduce the accuracy of classification. Counter-measures like this do though involve significantly increased costs to the attackers. Having multiple suicide attackers increase losses with no increase in the damage inflicted. Similarly, use of mannequins may give the impression of a second occupant, but there are practical responses to this. Take the best heuristics can be quickly updated to cope with changes and training and techniques may be used to recognise deceptions, such as the use infrared aids. Decision trees have the major advantage that they can be quickly altered in the light of changes in the environment, integrating or removing cues for decision making when needed. Fundamentally though, there is a need to recognised that in 'large-world' conditions, no perfect processes of categorisation exists. This ideal seems to have crept in from the mis-application of 'small-world' models. In these, it is always possible to 'tweak' the model and its parameters to obtain better fitting. However, this does not translate into a world of uncertainty and intractability (Fischbacher-Smith, 2015, 2016). Fortunately, there are a range of heuristics here that can be effective in dealing with just these conditions (Gigerenzer and Brighton, 2009). There is also clear scope to improve the application of these. This can be achieved by better structuring of environments and training, which facilitate and build on naturally occurring strengths.

Summary and conclusions

How to address risk in relation to the varied forms of politically motivated violence remains a focus of live debate in forensic practice, with no universally agreed definition of risk. The definition adopted here follows Knight (1921) in seeing risk as a measurable quality of the likelihood of something happening: either in terms of *a priori* probability or a relative frequency estimate of probability. This depends on being able to define the possible states of a system. Uncertainty refers to cases where all the states of the system are not known meaning there is no sensible way to calculate or estimate probability empirically.

Risk assessment is defined here as a process of using 'risk factors' or 'risk correlates' of various kinds to estimate the likelihood of an outcome occurring in a population. Two approaches to this have come to dominate forensic practice and have been described as actuarial and checklist-based. Actuarial approaches draw on formal analysis to determine estimates of probability. Checklist-based assessments involve descriptive assessments of likelihood and might more accurately be characterised as assessments of uncertainty. Both approaches make contested claims to improve significantly on expert judgement and have been widely and increasingly applied across forensic practice. These methods have recently been transplanted to areas of politically motivated violence. This extension appears to rest on poorly founded assumptions, and there is limited evidence of validity or utility of these methods. There is a lack of knowledge and understanding around valid indicators of risk in terrorism and other areas of politically motivated violence. This requires a shift in research to identifying robust risk factors and correlates. There is also a need for credible independent research to validate and develop these for use in practice.

Claims that people are generally irrational and easily misled appear to have strongly influenced forensic practice in this area. This has been associated with a wider adoption of statistical reasoning in cognitive psychology and a misplaced stress on cognitive illusions, as divergences from solutions based on theoretical models. It is surprising that such an anti-psychological approach, focussed on human failings, has been so influential. As well as detracting from the research traditions in cognitive psychology that could inform this area of practice, this has also contributed to neglect of wider environmental, social and economic drivers in decision making.

Making substantive progress here needs to recognise that many areas of politically motivated violence involve uncertainty rather than risk. Others will be intractable, meaning that future states and consequences of actions are known, along with all the probabilities but even so optimal solutions are not attainable. Under such conditions, heuristics can improve decision making, based on acceptance that classification needs to recognise the unstable and sometimes intractable nature of the world. This requires a clear shift towards work on effective heuristics decision making, the use of which can be aided by changing environments to aid better decision making. Heuristics also have some critical advantages, including transparency, accuracy and building on natural inbuilt skills that require little conscious efforts.

This can be illustrated by looking at a real-world example (Katsikopoulos, Simşek, Buckmann et al., 2020) concerning military checkpoints and suicidal terrorist attacks using explosive devices. This involves categorising traffic into hostile and not-hostile groups with life and death implications. This clearly addresses uncertainty and traditional approaches using checklist-based assessment here worked poorly. Battle Damage Assessment Reports suggested personnel were in fact using single cue 'compliance heuristic,' based on the vehicle complying or not complying with instructions, leading to multiple casualties. This was compared to an alternative heuristic using three cues: whether the vehicle had multiple occupants, whether the driver complied with instructions and whether there were any further valid threat cues such as specific intelligence reports. This 'Checkpoint Tree' used a take the best heuristic, assessing each cue in order, in the form of a binary question. Evaluation here suggested a very marked casualties when using this heuristic. This suggests that significant improvements in practice are possible using heuristics that are generally effective in dealing with such problems.

References

Allison, G. T. and Zelikow, P. (1971). *Essence of Decision: Explaining the Cuban Missile Crisis*. Boston: Little, Brown.

Aven, T. (2015). *Risk Analysis*. Chichester: John Wiley.

Aven, T. and Renn, O. (2009). The role of quantitative risk assessments for characterizing risk and uncertainty and delineating appropriate risk management options, with special emphasis on terrorism risk. *Risk Analysis: An International Journal*, *29*(4), 587–600.

Bagwell, R. (2008). The Threat Assessment Process (TAP): The Evolution of Escalation of Force (April 2008). The Army Lawyer, April 2008, DA PAM 27-50-419, Available at SSRN: https://ssrn.com/abstract=3022835

Behavioural Insights Team. (2010). *Applying Behavioural Insight to Health*. London: Cabinet Office.

Biau, G. and Scornet, E. (2016). A random forest guided tour. *Test*, *25*, 197–227.

Bischof, G., Karner, S., and Ruggenthaler, P. (Eds.) (2009). *The Prague Spring and the Warsaw Pact Invasion of Czechoslovakia in 1968*. Lanham: Rowman and Littlefield.

Braddock, K. (2019). *A Brief Primer on Experimental and Quasi-Experimental Methods in the Study of Terrorism*. The Hague: International Centre for Counter-Terrorism.

Brighton, H. and Gigerenzer, G. (2015). The bias bias. *Journal of Business Research* , *68*, 1772–1784.

Bunn, M. and Sagan, S. D. (2014). *A Worst Practices Guide to Insider Threats: Lessons from Past Mistakes*. Cambridge: American Academy of Arts and Sciences.

Burke, B., Martens, A., and Faucher, E. (2010). Two decades of terror management theory: a meta-analysis of mortality salience research. *Personality and Social Psychology Review*, *14*, 155–195.

Chopin, N. and Papaspiliopoulos, O. (2020). Introduction to state-space models. In N. Chopin and O. Papaspiliopoulos, (Eds.), *An Introduction to Sequential Monte Carlo*. Cham: Springer. https://doi.org/10.1007/978-3-030-47845-2_2

Coid, J. W., Kallis, C., Doyle, M., Shaw, J., and Ullrich, S. (2015). Identifying causal risk factors for violence among discharged patients. *PloS one*, *10*(11), e0142493.

Cotter, K. (2023). "Shadowbanning is not a thing": black box gaslighting and the power to independently know and credibly critique algorithms. *Information, Communication & Society*, *26*(6), 1226–1243.

Crenshaw, M. (1981). The causes of terrorism. *Comparative Politics*, *13*(4), 379–399.

Crighton, D. (2023). *Risk Assessment in Forensic Practice*. London: Routledge.

Crighton, D. A. and Towl, G. J. (2008). Principles of risk assessment. In D. A. Crighton and G. J. Towl (Eds.), *Psychology in Prisons*. Oxford: Blackwell.

Cronbach, L. J. and Meehl, P. H. (1955). Construct validity in psychological tests. *Psychological Bulletin*, *52*, 281–302.

Daddis, G. A. (2012). The problem of metrics: assessing progress and effectiveness in the Vietnam War. *War in History*, *19*(1), 73–98.

Daston, L. (1995). *Classical Probability in the Enlightenment*. Princeton: Princeton University Press.

Dawes, R. M. and Corrigan, B. (1974). Linear models in decision making. *Psychological Bulletin, 81*(2), 95–106.

Dawid, A. P., Musio, M., and Murtas, R. (2017). The probability of causation. *Law, Probability and Risk, 16*(4), 163–179.

Descartes, R. (1644/2006). *Principles of Philosophy*. Cambridge: Cambridge University Press.

Department of Defense. (2010). *Protecting the Force: Lessons from Fort Hood—Report of the Department of Defense Independent Review*. Washington: Department of Defense. Retrieved from https://archive.org/details/ProtectingTheForceLessonsFromFortHood

Dressel, J. and Farid, H. (2018). The accuracy, fairness, and limits of predicting recidivism. *Science Advances, 4*(1), eaao5580.

Elliott, I. A., Randhawa-Horne, K., and Hambly, O. (2023). *The Extremism Risk Guidance 22*. London: OGL.

Emery, J. R. (2021). Moral choices without moral language: 1950's political-military wargaming at the RAND Corporation. *Texas National Security Review, 4*(4), 12–34. Available online https://repositories.lib.utexas.edu/server/api/core/bitstreams/990f44b5-de98-47ec-92aa-aeb8f90f3f99/content. Retrieved January 31, 2025.

Erickson, P., Klein, J., Daston, L., Lemow, R., Sturm, T., and Gordin, M. D. (2013). *How Reason Almost Lost Its Mind. The Strange Career of Cold War Rationality*. Chicago: University of Chicago Press.

Ferguson, A. (2010). Nudge nudge, wink wink: behavioral economics – the governing theory of Obama's nanny state. The Weekly Standard. 19 April.

Fischbacher-Smith, D. (2015). Through a glass darkly: expertise, evidence, and the management of uncertainty. *Risk Management, 17*, 352–372.

Fischbacher-Smith, D. (2016). Framing the UK's counter-terrorism policy within the context of a wicked problem. *Public Money & Management, 36*(6), 399–408.

Fischbacher-Smith, D. and Smith, L. (2015). Navigating the 'dark waters of globalisation': global markets, inequalities and the spatial dynamics of risk. *Risk Management, 17*, 179–203.

Feynman, R. P. (1974). Cargo cult science. *Engineering and Science, 37*(7), 10–13.

Friedman, D., Issac, R. M., James, D., and Sunder, S. (2014). *Risky Curves: On the Empirical Failure of Expected Utility*. London: Routledge.

Friedman, M. (1953). *Essays in Positive Economics*. Chicago: University of Chicago Press.

Freilich, J. D., Chermak, S. M., Belli, R., Gruenewald, J., and Parkin, W. S. (2014). Introducing the United States Extremist Crime Database (ECDB). *Terrorism and Political Violence, 26*, 372–384.

Gaissmaier, W., and Gigerenzer, G. (2012). 9/11, Act II: A fine-grained analysis of regional variations in traffic fatalities in the aftermath of the terrorist attacks. *Psychological Science, 23*(12), 1449–1454.

Garrett, B. L. and Monahan, J. (2020). Judging risk. *California Law Review, 108*, 439–493.

Gill, P., Horgan, J., and Deckert, P. (2014). Bombing alone: tracing the motivations and antecedent behaviors of lone-actor terrorists. *Journal of Forensic Sciences, 59*, 425–435.

Gigerenzer, G. (2008). Why heuristics work. *Perspectives on Psychological Science, 3*(1), 20–29.

Gigerenzer, G. (2010). *Rationality for Mortals: How People Cope with Uncertainty*. New York: Oxford University Press.

Gigerenzer, G. (2024). The rationality wars: a personal reflection. *Behavioural Public Policy*, 1–21. https://doi.org/10.1017/bpp.2024.51

Gigerenzer, G. and Brighton, H. (2009). Homo heuristicus: why biased minds make better inferences. *Topics in Cognitive Science*, *1*(1), 107–143.

Gigerenzer, G. and Gaissmaier, W. (2011). Heuristic decision making. *Annual Review of Psychology*, *62*(1), 451–482.

Gigerenzer, G. and Hoffrage, U. (1995). How to improve Bayesian reasoning without instruction: frequency formats. *Psychological Review*, *102*(4), 684–704.

Gigerenzer, G. and Murray, D. J. (2015). *Cognition as Intuitive Statistics*. New York: Psychology Press.

Gigerenzer, G., Todd, P. M., and The ABC Research Group. (1999). *Simple Heuristics that Make Us Smart*. New York: Oxford University Press.

Ginges, J., Atran, S., Sachdeva, S., and Medin, D. (2011). Psychology out of the laboratory: the challenge of violent extremism. *American Psychologist*, *66*, 507–519.

Goldstein, D. (2010). *On Fact and Fraud: Cautionary Tales from the Front Lines of Science*. New Jersey: Princeton University Press.

Gregory, R. L. (1997). Knowledge in perception and illusion. *Philosophical Transactions of the Royal Society of London. Series B: Biological Sciences*, *352*(1358), 1121–1127.

Gruenewald, J., Chermak, S., and Freilich, J. (2013). Distinguishing "loner" attacks from other domestic extreme violence: a comparison of far-right homicide incident and offender characteristics. *Criminology and Public Policy*, *12*, 65–91.

Gunaratna R. (2002). *Inside Al-Qaeda*. London: C. Hurst and Co.

Hearst, M. A., Dumais, S. T., Osuna, E., Platt, J., and Scholkopf, B. (1998). Support vector machines. *IEEE Intelligent Systems and Their Applications*, *13*(4), 18–28.

Hertwig, R., Leuker, C., Pachur, T., Spiliopoulos, L., and Pleskac, T. J. (2022). Studies in ecological rationality. *Topics in Cognitive Science*, *14*(3), 467–491.

Ho, E., Rajagopalan, A., Skvortsov, A., Arulampalam, S., and Piraveenan, M. (2022). Game theory in defence applications: a review. *Sensors*, *22*(3), 1032. https://doi.org/10.3390/s22031032

Ilbas, P. (2012). Revealing the preferences of the US Federal Reserve. *Journal of Applied Econometrics*, *27*(3), 440–473.

Inhelder, B. and Piaget, J. (1958). *The Growth of Logical Thinking from Childhood to Adolescence: An Essay on the Construction of Formal Operational Structures*. London: Routledge.

International Organisation for Standardization (ISO). (2018). *Risk Management Guidelines*. Geneva: International Organisation for Standardization.

Jones, A. J. (2004). New tools in non-linear modelling and prediction. *Computational Management Science*, *1*(2), 109–149.

Katsikopoulos, K. V., Simşek, O., Buckmann, M., and Gigerenzer, G. (2020). *Classification in the Wild the Science and Art of Transparent Decision Making*. Cambridge: MIT Press.

Keller, N. and Katsikopoulos, K. V. (2016). On the role of psychological heuristics in operational research; and a demonstration in military stability operations. *European Journal of Operational Research*, *249*(3), 1063–1073.

Keynes, J. M. (1921). *A Treatise on Probability*. London: Macmillan.

Keynes, J. M. (1937). The general theory of employment. *Quarterly Journal of Economics*, *51*, 209–223.

Knight, F. H. (1921). *Risk, Uncertainty and Profit*. Boston: Hart, Schaffner and Marx.

Körding, K. P. and Wolpert, D. M. (2004). Bayesian integration in sensorimotor learning. *Nature*, *427*(6971), 244–247.

Kraemer, H., Kazdin, A., Offord, D., Kessler, R., Jensen, P., and Kupfer, D. (1997). Coming to terms with the terms of risk. *Archives of General Psychiatry*, *54*, 337–343.

Kraemer, H. C., Stice, E., Kazdin, A., Offord, D., and Kupfer, D. (2001). How do risk factors work together? Mediators, moderators, and independent, overlapping, and proxy risk factors. *American Journal of Psychiatry*, *158*(6), 848–856.

Kroner, D. G., Mills, J. F., and Reddon, J. R. (2005). A coffee can, factor analysis, and prediction of antisocial behavior: the structure of criminal risk. *International Journal of Law and Psychiatry*, *28*(4), 360–374.

Kruglanski, A., Crenshaw, M., Post, J., and Victoroff, J. (2008). What should this fight be called? Metaphors of counterterrorism and their implications. *Psychological Science in the Public Interest*, *8*, 97–133.

LaFree, G. (2013). Lone-offender terrorists. *Criminology and Public Policy*, *12*, 59–62.

LaFree, G. and Dugan, L. (2007). Introducing the global terrorism database. *Terrorism and Political Violence*, *19*(2), 181–204.

Le Grand, J. (2022). Some challenges to the new paternalism. *Behavioural Public Policy*, *6*(1), 160–171.

Lloyd, M. and Dean, C. (2015). The development of structured guidelines for assessing risk in extremist offenders. *Journal of Threat Assessment and Management*, *2*(1), 40–52.

Lundberg, G. A. (1926). Case work and the statistical method. *Social Forces*, *5*, 61–65.

Maier, M., Bartos, F., Stanley, T. D., Shanks, D. R., Harris, A. J. L., and Wagenmakers, E.-J. (2022). No evidence for nudging after adjusting for publication bias. *PNAS*, *119*(31): e2200300119.

McCauley, C., and Moskalenko, S. (2011). *Friction: How Radicalization Happens to Them and Us*. New York: Oxford University Press.

McCauley, C., and Moskalenko, S. (2014). Toward a profile of lone wolf terrorists: What moves an individual from radical opinion to radical action. *Terrorism and Political Violence,, 26*, 69–85.

Meehl, P. E. (1954). *Clinical versus Statistical Prediction: A Theoretical Analysis and a Review of the Evidence.* Minneapolis, MN: University of Minnesota Press.

Meehl, P. E. (1956). Symposium on clinical and statistical prediction: The tie that binds. *Journal of Counselling Psychology*, *3*(3), 163–164.

Meehl, P. E. (1967). Theory-testing in psychology and physics: a methodological paradox. *Philosophy of Science*, *34*(2), 103–115.

Meehl, P. E. (1978). Theoretical risks and tabular asterisks: Sir Karl, Sir Ronald, and the slow progress of soft psychology. *Journal of Consulting and Clinical Psychology*, *46*(4), 806–834.

Mertens, S., Herberz, M., Hahnel, U. J., and Brosch, T. (2022). The effectiveness of nudging: A meta-analysis of choice architecture interventions across behavioral domains. *Proceedings of the National Academy of Sciences*, *119*(1), e2107346118.

Milstein, J. S. (1974). *Dynamics of the Vietnam War: A Quantitative Analysis and Predictive Computer Simulation*. Columbus, OH: Ohio State University Press.

Moffitt, L. J., Stranlund, J. K., and Field, B. C. (2005). Inspections to avert terrorism: robustness under severe uncertainty. *Journal of Homeland Security and Emergency Management*, *2*(3), 1–19.

Monahan, J. (2012). The individual risk assessment of terrorism. *Psychology, Public Policy, and Law*, *18*, 167–205.

Monahan, J. (2016). The individual risk assessment of terrorism: Recent developments. In G. LaFree and J. D. Freilich, J. D. (Eds.). .), *The Handbook of the Criminology of Terrorism.* New York: John Wiley.

Monahan, J., and Skeem, J. (2014). The evolution of violence risk assessment. *CNS Spectrums*, *19*, 419–424.

National Offender Management Service. (2016). *Public Protection Manual*. London: OGL.

Orehek, E., Sasota, J., Kruglanski, A., Dechesne, M., and Ridgeway, L. (2014). Interdependent self-construals mitigate the fear of death and augment the willingness to become a martyr. *Journal of Personality and Social Psychology*, *107*, 265–275.

Peterson, C. R. and Beach, L. R. (1967). Man as an intuitive statistician. *Psychological Bulletin*, *68*, 29–46.

Piaget, J. (1962). *The Origins of Intelligence in the Child*. New York: Norton.

Pressman, D. E. and Flockton, J. (2014). Violent extremist risk assessment: issues and applications of the VERA-2 in a high-security correctional setting. In A. Silke (Ed.), *Prisons, Terrorism and Extremism*. London: Routledge.

Pyszczynski, T., Abdollahi, A., Solomon, S., Greenberg, J., Cohen, F., and Weise, D. (2006). Mortality salience, martyrdom, and military might: The great Satan versus the axis of evil. *Personality and Social Psychology Bulletin*, *32*, 525–537.

Rizzo, M. J. (2023). The antipaternalist psychology of William James. *Behavioural Public Policy*, 1–26. https://doi:10.1017/bpp.2023.20

Ronfeldt, D. and Arquilla, J. (2001). Networks, netwars and the fight for the future. *First Monday*, *6*(10). https://doi.org/10.5210/fm.v6i10.889

Russell, B. (2001). *The Problems of Philosophy*. Oxford: Oxford University Press.

Sageman, M. (2008). A strategy for fighting international Islamist terrorists. *The Annals of the American Academy of Political and Social Science*, *618*(1), 223–231.

Sageman, M. (2014). The stagnation in terrorism research. *Terrorism and Political Violence*, *26*, 465–580.

Sarbin, T. R. (1944). The logic of prediction in psychology. *Psychological Review*, *51*, 210–228.

Savage, L. J. (1954). *The Foundations of Statistics* (2nd edition). New York: Wiley. 1972.

Schelling, T. C. (1960). Meteors, mischief, and war. *Bulletin of the Atomic Scientists*, *16*(7), 292–300.

Schick, J. M. (2016). *The Berlin Crisis, 1958-1962*. Philadelphia: University of Pennsylvania Press.

Schouten, R. and Saathoff, G. (2014). Insider threats in bioterrorism cases. In J. R. Meloy and J. Hoffmann (Eds.), *International Handbook of Threat Assessment*. New York: Oxford University Press.

Siegler, R. S. (1999). Strategic development. *Trends in Cognitive Sciences*, *3*(11), 430–435.

Simon, H. A. (1977). *Models of Discovery: And Other Topics in the Methods of Science*. Dordrecht: Springer Netherlands.

Simon, H. A. (1978). Rationality as process and as product of thought. *The American Economic Review*, *68*(2), 1–16.

Simon, H. A. and Newell, A. (1958). Heuristic problem solving: the next advance in operations research. *Operations Research*, *6*(1), 1–10.

Simonsohn, U., Simmons, J. P., and Nelson, L. D. (2021). Evidence of Fraud in an Influential Field Experiment About Dishonesty. https://datacolada.org/98 [7 January 2025].

Skinner, B. F. (1971). *Beyond Freedom and Dignity (1971)*. New York: Bantam, Vintage Book.

Tajfel, H. and Turner, J. C. (1979). An integrative theory of intergroup conflict. In S. Worchel and Austin, W. G. (Eds.), *Psychology of Intergroup Relations*. Monterey: Brooks/Cole.

Taleb, N. N. (2015). *The Black Swan: The Impact of the Highly Improbable*. New York: Random House.

Taylor, M., Roach, J., and Pease, K. (Eds.) (2015). *Evolutionary Psychology and Terrorism.* New York: Routledge.

Thaler, R. H. and Sunstein, C. R. (2008). *Nudge: Improving Decisions about Health, Wealth, and Happiness.* New Haven: Yale University Press.

Todd, P. M. and Gigerenzer, G. (2007). Environments that make us smart: ecological rationality. *Current Directions in Psychological Science, 16*(3), 167–171.

Towl, G. J. and Crighton, D. A. (1996). *A Handbook of Psychology for Forensic Practitioners.* London: Routledge.

Turner, J. C. (1975). Social comparison and social identity: some prospects for intergroup behaviour. *European Journal of Social Psychology, 5*(1), 1–34.

van der Heide, L., van der Zwan, M., and van Leyenhorst, M. (2019). *The Practitioner's Guide to the Galaxy – A Comparison of Risk Assessment Tools for Violent Extremism.* The Hague: International Centre for Counter-Terrorism.

van Der Vegt, G. S., Essens, P., Wahlström, M., and George, G. (2015). Managing risk and resilience. *Academy of Management Journal, 58*(4), 971–980.

von Neumann, J. and Morgenstern, O. (1947). *Theory of Games and Economic Behavior (2nd Edition).* Princeton: Princeton University Press.

von Neumann, J. and Morgenstern, O. (1953). *Theory of Games and Economic Behavior (3rd Edition).* Princeton: Princeton University Press.

Wald, M. S. and Woolverton, M. (1990). Risk assessment: the emperor's new clothes? *Child Welfare: Journal of Policy, Practice, and Program, 69*(6), 483–511.

Wiest, A. (2003). *The Vietnam War 1956-1975.* London: Routledge.

Wilson, P. (2020). Academic fraud: solving the crisis in modern academia. *Exchanges: The Interdisciplinary Research Journal, 7*(3), 14–44.

Woo, G. (2002). Quantitative terrorism risk assessment. *The Journal of Risk Finance, 4*(1), 7–14.

Woo, G. (2021). Expert Judgement in Terrorism Risk Assessment. In A. M. Hanea, Nane, G. F., Bedford, T., French, S. (Eds.). *Expert Judgement in Risk and Decision Analysis. International Series in Operations Research & Management Science, vol. 293.* Cham: Springer. doi.org/10.1007/978-3-030-46474-5_22

Yang, M., Wong, S. C., and Coid, J. (2010). The efficacy of violence prediction: a meta-analytic comparison of nine risk assessment tools. *Psychological Bulletin, 136*(5), 740–767.

Concluding thoughts

Definitions are central to effectively addressing the area of politically motivated violence, whether this comes from state actors or non-state actors. In the absence of clarity, discussions in this area can easily become confused and muddled, with the multi-disciplinary nature of the field adding an extra layer of complexity. Failing to do this has led to confusions over what constitutes violence as well as what is meant by the 'state.' As a result, many debates in this area appear to have taken place at cross purposes. There is no need for this. All of the relevant concepts involved have been carefully defined somewhere in the academic literature. Such definitions can be drawn on, providing a useful foundation for further work and making communication easier. Good operational definitions here allow for more effective systematic inquiry and forms an important foundation to scientific study.

The first important distinction concerns aggression and violence. A variety of approaches have been taken to this and the most common has been the use of exemplar-based definitions. These dominate legal systems around the world and serve an important function. For the purposes of research and practice development though, this approach does not work well. Exemplars of 'violence' have differed over time and place and continue to do so. Identical behaviours can be differently categorised using exemplar-based approaches, meaning that this approach does not provide a firm foundation for the application of scientific method. Use of health-based models improve this but do not fully address the problem. Social and Bio-psychological approaches appear more effective in defining violence for this purpose. These define aggression in terms of its function and near universality. Aggression involving behaviours that have value in terms of interactions. Violence is distinguished from aggression by its non-essential, unwanted, harmful and intentional nature.

There has been considerable debate over the notion of state violence and whether this can or should ever be described as terrorism. As noted in the preface, states routinely use violence. Indeed functional states can be seen to rest on their monopoly on the legitimate use of violence, both internally and externally: which may be acquiesced to, legitimated or challenged. States may also engage in clearly illegitimate violence and the issue of how to describe this has been contentious.

DOI: 10.4324/9781003429579-7

Arguments have been made for a fundamental distinction here between state and non-state actors, with the use of terms such as 'state atrocities' or 'state repression' rather than terms such as 'state terrorism.' Such views have stressed a distinction between state acts and acts of politically motivated non-state actors, seeing benefits in studying these separately. This often seems to involve making distinctions without a difference and, given that notions such as 'terrorism' were first coined to describe state activities, appears odd. Views that suggest similar behaviours and acts should be similarly categorised seem more compelling. They are also more promising as a basis for better systematic study and policy development.

Defining the 'state' also seems important. States can usefully be seen as social constructs that involve a distinct and sustained identity, based on legal order and some form of political system. As such states are seen to involve a social contract, based on the states monopoly on public power and the legitimate use of violence, granted to deal with the central problem of maintaining social order. Notions of state are on occasion erroneously and unhelpfully conflated with transitory governments but conceptions of the state extend far beyond this.

Functional states moderate use of public power and violence through efforts to increase legitimacy and balance the growing self-interest seen in elite groups. This traditional view of the state though has been under increasing stress. The effects of increased globalisation and marketisation have often served to reduce public state power, replacing this with international legal and economic agreements. These have often lacked accountability and legitimacy, replacing this with autonomous and disembedded markets. This risks breaking the social contract between states and citizens, driving emergence of violence by non-state actors.

The United Kingdom (UK) has been used as a case study of responses to politically motivated violence. The UK has a long history here, most recently in addressing this emerging from Northern Ireland and in response to trans-national ideologically motivated violence. The response to the later has involved a common policy framework called Contest, which mirrors the approach of the European Union. This gives increased emphasis to tackling what appear causal factors of 'extremism' and 'radicalisation,' stressing psycho-social assessment and interventions to address these, alongside more traditional detection and deterrence. This shift and the 'prevent' aspect of the Contest framework have come in for particular criticism, leading to extensive changes and revisions. Concerns though remain. The use of a 'dragnet' approach here has been associated with administrative overloading of processes with false positive cases. Responsibility for this has been devolved to local government but expertise and resources have generally not followed. The assessments and psycho-social interventions created centrally lack evidence of efficacy. Both can be seen as failing and heavily marketised approaches, transposed from very different clinical and correctional settings. These have failed to address many of the considerable differences involved.

These failures can be seen as a result of wider changes and concerns. As a relatively young discipline, forensic practice has already amassed a troubling history of professionally unethical practices. These have included unethical and inappropriate support for states, state actors and state supported actors. Serious failings of this kind provide considerable scope for learning and reflection on ethics and the criticism of an emergence of 'guild ethics,' that covertly seek to balance ethical requirements against and professional self-interests.

Two major areas have been addressed where forensic practice has made its most significant contributions. The first of these addresses 'profiling.' This captures systematic efforts to identify and predict characteristics and its use in security and intelligence settings dates back to the work of the United States Office of Strategic Services (OSS) profiling of world leaders, during World War II. The scope of this work has expanded greatly to include efforts to identify unknown perpetrators and predict likely characteristics of individuals and acts. This has thrown up unique challenges but also opportunities stemming from exponential growth in capacity to gather and process data based on 'data mining' techniques.

Profiling of individual psychological reactions has become a part of layered security measures in settings that may be targeted for attack, such as ports and airports. These rely on assessment of 'body language,' typically on indicators of stress and anxiety. This application of profiling has been criticised for being based on weak evidence and poorly founded assumptions. Despite widespread use independent evaluation of efficacy or utility of these methods has often been lacking.

Profiling of terrorists in other areas has been limited and has developed comparatively recently. This seems to be linked to past research findings, which suggested that terrorists did not differ from the general populace in terms of demographic or psychological characteristics. More recent developments have questioned whether this still hold true. Psychological profiling has also moved away from focussing on psychopathology. In combination, these changes have led to a growth of the research into profiling and its wider application to terrorism and related areas. Drawing largely on statistical methods of analysis, this work has suggested differences in terms of the profiles of actors, methods used and behaviours during incidents. This work suggests that these methods have significant potential to improve practice and to be developed further.

The specialist area of terrorist hostage incidents has also been a focus for research and practice development. Work here has suggested a significant degree of predictability in behaviours and as a result the ability to develop useful profiles of incidents and perpetrators. This has suggested the presence of structures underlying these types of incidents, that seem to be based on the rational decision-making of perpetrators and those linked by command or control relationships. Methods of psychological profiling therefore appear relevant to this form of hostage taking, with the potential to develop effective models for practice and further research.

Evaluating the accuracy and utility of profiling in areas of politically motivated violence presents serious challenges. Much of the available data has been and continues to be inaccessible to independent researchers, whilst organisations holding data often lack the skills to undertake necessary and credible research. This has been partially mitigated by the development of accessible databases such as the ECDB and GTD which pool data in this area and make this available to researchers. This has been associated with significant advances in the quality of research and utility of work in this area. It cannot though fully address the large amount of classified data which has not benefitted from high quality analysis.

How best to address the risk and uncertainty that surrounds the varied forms of politically motivated violence remains a live debate in forensic practice. There is no universally agreed definition of risk but this is seen here as a measurable quality of the likelihood of something happening. This can be seen to take two forms, either an *a priori* probability or a relative frequency estimate of probability. Both depend on the ability to define the possible states of a system, allowing calculations of probabilities that sum to 1. For situations where this is not true and all the states of a system are not known, there is no way to calculate or estimate probability empirically. These cases involve uncertainty not risk.

Risk assessment has generally been defined in forensic practice as a process of using 'risk factors' or 'risk correlates' to estimate the likelihood of an outcome occurring in a population. Two methods have come to dominate and these have been described as 'actuarial' and 'checklist-based.' Actuarial approaches draw on formal analysis to determine a numerical estimate of probability. Checklist-based approaches normally involve descriptive assessments of likelihood. Both approaches make contested claims to improve significantly on expert judgement and have been widely marketed and applied across forensic practice.

Both methods have quite recently been transplanted to areas of politically motivated violence. This extension appears to rest on poorly founded assumptions, with little evidence of the validity or utility of these assessments. This is unsurprising given the lack of knowledge and understanding around valid indicators of risk for politically motivated violence. A first step, before developing risk assessments in some of these areas, is the identification of robust risk factors and correlates.

Claims that people are generally irrational and easily misled appear to have strongly influenced forensic practice in this area. This stems from a comparatively recent adoption of statistical reasoning in cognitive psychology and a misplaced stress on cognitive illusions, based on divergences from solutions based on formal theoretical models. That such an anti-psychological approach, with its focus on human failings, has been so influential in forensic practice is surprising. It has detracted from the research traditions in cognitive psychology that could have usefully informed this area of practice, as well as contributing to neglect of the role of wider social and economic drivers in decision making.

Making substantive progress here, needs a recognition that in many areas of politically motivated violence it is not possible to define all the possible states of a system. These involve dealing with uncertainty rather than risk. Others instances will involve intractability: where future states and the consequences of actions are known, along with all the probabilities but even so optimal solutions are not attainable. Under both conditions, heuristics can improve decision making, based on an acceptance that classification needs to take place in a sometimes uncertain and intractable world. These also have critical advantages, including transparency, accuracy and building on natural inbuilt skills that require little conscious efforts. Effective heuristics decision making can though be greatly aided by changing environments, in ways that aid better decision making, such as presenting informa-tion in ways that make it easier to draw of these inbuilt skills.

There are many real-world examples of this. The one chosen in this text as illus-trative looked at the use of heuristics in decision making at military checkpoints in an active conflict zone, subject to suicidal terror attacks using explosive devices. Personnel here need to quickly categorise incoming traffic into hostile and non-hostile groups, with life and death implications. This involves uncertainty rather than risk, since there is no way to calculate all the possible states and the estimated probability of these. Traditional approaches using checklist-based assessment here worked poorly, with Battle Damage Assessment Reports showing that personnel were in fact using a single cue 'compliance heuristic': whether vehicles did or did not comply with instructions. This resulted in 204 civilian casualties. Development of an alternative using more cues in the form of a 'Checkpoint Tree' and using a take the best heuristic, which assessed cues in order of significance, proved effective. Evaluation here suggested an upper limit of 78 casualties from use of this, suggesting considerable improvement.

Overall it can be observed that forensic practice has much to offer in addressing some aspects of politically motivated violence more effectively. There is encour-aging evidence of progress in practice, where this has been able to build on credible research. To take this forward needs a willingness to face up to a lot of bad practice. Past ethical failings need to be recognised and remembered if learning is to occur. There is also a need to discard a lot of the 'cargo cult' science in forensic practice and replace this with the real thing.

Index

For Product Safety Concerns and Information please contact our EU
representative GPSR@taylorandfrancis.com
Taylor & Francis Verlag GmbH, Kaufingerstraße 24, 80331 München, Germany

www.ingramcontent.com/pod-product-compliance
Lightning Source LLC
Chambersburg PA
CBHW070336270326
41926CB00017B/3886